AF448667

Sports and Life
An Olympian's View

by John Morton

Published in the United States of America

Most of the work contained herein was originally published in the following publications; reprinted with permission:
 Vermont Public Radio's Commentary Series
 Vermont Sports Today
 Middlebury College Magazine
 Dartmouth Medicine

Printed in the United States of America
ISBN: 979-8-218-31569-6

Work set in Book Antiqua.
Book and cover design by Emily Newton.

Cover photos:
 Top left: John Morton (credit MarathonFoto)
 Top right: Julie, John, and Kay Morton, dog Rosie
 Bottom left: John and Kay Morton
 Bottom center: John Morton
 Bottom right: John Morton (credit Hugh Brown)

This book is dedicated
to the latest generation in a family of sports enthusiasts:
Kaj, Hazel, Luca, Zaen, Clara and Emeline, who have already
demonstrated a love for skiing, biathlon, hiking, fishing, swimming,
cycling, soccer, snowboarding, ice hockey, running and dance.

Reviews for *Sports and Life*

A reasonable question is, what's the point of our lives? And one reasonable answer is the sheer pleasure of moving across the surface of this earth--by foot, on bikes, in a canoe. You name it and John Morton has not only done it, he has a great yarn to share about it; for anyone who really loves sport, this book will charm, enlighten, amuse and motivate you!

— Bill McKibben
Internationally recognized author, educator and environmentalist.

Sports and Life is a splendid collection of eclectic vignettes from a man well-known to the sports world and those of us who have known him through his writing and commentaries on public radio. Subjects range from his familiar world of sports to forays into bird watching and gardening. He also includes some deep political stands on climate, gun control, and drug usage in sports.

His writing style is filled with colorful and concise descriptions, (often with an unusual wrinkle to the subject at hand), subtle humor, humility, and a word of kind advice at the end of many entries.

His longest pieces are about his cardiac surgery (a must read) and going on an Outward Bound expedition to the Tien Shan mountains with a small group of fellow Vietnam veterans and Russian "Afghantsi." The latter was an intense bonding experience designed to address the common thread of PTSD while showing us a pathway to peace with our "enemies" through shared challenges.

— Jed Williamson
Former Executive Director, U.S. Biathlon Association; former Director, Outward Bound; President Emeritus, Sterling College; past President, now Honorary President, American Alpine Club

---

I met John Morton the day he walked into L.L. Bean headquarters in 1992, a 7-time Olympian as an athlete and coach, to pitch the company on becoming sponsors of the U.S. Biathlon Team. I remember being immediately impressed by his humility, his integrity and how comfortable he was with who he was. In the 31 years since, my admiration and respect for Morty has only grown.

He was instrumental, along with an equally inspiring colleague, Max Cobb, with helping me start the Maine Winter Sports Center, which invested $48 million into using skiing and the Olympic movement to create a new economic and community development model for rural locations in Maine. We were able to attract some of the brightest young minds in the ski world, from some of the top colleges in the country to move to Aroostook County, Maine, one of the most isolated and economically challenged regions of New England. My role model for hiring these coaches was whether they shared Morty's attributes for honesty, humility, and a commitment to excellence.

But Morty is not just an accomplished athlete. He has written a number of books as well as being a frequent contributor to Vermont Public Radio. His writing and speaking have always shown a thoughtful man who cares deeply about things that matter and has an uncommon story-telling skill in conveying his thoughts.

— Andy Shepard
Founder and former CEO, Maine Winter Sports Center; former General Manager, Saddleback Mountain, Rangeley, ME

John's sense of humor, humanitarian world view creates bridges and furthers one's understanding of ourselves in the context of larger community. It is an engaging read.

— Perry F. Williamson
The Hurricane Island Outward Bound School's first female instructor

---

John Morton is a gifted story-teller who has a wealth of wonderful stories to share!

His topics range from dally life in Vermont to expeditions and adventures further afield. They include his time in the military, his years of coaching college skiing, his role as a parent and grandparent, and his love of sport.

John can take even a fairly "normal" experience and turn it into a story, thanks to his keen observations of both people and places, his warm sense of humor, and his sense of humility—he is not afraid to make fun of himself.

—Judy Geer
Three-time Olympic rower; former president, New England Nordic Ski Association; co-owner, Craftsbury Outdoor Center

---

An engaging medley of life. Morton reflects on the sports he has participated in as an observer, recreational participant, Olympic competitor, and collegiate coach. His memoir, a collection of essays written over the years, is rooted in those times, but it's also about the diverse and impassioned people he met along the way, interspersed with observations about his personal life. The essays are refreshing, hopeful, funny, introspective, and entertaining. The book is a page turner, not because it's a cliffhanger, but because it's such an enjoyable read.

—Kate Carter
Founder, publisher, editor, Vermont Sports Today

Once again author John Morton has hit a home run in his latest book. In typical Morton fashion, his erudite writing takes us on an Olympian journey, that resonates deeply with anyone who loves the outdoors. He takes us to the ramparts of Mount Everest, the Iditarod sled dog race and comments on contemporary outdoor sporting culture, covering thoughts as diverse as Joe Paterno and Lance Armstrong to the advancement of sports for women and young girls. He covers a wide swath of interesting and compelling topics. His typical fluency is again on display in this thought-provoking work. If you are looking for the perfect gift, I highly recommend this book that resonated deeply with me. I simply couldn't put it down. I consider it an essential read for those looking for a book where sport and culture blend.

—Peter Graves
Thirteen- time Olympic Games Commentator, member of the U.S. Ski and Snowboard Hall of Fame

---

John Morton is an extraordinary guy- upbeat, friendly, active, and generous to a fault. So it's no surprise that this collection of his stories and reminiscences is among my favorite reading, especially when I need a pick-me-up and a reminder how wonderful it is to be alive on this earth.

—Willem Lange
Former instructor, Outward Bound; newspaper columnist; public television personality; adventurer

Table of Contents

FAMILY   149

COMMENTARY ON SPORTS AND LIFE249

Introduction

In 1994 I was offered the opportunity to submit short essays on "off-beat sports" to Vermont Public Radio (VPR, recently rebranded Vermont Public) for broadcast as part of their Commentary Series. With the patient guidance of Betty Smith-Mastaler who produced the series, I wrote and recorded stories and commentaries for the next decade. After the first year, Betty said my commentaries could be on any subject that caught my interest. Not long thereafter, I approached Kate Carter, the founder and publisher of the monthly newspaper *Vermont Sports Today*. Both Betty and Kate agreed to let me recycle my VPR commentaries as monthly columns in *Vermont Sports Today*, which I did for almost 20 years.

In 2020 I gathered many of the commentaries and articles dealing with skiing into a volume titled *Celebrate Winter*. This current volume contains most of the remaining articles and stories, which deal with everything but skiing. To create some sort of order to the stories, I divided them into three sections. The first section contains stories and commentaries dealing with my personal sporting experiences. In the second section, I expand the scope to stories about family. In the third section, the commentaries and essays are observations on topics of sports and life, generally beyond the family. The stories are roughly chronological within each section.

Because of the three distinct sections, there may be some confusion about the chronology of the stories. I attended Tilton School, graduating in 1964, followed by four years at Middlebury College, then four years in the army (three in Alaska, one in Vietnam). I married my college classmate, Mimi Seemann, in 1969, and our daughter, Julie, was born in 1977. After teaching and coaching for four years in an Anchorage high school, we moved back east, where I coached the Dartmouth Ski Team for 11 years. In 1990 I gave up my coaching job and established Morton Trails, a recreational trail design consulting business. In 1998, Mimi passed away from cancer. In 2001 I married Kay Howell, who had two children, Nelle and Blair. Kay and I are currently entertained (and sometimes worn out) by six wonderful grandchildren, to whom this book is dedicated.

Since the commentaries and articles appeared over the course of a couple of decades and dealt with a wide variety of topics, I often provided a bit of background, which in a collection like this may seem repetitive. I apologize for that.

A LOVE OF SPORTS AND THE OUTDOORS

Pond Hockey

Some of my most enjoyable hours in the wintertime have been spent playing pond hockey. I don't mean the slam-bang, fully-padded, Zamboni-manicured version of hockey you see on television; I'm talking about old-fashioned, pickup games played on neighborhood frog ponds.

The surface might have been larger or smaller than a regulation rink, depending upon recent snowfalls and how many kids showed up with shovels. Silky smooth ice was rare, but the bumps and ripples which Mother Nature provided made us better skaters. And those random cracks which commonly bisect pond ice added lots of entertainment. Without fail, some hotshot skater racing full tilt for the opposing goal would catch a blade in a crack and sprawl spread-eagled on the ice, while the rest of us hooted and cheered.

What really set our games apart were the unusual teams we produced. You could usually count on a couple of experienced hockey players showing up, adults who had played in college or older high school kids who had done a lot of skating. There seemed to be an unwritten rule that the really good players wouldn't take any shots at the goal, but instead would set up scoring opportunities for their less able teammates.

Occasionally however, when the teams were evenly matched or the action got a little rough, we "rookies" were treated to a battle of the hotshots, when former college players focused intensely on each other, ignored the rest of us, and demonstrated a speed on skates and an agility with the stick that left us spellbound.

At the other end of the ability scale were the younger kids, some of whom didn't even have skates. These squirts were regarded as moving obstacles on the ice, a minor nuisance to be avoided when attacking your opponent's goal. Occasionally, one of these little, snow-suited, ice-shufflers would fall on the puck, robbing a more skillful player of a certain goal. The resulting celebration would make you think the little kid had just been declared the MVP of the Stanley Cup playoffs.

Between the former college stars and the miniature Michelin men were the rest of us, a mixture of various ages, sizes, shapes, and abilities.

We practiced Women's Liberation long before we knew what it was. A spunky girl in figure skates who could go like the wind would always be picked ahead of some lazy guy we knew would tucker out twenty minutes into the game.

Occasionally we had to contend with a family dog as well. But this wasn't as much of a nuisance as you might imagine. Like the little kids, dogs were moving obstacles, part of the challenge of the game. When a dog snatched the puck and bolted for the nearest snowbank, it provided a welcome time-out in the hockey action until the puck was recovered.

Pond hockey was never boring, but the source of excitement was seldom predictable. Sometimes, kids would get too engrossed in the game and it would end in a fist fight. It was also common for one of us to trip over our own skates, slam down on the ice, and come up with a split lip or a bleeding scalp. But our most memorable day occurred when a well-intentioned hockey fan, in his new, plow-equipped International Scout, pulled off the road to enlarge our skating area. We stood back and cheered as he dropped the plow and headed for the pond. Our cheers caught in our throats when a loud C R R A A C K . . . resounded across the ice, and the front end of the Scout slowly settled beneath the surface. The driver scrambled from the cab, red-faced with anger and embarrassment. As he stormed off on foot, we stared at the partially submerged truck, afraid to skate closer because of the thin ice.

Before long the driver was back with a friend in a four-wheel-drive pickup. Within minutes they had retrieved the Scout from the pond, and amazingly, had it running again.

With his good humor restored, the driver warned us to stay away from the hole in the ice, hopped in his Scout and headed down the road. As he thanked his friend in the pickup, we heard him say he was headed to the village service station, just to be sure the Scout hadn't been damaged by its icy bath.

We heard the rest of the story a day or so later. Apparently, the fellow drove his Scout to town and pulled into the Gulf station. Unfortunately, the brakes were frozen solid and he went through the overhead door of the first bay at a pretty good clip. But it wasn't all bad luck. The mechanics were on a coffee break in the office, the first bay wasn't occupied by another car at the time, and the snowplow saved the Scout's front end from major damage. In fact, when it finally stopped, the Scout was pretty well positioned over the lift for the brake-thawing operation.

Sports and Life

The Agony of Tennis

Tennis is one of the most popular participation sports in America. Anyone can play, from young kids to senior citizens. And it's not just a fair-weather game anymore. People play tennis in cities from Anchorage to Boston all winter long, thanks to beautiful, indoor tennis clubs.

I used to play quite a lot of tennis. I grew up not far from a court where I was encouraged to learn the game. Though I never had formal lessons, by the time I was in high school, I could get the ball back over the net consistently, and most of my serves went in.

The school I attended had a tennis team every spring. The top six guys played on the varsity, while the rest of us comprised the j.v. The school scheduled eight matches on Saturdays throughout April and May. The format was always the same; our top six guys would play singles against the opposing school's top six, then those same athletes would pair up against each other and play three doubles matches. The school which won the majority of the nine contests was declared the winner. If the players from each school were evenly matched, and the games were close, it became a long day of tennis.

We were blessed with several very good players. A couple of the guys had been in youth programs since they were toddlers, and our top player was a nationally ranked junior. Normally, between Sunday and Friday, we would play inter-squad matches to determine who the six varsity and the six j.v. players would be for Saturday's competition.

Although I didn't have the classic strokes of the experienced players, I somehow managed to be among the top six j.v. players for every match during my freshman and sophomore years. Even more miraculously, I earned a spot on the varsity every weekend during my final two years. In four years of high school tennis, I never missed a Saturday. Two years of j.v. and two years of varsity: thirty-two consecutive singles matches. And I lost... every one of them!

It was uncanny, how week after week I managed to earn a spot on our traveling team, only to be defeated by my opponent from a rival school. Before long, my teammates would automatically tally my match in the loss column, even while we were warming up. By junior year, the coach would seed me first against the other schools, although I had only earned the fifth or sixth spot on our squad. I guess he figured if I was going to lose my match anyway, I might as well lose big, and maybe the other guys on our team could sneak out a victory or two.

My senior year we played Kimball Union Academy and I drew a player who must have had polio as a child. He had one leg that was several inches shorter than the other, and as we warmed up, he hobbled awkwardly around the court. *Finally*, I thought, after three years of defeats, I'm going to win a singles match!

The kid with the bum leg from K.U.A. was the best tennis player I ever faced. I could barely *see* his serves. Getting them back over the net was out of the question. When I served, he drilled his return to my baseline and hobbled to the net. If somehow I managed to get his shot back, he was waiting with an overhead slam that would have put me in the hospital if it had hit me. It was a quick match: six-love, six-love. And you should have seen that kid play doubles!

I finished out my senior spring on the varsity, and my record remained unblemished: thirty-two consecutive singles losses. The tennis coach made a special appearance at the school's commencement ceremony that year, just to be certain I was really graduating.

I love sports. They've been a central part of my entire life. I've actually been pretty successful in a couple of different sports, including a handful of age-group National Championships and two trips to the Winter Olympics as a competitor. But I'm afraid my one athletic achievement which will remain unchallenged is my high school tennis record. It kind of keeps me humble.

Glory Days on the Gridiron

It's that time of year again. For some inexplicable reason I waste three hours every Monday night watching Goliaths on steroids pulverize each other.

As a high school freshman I weighed 138 pounds. Since I couldn't kick, throw, or catch a football, I wound up playing right guard. Linemen practice by slamming into blocking sleds hour after hour, those contraptions you've seen the pros push across the field, usually with a coach along for the ride, yelling, "DRIVE... DRIVE... DRIVE, DIG... DIG... DIG." In my case the sled never budged. Instead, the recoil from the padded steel often bounced me back into teammates who were waiting their turn.

My pads and helmet never fit properly, which made it difficult to run and nearly impossible to see. But a right guard doesn't see much anyway. Facing off at the line of scrimmage, my view was filled with the sweating, mud-streaked faces and the bleeding knuckles of gigantic, opposing linemen.

We did a lot of yelling. We barked in cadence during our pregame warm up. We roared at the kickoff. We shouted and slapped our knee pads after every huddle, and we growled ferociously when we attacked the enemy. My head throbbed and my ears rang for days following every game. I figured it was from banging helmets all afternoon, but it might have been from all that yelling.

In four years of high school football, I was involved in three memorable plays. The main function of the reserve squad was to scrimmage the varsity. The assistant coach who supervised us bench-warmers, lived to upstage the head coach and the first-string offense. This rarely happened since most of the starters were experienced post-graduates (P.G.s) who had played for strong high school teams in Massachusetts and Connecticut.

During one of those scrimmages, the player across from me was a P.G. who weighed about 240 and stood six foot four inches. Although he was just walking through his blocking assignment, the offense had no problem running play after play right through my position. The defensive coach grabbed me by the face mask and hissed, "Are you gonna let that buffalo trample you all afternoon? Get the jump on him! Hit him low and hit him hard!"

The next play, I exploded off the line, buried my helmet in the P. G.'s gut, and drove him into their quarterback. When I emerged from the pileup, the head coach was scowling. My block had knocked the wind out of my opponent, but as he staggered back to their huddle, I heard him wheeze, "Run dat play again."

The only thing I remember after that is the blur of the P. G.'s forearm slamming me under the chin, and waking up later on the sidelines. My teammates said it was awesome. I did a complete back flip in the air, landing on my face in the dirt. Blood gushed from my nose all over my practice jersey. I was so proud of that stain, I wouldn't let them wash the shirt 'til the season was over.

My second football highlight actually took place in a game. As a defensive linebacker, I charged our opponents, expecting to get crushed as usual. But someone missed a block and I found myself face to face with their punter, who was holding the ball at arm's length, ready to launch it. My momentum carried me into the ball at the instant his foot made contact, in effect, kicking me and the ball back toward the scrimmage line. Doubled over and gasping for air, I clutched the ball to my stomach. The opposing coach screamed, "Roughing the kicker," but the officials had a pretty clear impression of who'd been roughed up. I was credited with blocking a punt and recovering a fumble. It was the only time in four years that I touched the ball during a game.

My final football experience took place early senior year. In the first preseason scrimmage, our coach called an "82 right," the play in which the right guard leads the ball carrier around the end, and theoretically throws the strategic block which breaks the runner free to sprint for a touchdown. It was an offensive guard's only chance for glory.

The quarterback barked the signals, the ball was snapped, I pivoted to my right, but before I could take a step, the opposing linebacker crunched my foot on his way in to maul our halfback. I heard a loud SNAP, and hobbled off the field with a broken ankle. I spent that fall on the sidelines in a cast: an insignificant casualty, dwarfed by roaring warriors.

Come to think of it, maybe that's why I can't resist Monday Night Football; I can finally see what the heck is going on. And, of course, I can turn down the volume whenever I like.

Track and Field Friends

I was recently reminded of a couple of old friends. My stepson is on his high school track team, so I have attended a few of his meets this spring. I had forgotten what a three-ring circus a track meet can be. I admired the determination of the young javelin throwers, many of whom struggled to stick the spear in the turf. I held my breath as a lanky boy led most of the 1,600-meter race, with laces flapping wildly from both shoes. And I was almost beaned by a discus that was launched 180 degrees off its intended course.

More than thirty years ago, I ran track in college. Sort of. Middlebury didn't have much of a track team in those days, although there were one or two truly outstanding athletes. This meant the otherwise easygoing track coach spent the final weeks of winter frantically cajoling Middlebury students to go out for track and field so that his ringers would have a team on which to participate. As a Nordic skier, I was running in the spring anyway, so training with the track guys wasn't a problem, and racing the mile and the two-mile at the meets simply added spice to the training.

But what began as a favor to the coach quickly began to pay unforeseen dividends. There were some wonderful guys on the track team, and several have remained lifelong friends. Glenn Govertsen was strong and fast, which made him successful at most of the events. Since I was entered in only the two distance races, I became Govertsen's agent. While he prepared for the 200-meter dash, for example, he'd send me across the field to see what heights the pole vaulters and high jumpers were clearing. When his name was called in the rotation, I'd announce to the officials that Glenn "passed," until the competition reached the height at which he wanted to start.

I have two vivid memories of Govertsen as a track athlete. The first is sitting in the grass changing his shoes. He was constantly changing his shoes. I'll bet he had half a dozen pair. Since it was common for the field events to be interrupted by a sprint, Glenn spent most of the track meet lacing and unlacing shoes.

The second image is of Govertsen exploding out of the blocks in a sprint and collapsing to the cinders in agony. None of us watching that day learned the details until later, but Glenn was so strong that the contraction of his thigh muscles at the sound of the gun fractured his femur.

Another college track personality who became a loyal friend was Art Coolidge. Art was a brilliant student majoring in math or physics (probably both), had a devilish sense of humor, and weighed 120 pounds, soaking wet. I'm sure he was teased about his size, but he usually got the last laugh. In the football training room, there was a lavish array of supplies: athletic tape, foot powder, Skin Lube to prevent chafing, and Atom Balm, which provided that deep-heating relief for sore muscles. One of Art's most daring pranks was to switch the Skin Lube and the Atom Balm, knowing that the 270-pound defensive tackle who put Atom Balm in his jock could have broken Coolidge in half, had it been discovered who made the switch.

Art was a gifted runner, far ahead of the rest of us who plodded through the distance events. But track is not just about outstanding individual performances, and Art knew that. In a close meet with arch rival, Norwich University, as we warmed up for the two-mile, Coolidge overheard the Norwich coach instruct his top runners to "stick with the leader, no matter what." Art grinned and reminded Middlebury's distance men to "stay on your pace schedules, I'll bring the cadets back to you."

The gun went off and Coolidge was away like a rabbit with the Norwich cadets in hot pursuit. After sprinting for a lap or two, Art would throttle back, and the rest of us would gain ground. After three or four of these sprints, he had the cadets worn to a frazzle. Then he dropped back on the final lap and talked his Middlebury teammates past the baffled cadets. Middlebury won the entire meet.

After college, Art continued running. He was the top American in the 1971 Boston Marathon, finishing seventh overall. He was a leading contender for the '72 Olympic Team until an injury forced him to withdraw from the trials.

I'm glad my stepson went out for track. It has brought back some great memories for me, and I have no doubt he's creating some great memories for himself.

14

Bee Hunting

Every summer we seem to have a stretch of weather when the temperature approaches triple digits, the air is thick with haze, and there's not a breath of wind. Those oppressively hot summer days are perfect for one of Vermont's oldest and most exciting sports.

Beekeeping is a happy, symbiotic relationships in which both parties benefit; the prudent beekeeper can harvest a supply of honey and beeswax, while the bees enjoy a residence relatively secure from their traditional enemies: fire, disease, and wild animals. But the ancient instinct for survival is strong, and even domestic colonies can't resist the temptation to swarm, an annual urge which compels honeybees to raise a second queen who will take 40 percent of the hive's population and find a new home. These swarms set up housekeeping anywhere that offers protection: abandoned buildings, junk cars, or when they are available, hollow trees.

A hot summer day, when the nectar is flowing, is perfect for bee hunting. The hunt begins in a remote field of wildflowers, preferably several miles from any domestic bee hives. The hunter sets out an irresistible lure for his quarry: diluted honey on a piece of honeycomb. Soon worker bees gather, tank up on the sweet mixture, and struggle to get airborne. They circle like overloaded 747s to gain altitude before zipping off to their colony on the proverbial beeline. Some bee hunters get fancy and mark workers with carpenter's chalk so a round trip can be timed, thereby providing an estimate of the distance to the hive.

This is where the excitement begins. When several bees seem to be flying off in the same direction, it's time to carefully close the honeycomb lure, including the bees still feasting on it, into an old shoe box. Honeybees are usually docile while working a good source of nectar, but they aren't thrilled about being imprisoned in an old box.

Holding the furiously buzzing container very carefully, the bee hunter heads off across the fields and through the woods on the beeline. After covering a half a mile or so, it's time to release the bees. Placing the box up on a stump or a fence post and gently removing the cover, the hunter slowly ducks out of the way. The liberated bees will climb and circle to orient themselves before making a new beeline back to their colony. Within minutes they'll return with reinforcements. If they appear to be headed in a new direction, the hunter replaces the cover on the shoe box, and heads off on the new line.

Eventually it becomes a treasure hunt, carefully searching the sun-dappled leaf canopies of majestic old hardwood trees and listening intently for the humming of the hard-working insects. The bees seem to favor living, rather than dead trees, and maples, beeches or oaks provide the best cavities for wild swarms. A hundred years ago, anyone who carved their initials on a bee tree owned it, but today it's much safer to consult the landowner before attempting to extract the treasure once it's located.

It's the final stage of this sport which provides the real excitement, requires some courage, and inflicts a certain amount of pain. The bee hunter returns to the tree loaded down with equipment. It's helpful to have an assistant for this aspect of the sport, but once they've gained some experience, assistants are hard to find.

It's usually necessary to cut the tree down with a chain saw. Although the wild colony will be better off installed in a conventional hive box, the bees don't understand this yet, and an army of angry workers will pour out of the tree to defend it. This is the most stressful part of the sport if you happen to be a participant, but very entertaining if you are observing from a safe distance. Once the tree is on the ground, the bee hunter reveals the golden treasure with a splitting maul and wedges. Large sections of honeycomb filled with brood cells are placed in a hive box to attract the queen.

At this point the air is thick with bees and it's very clear that they're angry. It's been said that bee venom has a positive effect on arthritis. If that's actually true, this is where the bee hunter gets cured for life. Soon the queen will discover the hive box and signal her workers that a new home has been found. Thousands of bees will be drawn to the box as if by magic, and will set to work establishing the new colony. A few nights later, after dark when the bees are clustered safely inside, the bee hunter returns with a pack frame to lug the treasure home.

So, if you're looking for some innovative way to amuse the kids on one of those sultry summer days, consider taking them out on a bee hunt. Just don't tell them where you got the idea.

Motorcycles

Summertime. The weather is hot, the roads are dry, and I want a motorcycle! When I was a kid, my dad came home one bright, summer day with a classic: a powerful Indian with turquoise fenders and a leather saddle fit for a thoroughbred. I sat on his lap as we roared around the neighborhood.

In college, motorcycles reappeared every springtime as reliably as the daffodils. After five months imprisoned in classrooms by snow and ice, many of my friends celebrated the return of warm weather by exploring Vermont's back roads on two wheels, at 80 miles an hour.

In those days of turmoil on college campuses, all-night vigils to protest the war in Vietnam, and demonstrations in support of racial integration, a third dispute divided college students: the rivalry between European and Japanese motorcycles. Honda, Kawasaki, and Suzuki were flooding America with fast, flashy machines. Their only drawback was the high-pitched whine of their engines, which inspired the derisive nickname, "rice grinders." Triumphs, BSAs, and BMWs on the other hand, were identifiable by a deep, throbbing roar, synonymous with power.

I had a friend in college who disassembled and rebuilt his Norton in his dorm room every winter to be certain it would run smoothly in the spring. When the weather finally got warm, he would rise at dawn (not typical for your average college student) and explore rural Vermont on his beautiful silver machine, returning just in time for late morning classes, his face wind-burned and bugs in his teeth. It was a spiritual experience for him.

Those were the days of discount airfares to Europe, youth hostels, and Eurail passes. A resourceful college student really could see the sights of Europe on five dollars a day. A popular variation on that travel theme was to buy a new Triumph in England or a BMW in Munich, and explore Europe on your new motorcycle.

I couldn't swing the plane ticket and the bike, so I settled for hitch-hiking. But at a tiny youth hostel in central Norway, I met Graham Bailey, a British motorcycle policeman on holiday, touring Scandinavia on his

Vincent 1000. I spent several days marveling at the unforgettable scenery of the Norwegian fjords astride the 747 of motorcycles, driven by one of the few Englishmen who routinely averaged better than 100 miles per hour on the famous Isle of Man racecourse. Needless to say, I was hooked.

As a London policeman, Graham Bailey said he could find me the motorcycle of my dreams at a bargain price from the police impound lot. When the right bike turned up, he would simply buy it, crate it, and ship it to me.

Back at college that fall, during a rough-and-tumble soccer game, I collided with another player and injured my foot. As I waited in the emergency room to be treated, an ambulance arrived with the victim of a motorcycle accident, and I had a front-row seat as a team of doctors and nurses tried frantically to save his life. I had never seen so much blood. The next day, I phoned Graham Bailey in London and canceled my order.

It was not until many years later that my interest in motorcycles was rekindled. I was almost forty, a mature, responsible family man, when I spotted an ad for a 1968 Triumph. It had been lovingly cared for and the price was reasonable. I couldn't resist.

The day I brought it home, I had to try it out. After all, how could I pass the test for an operator's license until I had spent a little time in the saddle? Besides, Thetford is blessed with an extensive network of back roads, and virtually no traffic. Except on that day. On a lonesome stretch of dirt, I passed a State Trooper. It was the first time I'd ever *seen* a Trooper in our town. He was headed in the other direction, and the road was narrow. I thought he might have failed to notice my unregistered bike, but no such luck. I got a ride home in his cruiser, which gave my wife a real scare as we pulled into the yard. I also got a ticket for operating an unregistered motor vehicle without an operator's license.

But I can take a hint. I just wasn't meant to have a motorcycle. That's okay, I've probably had more than my share of fun and excitement anyway. It's just that, on those hot, summer days...

I hope you folks roaring down the highway with the wind in your face are really enjoying yourselves.

Sailing

Ah… July. The hot sun sparkling on the water and a gentle breeze conjures up memories of sailing. For many, those memories are of blissful hours listening to the lap of the waves and the slap of the canvas. Not for me.

My introduction to sailing occurred at my cousin's place on Cape Cod, before I was a teenager. Stevie was a year older, the son of a naval officer and very confidant around the water. We had been allowed to take out his sailing dinghy without adult supervision, a thrilling prospect. The boat was so small, we were constantly shifting our positions to keep it from flipping. After a wonderful afternoon of zig-zagging across the salt water estuary, we returned triumphantly to the dock and our assembled parents and siblings. As Stevie skillfully guided us to the float, he instructed me to "sit on that gunnel." Instinctively, I did what I was told, as I had all afternoon. The dinghy came to a stop, Stevie stepped onto the dock, and I flipped into the water. When I surfaced, I was greeted by gales of laughter from the crowd of relatives and Stevie's smug grin, confirming that he had set me up.

Almost a decade later, after several weeks of tough summer training with my friend and skiing rival, Ned Gillette, he suggested a break. His dad, a dedicated weekend sailor, had entered a three-day race, and needed a crew. Ned assured me that physical fitness and a positive attitude were more important than sailing experience for this friendly competition. The race began at a fancy yacht club in Manchester-by-the-Sea, northeast of Boston, and I should have known by the size and splendor of the sailboats that this was not just a "friendly competition."

During the first leg, across Massachusetts Bay to the tip of Cape Cod, I was grilled for hours on the name and function of every rope and sail on the boat. It made the S.A.T. seem like a pop quiz. At Provincetown, we rounded a buoy and our mild-mannered skipper nearly went berserk because we were a little clumsy getting the spinnaker up. We roared into the night heading for some whistle buoy which seemed to be halfway to Ireland. I was awakened in the pitch dark for my four-hour watch, and cautioned to be absolutely silent. The wind had died and we were drifting through a dense fog. In the distance, we could hear the illusive whistle buoy as well as the fog horns from several of our rival boats. Ned's dad had demanded absolute silence because he didn't want to lead any of his competitors to the buoy. For what seemed like hours, we peered anxiously into the fog, searching for the marker and prepared to fend off other boats.

I don't remember how we finished in that race. I do know, however, that in the four decades since, during which I have participated or coached in hundreds of skiing events, including several Winter Olympic Games, I have never experienced a more intense, gut-wrenching determination to win. "Friendly competition"…my foot!

It took me another decade to return to sailing. As the Dartmouth ski coach, I was provided access to the college's sailing club on nearby Lake Mascoma. My sister's husband had grown up on a lake in Michigan, so I cajoled him into giving me a lesson. Unfortunately, the Dartmouth sailing dinghies were as unstable as my cousin Stevie's. My brother-in-law and I weren't far from the dock when we went over for the first time. A gracious club member in a motor launch came to our rescue, and we were soon underway again. But the winds on Lake Mascoma can be fickle, and we flipped again. After our fourth or fifth capsizing, the club member gave up on us. I don't think I advanced my sailing skills that day, but we got a lot of practice bailing.

Then there was the weeklong Outward Bound course in Maine's Penobscot Bay back in September '91. It was part of an innovative project joining American Vietnam vets with Soviet veterans of their war in Afghanistan. You've heard about the Outward Bound approach: put a bunch of people in a stressful situation, way out of their comfort zone, and let them work it out. Most of the Soviets had never even seen the ocean before! You get the picture.

For the past several summers, my wife's older brother has been after us to join his family for a relaxing sail on Lake Champlain. I'd love to accept, but I'm not sure I could stand the stress.

Skydiving

After almost thirty years, the sight of massive summer thunderheads still reminds me of my most exciting sports experience. I had just gone into the U.S. Army, and was stationed at Fort Benning, Georgia. It was 1968, with the Vietnam War in full swing. There was a long waiting list for Airborne School, and many of the soldiers who were desperate to become paratroopers were turned away, including a Citadel graduate who lived across the hall. He never gave up on his dream of an Airborne assignment, but in the meantime, he discovered the Fort Benning Sport Parachute Club.

He talked me into attending the club's orientation for new students. The format was simple: a series of evening classes, a few weekends of static line jumps where the parachute is opened automatically as the student exits the aircraft, and finally, the opportunity to free fall out of an airplane. I kept thinking, if this gung-ho Citadel grad can handle this, I suppose I can. So, we signed up for skydiving jump school.

The evening classes concentrated on three aspects of skydiving: malfunctions, packing the chute, and landings. The instructors were obviously trying to frighten the weak and timid out of the class, but the honor of my friend's southern military family kept us in it. We learned about streamers, May Wests, and several other varieties

of "trash," Airborne slang for a parachute which deploys incorrectly. Skydivers pack their own parachutes, so if your chute doesn't open properly, it's nobody's fault but your own. The classes devoted to packing the parachute commanded everyone's undivided attention.

Finally, we practiced the Parachute Landing Fall: "Feet and knees together, legs slightly bent, absorb the shock, then collapse to your side." For a couple of weeks, we were hopping and rolling off everything in sight: front steps, picnic tables, first-floor windows.

Then one hot Sunday morning at Fort Benning's airfield, we boarded an ancient, single-engine army Beaver for our first jump. The fuselage had a gaping hole where the side door had been. Prop wash and exhaust fumes blasted us, as the old plane struggled to gain altitude. Finally, the jump master snapped our static lines to a hook above the door, and unceremoniously pushed us out like sacks of potatoes. The glide to earth was peaceful and strangely silent after the deafening roar of the airplane. Landing was remarkably similar to our hops off the picnic table.

Within a couple of weeks, my Citadel friend and I had survived four "hop and pops." In those days, the fifth static line jump and the first free fall were supposed to occur on the same day. Massive thunderheads were building in the Georgia heat on the Sunday we were to become real skydivers.

"Now look you guys, we'll take you right up for your fifth static line, then get those chutes packed quick so we can get the free fall in before the weather gets nasty."

As we roared skyward, the approaching thunderheads towered above us. Moments later, when we hit the gravel and gathered up the armload of fabric, the jump master shouted above the wind.

"I've saved space for you guys on the next lift. Get 'em packed and let's go!"

The sky was ominously dark, and my pulse was throbbing in my ears. My first free fall... into a thunderstorm! The wind whipped the nylon as I tried to untangle the lines and fold the fabric. Nervously, I stuffed the folded mass into the backpack and threaded the rip cord. As the jump master hustled us to the loaded airplane, a nagging suspicion gnawed at my stomach. Over the roar of the engine, I shouted to the jump master, "I'm not sure about my packing job. Will you take a look?"

A look of frustration crossed his face, but safety was so firmly ingrained, he nodded and dragged me away from the prop wash. In seconds, he had the pack on the ground, the fabric unfurled, and was running his fingers down the critical risers. When he reached a tangle in the lines, he looked up with a smile, "Good instincts, soldier, you've packed yourself a streamer for sure. You dying to try out your reserve 'chute on your first free fall, or what?"

Right there on the runway, he coached me through a proper repacking job, and within minutes I was crammed back into the old airplane. The joy of free falling is just that, the indescribable adrenalin rush of falling, unencumbered, toward the earth. Deploying the parachute is little more than a necessary requirement to ensure a safe landing. That day in Georgia, however, I set records for the shortest free fall in history. The feeling of the abrupt tug as the canopy opened remains one of the greatest sensations of my life. Almost thirty years later, my pulse still races when those summer thunderheads roll in, but here on the ground they never seem quite as menacing.

Sports and Life

Pelé

In the autumn of 1968, I was a brand-new second lieutenant assigned to the Infantry School at Fort Benning, Georgia. The executive officer of our company had played soccer in college, and shouted with excitement when he noticed that Atlanta's professional soccer team, the Chiefs, would be hosting the famous Santos from Brazil. The rest of the soldiers in the office regarded Mike's enthusiasm with amusement. Football, basketball, and stock car racing were the only sports which aroused that kind of excitement in Columbus, Georgia.

"Hey guys, they're playing a night game. We could leave after work and make it to Atlanta in plenty of time. I'll call and get tickets, who wants to go?"

Silence.

"Don't you guys know about the Santos? They're the best soccer team ever! Pelé, their star player, is the highest paid athlete in the world!"

"Who? You 'spect us ta believe some little Brazilian with one name makes more money than A.J. Foyt or Broadway Joe Namath? Come on, Mike!"

The Ex.O. stormed out of the office followed by laughter and a couple of parting shots at the game of soccer.

I caught up with Mike later, and told him I'd love to see the game. Although I had never played organized soccer, I had heard of Pelé. To be honest, I shared the disbelief of the others, that some little guy from south of the border, who played a sport largely unknown in the States, could command more for his athletic prowess than any of the sports heroes in America. If Pelé was for real, it would be worth the trip to Atlanta to see him play.

A couple of weeks later, four of us piled into Mike's car and headed north. In the warm Georgia evening, the orange glow of sunset faded, but the stadium and surrounding neighborhood was illuminated by hundreds of floodlights. There were so few cars in the parking lot, I was afraid we had come on the wrong night. But we entered the stadium to see soccer players warming up on the brilliant green turf, and a handful of fans gathered in the seats down next to the field.

The teams were taking practice shots at their goal keepers. The Atlanta team had several lanky Africans and a few rugged-looking Europeans. The Brazilians were compact, muscular, and fast. One at a time the players would take a pass from a teammate and drill the ball at the net. Their goalie would launch himself horizontally and snatch the ball to his chest or punch it far out onto the field. Pelé, wearing number 10 for the Santos, spent most of the warmup period chipping passes to his teammates

and retrieving shots that went over the net.

When the game began, the action consisted of crisp passing and skillful defense. The teams seemed equally matched. The Chiefs would threaten the Brazilians' goal, only to have the ball stolen and brought back down field by the Santos. As the first half wound to a close, Mike announced, "You guys want anything? I'm going to beat the rush to the hot dog counter."

Moments later, Pelé took a pass in front of the Brazilian goal. Looking half asleep, he dribbled the ball toward midfield. We were sitting high enough in the stands so that I could see what Pelé must have seen: the Chief's goalkeeper, out in front of his net, head down, smoothing the dirt with his feet. Pelé was still a few yards short of midfield, but without a windup, on the next step, he launched the ball high into the lights.

I remember looking for the referee, wondering if the first half had expired, but like magic, the ball came down out of the glare and struck the earth directly in front of the Atlanta goalie. In disbelief, he swatted helplessly as the ball bounced over his head, hit the crossbar, and ricocheted into the net.

There was shocked silence in the stadium, none of us really believing what we had seen. Then the place erupted. The small but loyal crowd of soccer fans had come to see the legendary Pelé do his stuff, and he hadn't let us down. As the ovation continued, the little Brazilian, still near midfield, faced the crowd, flashed a shy smile, and took a modest bow.

Soon, Mike returned, loaded down with hot dogs and Cokes. "I heard the cheering, wha'd I miss?"

I've thought about that game in Georgia quite a bit lately. I even considered getting tickets to one of the World Cup games in Boston. But almost thirty years ago in Atlanta, I had the amazing good fortune to watch Pelé, the greatest man who ever played soccer. I'm not sure even a World Cup game could top that.

Sports and Life

Hoops in Phung Hiep

In August of 1970, I stepped out of a stretched DC-8 into the intense sunlight and sweltering heat of South Vietnam. Often, it feels like yesterday, yet at other times, it could have been a previous life. I had been yanked directly from Alaska, where I was assigned to a small unit training for the Winter Olympics. Without a doubt, I was the most poorly prepared infantry officer in Vietnam. My previous two years on active duty had consisted of international biathlon competitions, skiing and shooting in weather conditions well below the freezing point. I had never commanded a military unit, I had never fired an M-16, and I'd had zero experience communicating on the radio. I was terrified by the prospect of calling in artillery or requesting a medevac.

So, consistent with many of the decisions our government made in Southeast Asia, and taking into account my total lack of useful experience, the U.S. Army made me an advisor to the Vietnamese, put me in charge of a five-man Mobile Advisory Team, and dropped us into a tiny village on the Mekong Delta. Our mission was "to win the hearts and minds of the people."

Unfortunately, by the time we arrived, the Viet Cong had already won their hearts and minds. In retrospect, the only reason we stayed out of serious trouble was because the local V.C. were confident of their victory. To openly confront us would have only prolonged the American withdrawal.

There weren't many options in the way of sport in the combat zone. I'm sure the big American units sponsored softball and volleyball tournaments within the relative security of their bases, and I know there were tennis courts in cities like Saigon and Can Tho. There were also stories of Americans water skiing behind river patrol boats, but I suspect that was more of a stunt than recreation. Nobody I knew in the Delta swam in the canals for the fun of it. We were doing everything we could to stay dry.

I do however, have one vivid sports memory from my tour in Vietnam. Our district capital, a busy town called Phung Hiep, located at the confluence of five canals, had a crude basketball court crammed between the open-air market and several humble homes. One evening our district senior advisor, a no-nonsense, former West Point football player, recruited five of us to take on the Vietnamese in a game of hoops. We walked from the protection of our compound to the center of Phung Hiep, where a crowd of eager Vietnamese spectators waited.

Five of us took positions on the court, while the sixth chambered a round in his M-16 and stood guard. Five wiry Vietnamese men stepped from the crowd and took positions at the other end of the court. There were no referees. The crowd of bright-eyed kids, mothers with infants on their hips, and ancient grandfathers completely surrounded the shabby, concrete court.

Major Haushill, who had brought the ball, tossed it to the Vietnamese, offering them first possession. It was immediately evident that they had played before. They were fast. Their passes were crisp and accurate. And although we towered over them, eventually one of the agile Vietnamese would break free, take a shot and score. There were no rebounds when the Vietnamese shot.

We took the ball to their end with the clumsy, lumbering strides of men in combat boots and jungle fatigues. We passed, and shot, and rebounded, high above the heads of our opponents, until finally, we scored. The game seldom broke that pattern. The spectators got into it, clapping and cheering when one of their heroes sunk a long shot, laughing politely behind their hands when we put up one of our frequent air balls.

The games were amazingly even, and Major Haushill usually called it quits as we ran out of daylight and he knew the score was tied. The Vietnamese played with fierce concentration, and they clearly relished the enthusiasm of their fans.

I can't remember if we shook hands after the games or not. There was little doubt, however, that at least a couple of our opponents were Viet Cong. It has caused me to wonder often during the decades since, how different everything would have been if we could have settled our conflict with them on the basketball court. If we could have walked away at sunset calling it a draw. If we could have saved all those lives.

Windsurfing

Back in the early 1970s, while I was living in Alaska, a German friend visited his childhood home in Garmisch and got all fired up about a new sport which had taken his native country by storm, windsurfing. He became hooked immediately and returned to Alaska with a brand-new sailboard and the exclusive rights to distribute the product in the 49th State.

Alaska promotes itself as "The Sportsman's Paradise," and few people who have lived there would dispute that claim, but I don't think they had boardsailing in mind when they coined that slogan. Great windsurfing requires wind and water, and of course Alaska has both in abundance. But there are a couple of drawbacks. For starters, even when the lakes aren't frozen solid, the water is so cold that fisherman figure if they fall in, they have seven minutes before hypothermia makes survival unlikely. And talk about wind. Chinooks roar in off the Pacific with such force that the Cook Inlet is whipped into a froth of whitecaps, and huge container ships remain docked until the winds subside.

Into this "Sportsman's Paradise" my German friend introduced windsurfing. He was so eager for me to try his new sport that he could barely wait until the middle of May when the ice melted in Big Lake, a couple of hours north of Anchorage. His instructions were brief: "Hey, you a skier. You haf great balance. Dis vill be easy for you. You fall a few times like everybody, den you gets the hang of it. You going love it!"

He was right about one thing, I fell a few times. Actually, I fell a lot. Even though he gave me a wet suit jacket, I spent so much time in the water that before long I was shivering uncontrollably. Because I was a stubborn athlete, and because my friend was German, we kept at it. My hands grew numb, my teeth chattered, and my knees were bruised from climbing out of that freezing water, back onto the board.

After an hour, we finally gave up. My friend was mystified: "I can't understand it, you're a skier, yes? Dis should not be so hard for you." Although ever since that day I've been embarrassed by my failure, I do take some comfort in the fact that his Alaskan sailboard dealership never caught on.

A few years ago, happily settled in Vermont, my wife, Mimi, and I were looking for a sport which we could enjoy together. Mimi loves the outdoors, especially hiking, canoeing, and camping. One of my fellow ski coaches at Dartmouth spent the off season supervising the college's Ledyard Canoe Club on the Connecticut River. Windsurfing had become a popular summer sport among the students. The club responded by providing lessons and offering a wide selection of sailboards for rental.

When Mimi suggested we take windsurfing lessons together, I suppressed my Alaskan nightmare, and reluctantly agreed. On a beautiful, warm, and totally calm summer day, we arrived at the river for our first lesson. Using a small rubber figurine on a miniature sailboard, my ski-coaching buddy went over the basic principles: how to balance on the board, how to hold the sail, how to lean into the wind, and the trickiest maneuver, moving around the sail to change directions. Understanding the fundamentals for the first time, I was feeling confident. His lecture concluded and we prepared to launch our boards. As Mimi went to change into her bathing suit, I helped Tim rig the windsurfers.

"We have only one learner's board," he said. "It's so big and stable we call it the White Elephant. A family of four could take it out on picnic, with no danger of tipping over. It'll be perfect for Mimi. She can concentrate on her sailing technique and never give a thought to balance. Once she gets the hang of it, we'll move her up to a lighter, more maneuverable board. Since you've tried windsurfing before, I'll put you on this new competition model which just arrived. You'll love it. Of course, it performs a lot better in a steady breeze. On a calm day like today it may seem a little tippy, but you'll get the hang of it."

Well, I didn't get the hang of it. Mimi rode the White Elephant across the glassy river like a pro, while I fell off and climbed back on the competition sailboard, time after time. As I struggled to control my temper, Tim gave me plenty of space and concentrated on encouraging Mimi.

She had a wonderful windsurfing experience. She loves to remind me that Tim called her the best student he had ever taught, a real natural for the sport.

I haven't totally given up on boardsailing. I wonder if they would rent the White Elephant at night, so I could fall off for a couple of weeks in private, until I got the hang of it?

In the Hall of the Mountain King

Well it's that time of year again. If you live near the woods (and most Vermonters do), you dress in the brightest clothes you can find. Perfectly normal people walk out to their mailboxes in outfits so colorful they would be the envy of the clowns in the Big Apple Circus. I'll bet half the dogs in the state spend the month of November in blaze orange vests. And more than once I've seen cows with large letters painted on their flanks, as if they just stepped off the page of a kindergarten reading book.

All these precautions are in anticipation of Vermont's most sacred ritual, deer-hunting season. Having survived the annual onslaught of leaf peepers from "down country," the locals now close up shop and head off to deer camp with a couple of loyal hunting buddies. I suppose being a Vermonter and not going deer hunting is like living in Colorado and not skiing, or spending your life in Hawaii and avoiding the beach.

My introduction to hunting occurred when I was twelve. A classmate's dad took the two of us to hunter safety classes, then to a gravel pit for shooting practice, and finally into the woods on opening day. It was cold, wet and foggy. Before long the excitement had worn off. My friend and I were soaked and shivering. We had had our fill of deer hunting. To his credit, my friend's father realized that a positive experience was more important than bringing home venison, so he stopped and built a small campfire to warm us up. It was the classic scene: the three of us stamping our feet around the smoky fire in the foggy drizzle, our rifles leaning against nearby trees, when a magnificent buck floated over a stone wall not fifty yards away, and stopped in confusion to stare at us.

My friend's dad reacted first of course, and before the deer could escape, we made the woods sound like the Battle of Gettysburg. I had a lever action 30/30. Later we discovered that in my excitement, I had ejected all four rounds from my rifle without ever pulling the trigger. Talk about buck fever!

After college, a tour of duty in the U.S. Army took me to Alaska. If hunting is an annual ritual in Vermont, it is a way of life in the 49th State.

The residents talk about two varieties of hunting, sport hunting and filling the freezer. Moose and caribou are plentiful, and the meat is delicious. But an Alaskan moose can easily weigh a thousand pounds, and the work involved in hiking out the meat is staggering. It was a great relief that moose season came only once a year.

But having filled the freezer, there was nothing to compare with the sport of hunting Dall sheep. These are the nimble animals which thrive in the jagged summits of Alaska's countless mountains. Simply being up in those peaks, far above tree line, surrounded by rocks and cliffs, is a significant challenge for any hunter. Dall sheep are blessed with phenomenal eyesight in addition to their uncanny dexterity on the sheer rock faces. Alaskans who hunt Dall sheep return home inspired and renewed, though frequently without an animal.

The year I left Alaska for Vermont, my schedule permitted one last sheep hunt. Two friends were eager to go along, so we hiked deep into the Talkeetna Mountains to a remote valley which had looked promising on the map and was spectacular on the ground. We set up a base camp on the soft tundra surrounded by jagged peaks, hanging glaciers, and picturesque alpine pastures. After four exhilarating days of scrambling over boulders and across crevasses, I rounded an outcropping of rock and stood face to face with a startled ram. For some unknown reason, rather than bolting to safety up the cliff, he stood transfixed, as we stared at each other. Perhaps if he had moved, I would have shouldered my rifle, for in a decade of Alaskan hunting, it was without question my easiest shot. Instead, as we studied one another, the title of a piece of Norwegian music filled my mind, "In the Hall of the Mountain King."

After several minutes, I retreated around the cliff, and back to base camp. Though I never fired a shot, it was my most memorable hunt.

Years later, after I was settled here in Vermont, I tried deer hunting a couple of times. I understand the magic of the ritual, and I love being out in the woods, but I saw far more hunters than I did animals. I guess I've been spoiled by the jagged peaks and the Dall sheep of Alaska. But it was worth it.

The Cosmic Message

Anyone who has spent time in the outdoors recognizes that Mother Nature often sends little messages to those alert enough to notice. The wind may subtly change direction long before threatening storm clouds are visible. The ice on a frozen pond cracks and shifts ominously as an overzealous skater ventures out.

Sometimes these natural signals send personal messages. Once, I was struggling through the final miles of a footrace, tired, weak, and feeling sorry for myself, when a large hawk swooped low over the road and perched on a nearby tree. As the hawk watched me run past, I was inspired by the strength and speed which the bird embodies. I picked up my pace and finished the race with a respectable time after all.

It is said that centuries ago, the Aztecs of Central America followed their spiritual leaders on a seemingly endless journey to establish a new home. When their leader finally observed an eagle drop from the sky, then take flight with a large snake in its beak, he declared the search over and established what has become Mexico City. These little signals occur frequently enough that I hesitate to discount them as pure coincidence.

Not long ago, I was working in the woods with my chain saw. As is often the case, Klister, the family black lab, was keeping me company. At lunchtime we returned to my truck, which was parked on a neglected logging road, bordered by a ditch. I filled the dog's dish with chow, set it next to the ditch, then hopped on the tailgate to enjoy my own lunch. Soon Klister was prancing around, eagerly anticipating whatever leftovers I might share with her. Finally, she stood still, straddling the shallow ditch and gazing at me expectantly. Between mouthfuls of my sandwich, I glanced in her direction and spotted a large snake directly beneath her. The snake was motionless, probably sensing danger from the dog. It reached from under Klister's chin to beyond her tail.

Normally alert and curious, Klister was totally oblivious to the snake directly beneath her. As I studied the scene, I noticed a large bulge a couple of inches behind the head of the snake. Ah ha, I thought, that explains it. The dog, doing her best to interrupt my lunch with her begging, has interrupted this snake's after dinner nap, and it's too groggy to move.

But as the seconds ticked by, I wondered if the snake wouldn't eventually come to its senses, and bite Klister out of self- defense. I dropped off the tailgate to get the unsuspecting dog away from the snake, but no luck. Anticipating a snack, Klister pranced eagerly, and a paw landed firmly on the snake. I jumped, and yanked the confused dog out of the ditch before she was bitten. Once the dog was safe, I turned back to the ditch and saw the snake, indented by the dog's paw, but minus the large bulge behind its head.

In fact, a few inches in front of the snake was a frog, appearing confused and disoriented. This frog can't possibly be alive, I thought. That bulge appeared to have been well into the snake's digestive tract, before Klister intervened. But when I put a finger down to the frog, it hopped away convincingly.

The snake, meanwhile, paying no attention to me, the dog, or the frog, slithered down the ditch in the opposite direction. By the time it disappeared in the grass, the dog print was no longer visible on its sleek anatomy.

This cosmic message has me stumped. A totally oblivious dog steps on a snake, saving the life of a frog, without injuring the snake, and miraculously, without being bitten herself. Both frog and snake calmly exit the scene in opposite directions, and the dog has no clue of the starring role she played in this life-and-death drama.

I suspect there's a profound omen here, but I'll be darned if I can figure it out.

The Simple Pleasures of the Winnipesaukee Relay

I love foot-running because it's so uncomplicated. A pair of shorts, a T-shirt, your running shoes, and you're ready to go. So, when a friend suggested we put together an eight-man relay team for the annual race around Lake Winnipesaukee, it sounded like a fun idea. With typical enthusiasm he gushed, "I've already talked with Jon, Bob and Joe. Including the two of us, we only need three more guys over forty, and we'll have a terrific masters team!"

In a moment of weakness, I agreed to serve as team captain. Finding three additional runners turned out to be more difficult than I had anticipated. It took scores of phone calls and some shameless begging, but eventually we had eight guys over forty willing to race.

The total distance of the relay was 65 miles: the shortest segment, 4 miles, and the longest, 11 miles. There turned out to be a macho appeal to the longer segments and several team members expressed the attitude "if I'm going all the way over to Winnipesaukee, I might as well get a decent workout."

Everyone seemed to have personal commitments and family obligations as well, which added to the confusion. One guy had to run the lead-off leg at 8 a.m., so he could get back in time to see his son's high school football game. Another fellow couldn't leave home until after a business meeting, and a third teammate was expected at his daughter's birthday party in the afternoon.

This led to the "transportation shuffle." Since many of the roads around Lake Winnipesaukee are narrow, the rules allowed each team only two support vehicles for dropping off and picking up runners at the seven tag zones. With commitments to football games, business meetings, and birthday parties, I needed a computer to figure out how each team member would get to his starting point and who would retrieve him after his race.

Then there was the distribution of the racing numbers, and the official release forms which had to be signed by each team member. Since our runners were scattered throughout the Upper Valley, and a couple were out of town on business, it was no simple task to get their signatures.

Just when I was beginning to get on top of the whole situation, two of the guys bailed out. Business commitments and a nagging injury had forced them to withdraw.

I called my friend with the discouraging news. "No problem," he said with characteristic optimism, "you start calling, I'll start calling, and we'll round up a couple more forty-year-olds."

Many phone calls later I successfully corralled a fifty-year-old friend. When I checked in with my enthusiastic teammate, he responded, "Great, then we're all set, 'cause I got someone too."

"Who'd you get?" I asked.

"A gal at work, but she's a good runner and she's over forty!"

By the morning of the relay I had little hope of anything working out. We would travel to Winnipesaukee in five vehicles, only two of which had the required traffic permits. By studying a course map, our runners were estimating when their teammates would reach the various tag zones, but none of us had actually ever run the course before. Our last-minute replacements had neither signed the release forms, nor received their race numbers from the original team members, who had been forced to withdraw.

Miraculously, everything worked out. Well, almost. Our masters men team wasn't disqualified because it included one woman. Somehow, everyone found their starting points on time, although Marcia ran her segment so fast that Joe was in the woods taking a pee when she arrived at the tag zone. Minutes later, as Marcia and I drove Joe's car to the end of his section, the timing belt failed and the car quit. While I hitchhiked to the nearest service station for help, the local police spotted the car, accused Marcia of parking illegally, and towed her away.

Our team finished the race, and we eventually recovered Marcia and the car. The insurance company might even reimburse Joe the six-hundred dollars it cost for towing and repairs.

I'm not sure we'll be competing in the Winnipesaukee Relay next year. As I mentioned earlier, what appeals to me about running is its simplicity. On the other hand, we have worked out some of the logistics, we know where all of the tag zones are, and Marcia runs faster than most of the men her age.

Sports and Life

44

The Finish Line

Until recently, I had always assumed it was much more exciting to participate in a footrace than to watch one. That changed a couple of years ago. Thanks to the efforts of a civic-minded parent named Dan Grossman, Thetford Academy was awarded the honor of hosting the New England High School Cross Country Running Championships. Winning the bid kicked off a tremendous community effort to design and build a new 5-kilometer cross-country course. In addition, it was necessary to recruit and train more than one hundred volunteers who would conduct a competition for five hundred of the best high school athletes in New England.

We made slow but steady progress as the big day approached. In his role as the event director, Dan became the commanding general of an eager army of community workers. Several weeks prior to the championship, he asked what assignment I'd like during the competition.

"Just keep me away from the finish line," I answered. "I know how many things can go wrong, so I'd rather be at the far end of the course."

"Wherever you want," he assured me.

November 14th was a classic Vermont autumn day: a clear blue sky and brisk, invigorating air. There was only one complication. The date, dictated to us by the New England Championship Committee, just happened to fall on opening day of deer-hunting season. Several of our experienced volunteers were apologetic, but nothing took priority over opening day of deer season.

As I headed to my post at the far end of the course, Dan approached, looking serious. Without preamble he announced, "Sorry, but I need you at the finish line." It was not a debatable request.

A dozen finish line volunteers were chatting as I explained that I had been reassigned to their crew. Due to the magnitude of the event, we had hired a professional timing service, so the head timer gave us our last-minute instructions.

"You folks have two important missions," he said. "The first is to keep the runners in order once they cross the line and head down the chutes; the second is to keep finishers from piling up and obstructing the finish line."

"No problem," a volunteer announced with confidence.

"Well, there's the potential for big problems! These are all good athletes and they're very competitive. You'll see one hundred runners cross this line within the same minute!" That was almost two every second! I began to feel sick to my stomach.

Soon the gun went off, and a throng of 250 high school girls scampered across the fields and into the woods. There were anxious remarks at the finish line. "Do they stay bunched up like that for the whole race?"

We had our answer seventeen minutes later when the leaders emerged from the woods, and charged toward us. The first fifteen girls graciously finished one at a time, congratulated each other while gasping for breath, and staggered down the chute in order. We volunteers exchanged glances. "This isn't so bad. We can handle this."

Then someone moaned, "Oh no," and we turned to see a pack of thirty girls sprinting down the home stretch. One of the leaders, wheezing and coughing, got two steps beyond the finish line and collapsed. The girls behind her tripped in a heap over the fallen athlete. We scrambled frantically to untangle the runners and sort them into the correct finish order: pushing some girls ahead in the line, dragging others back. A doctor ministered to the fallen competitor, while other volunteers deflected the incoming stream of exhausted runners around the obstruction.

Within minutes it was over. The finish line crew looked shell-shocked. Faces were pale, and eyes were wide with disbelief. No one spoke. The professional timer poked his head out of his van.

"Nice going folks, I think you kept them in order. That's a real accomplishment for your first big race."

"Will the boy's race be as bad is this one?" someone asked timidly.

"Oh this was just a warmup for the boy's race. The girls are polite and considerate. The boys will run over each other, and all of you, to be first down that finish chute."

He was right of course, though miraculously none of us actually got trampled, and somehow we managed to keep them all in order. His prediction of more than one hundred finishers within one minute turned out to be right on target.

Reluctantly, I have become a permanent fixture on the finish line crew, and have survived several championship events. It has given me an entirely new perspective on running.

If you know anyone who thinks footraces are boring, have them give Dan a call. He's always looking for fresh volunteers to work the finish line.

Running Through Mud Season

One of the things I really love about living in Vermont is the distinct seasons. Remember those warm, fragrant spring days, when entire hillsides are dressed in the delicate pastels of apple blossoms? How about the long, hot, summer days when Holsteins graze placidly in deep green pastures? Of course, a Vermont winter has its own brand of beauty: heavy icicles hanging from the roof of a red barn under a thick blanket of snow. And of course there's autumn, Vermont's famous fireworks display when the hardwoods put on a show which many say is unequaled on earth.

But there's another season here, which seldom makes it into the Vermont Life calendars. Long-time residents simply call it "mud season." It usually lasts from early March to late April. Nobody talks about enjoying mud season, it's more a question of just getting through, survival. Even the most avid winter sports enthusiasts among us have had their fill of snow and ice by late March. The snow gets heavy and wet, while the ice on the ponds becomes too risky. But it's far too sloppy for summer games like golf or tennis, and fishing season is still a month away.

A few Vermonters cop out and head south to Florida or Arizona, leaving the rest of us to muddle through mud season as best we can. I seriously question whether these traitors should be considered real Vermonters anyway. After all, part of living in Vermont is enduring a certain amount of hardship. We bump into these folks at the post office around the first of May, all suntanned in short-sleeved shirts, while the rest of us still don't trust the weather enough to give up our wool and flannel. No, leaving Vermont for mud season is not a morally acceptable survival technique.

But I've discovered two time-tested methods for beating the mud season blues. The first is typically Vermont, wrestling something of value from adversity: maple sugaring. If you've ever wondered why that golden liquid is so pricey, just stumble through a mud season, sugaring. It's very hard work! Often you're tromping for hours through a shin-deep crust gathering sap. Add to that the back-breaking work of hauling and pouring. Even when you get the sap to the sugar house, there's an endless pile of wood to be split and the constant stoking of the fire. Of course, if the sap's running well, you're boiling most of the night just to keep up. But sugaring is one heck of a way to get through mud season. By the time the sap stops running, the snow's gone and the daffodils are sprouting.

There's a second, legitimate way to survive mud season that isn't quite as tough as maple sugaring. Enter the Boston Marathon. For a hundred years the Boston Marathon has been held on Patriot's Day, a Monday in mid-April. Nobody runs a marathon without a little preparation, so you'll be training right through mud season.

Actually, training for the marathon up here in the Green Mountains is a tremendous advantage, psychologically. You're certainly not going to see anything on those famous 26 miles from Hopkinton to Boston more challenging than what you've already seen dozens of times during your training runs in March. Bad weather? Heck, I've started out on a long run the week after Saint Patrick's Day in shorts and a T-shirt, then barely made it home through a full-scale blizzard!

And all that hype you hear about Heartbreak Hill? If you train in Vermont, you won't be impressed. During my first Boston Marathon several years ago, I was dreading that ominous terrain feature, which I knew was about 20 miles into the race. I was relieved to discover that the infamous "Heartbreak" wouldn't even qualify as a hill here in Vermont.

Another wonderful benefit of running your way through mud season is that you really get to experience it. You'll stagger back home, numb from cold on those last days of winter, and sweating on those occasional, warm, spring days. You'll get to smell everything from woodstoves to pastures spread with fresh manure. You'll notice, maybe for the first time, extended minutes of sunlight, day after day. You'll hear the birds sing!

Perhaps one of the most unexpected benefits of my Boston Marathon Mud Season Survival Plan, is that you'll have more contact with your neighbors. In fact, if you run at the same time every day, you'll smile and wave at people in their cars whom you don't even know, and they'll smile and wave back.

Then you'll go to Boston in mid-April to run the marathon. The air down there will be rich with the smells of spring. You'll run in shorts. The fruit trees and flowers will be blooming. You'll get all caught up in the excitement of the event. But best of all, when you return to Vermont, it will be spring. You'll be in great physical shape for summer. And another mud season will be history. Hey, it works for me.

Sports and Life

Competitive Gardening

If there's one thing an endurance athlete hates, it's quitting. At some point in every long race, the blisters, the frost-nipped fingers or the overwhelming sense of fatigue makes dropping out seem like a very reasonable option. But every competitor knows that quitting once makes it even easier to drop out the next time that things get tough. So, endurance athletes hate to give up, at anything... ever.

For this reason, it's with shame that I am forced to admit that I've given up gardening. I simply can't stand the competition. Years ago, when I returned to Vermont from Alaska, I eagerly planted a massive vegetable garden. Growing vegetables in Alaska was for masochists. Oh, those postcards you've seen of seventy-pound cabbages from the Matanuska Valley, they're authentic, all right. Summer days with twenty hours of sunlight can do amazing things to some plants. But how many delicious recipes do you know for cabbage and Brussels sprouts? Then of course, there are the moose. Those giant cabbages are just appetizers for a typical Alaskan moose, and what they don't eat, they trample.

So, I was really excited about gardening when I returned to Vermont after ten years in the Land of the Midnight Sun. I rototilled half the open land on the property and spent fifty bucks on seeds. I hauled and spread several truckloads of cow manure. When the garden site was finally ready, I went wild! I planted three varieties of potatoes, four types of tomatoes, and five strains of sweet corn. I had pickling cucumbers and salad cucumbers. I started cantaloupe and watermelon. I had bib lettuce, leaf lettuce and iceberg lettuce. I went way overboard with peas and beans. I got so excited, I even planted stuff my family never ate, like beets and chard.

Having struggled with an Alaskan garden, I thought I was prepared for Mother Nature's challenges. I knew there would be days when I'd be engulfed by mosquitoes as I weeded, and no doubt there would be dry spells when I'd have to haul water until my hands hung below my knees. What I didn't anticipate was how methodically a woodchuck can clean off row after row of tender seedlings. I was amazed by how quickly I had cultivated a vast population of Colorado potato beetles. I learned firsthand about aphids, cut worms, and slugs.

But I fought hard against the bugs and worms because, miraculously, some of my seedlings were actually surviving! With great pride, I began to haul my homegrown delicacies to the kitchen for my wife and daughter. The first few zucchini were greeted with enthusiasm, but before long it was suggested that I should share some of my bounty with the neighbors. People were polite at first, but one crusty old friend was more candid. "You beginning gardeners are all the same," he said. "I appreciate your generosity, but what am I going to do with forty pounds of zucchini? I have a garden of my own, you know."

About that time the broccoli started coming in, and in my eagerness to get it on the table, I made an unfortunate mistake. There are these perfectly camouflaged, pale green worms, which are difficult to spot on the stalks of the plant. They're far more visible after they've been steamed with the vegetable. When my daughter found a couple of these delicacies on her plate, that was about it for garden-fresh produce, as far as she was concerned.

Then the deer moved in to help the woodchucks finish off anything that was still green. Although I was discouraged, the promise of row after row of tall, healthy, sweet corn kept me in the garden. But after three months of weeding, watering and watching the five varieties of towering corn mature, the raccoons took over. In one night they did about as much damage as a D-8 bulldozer. They couldn't eat it all, but they took one good bite out of every ear!

In retrospect, I might have been able to face all the challenges Mother Nature threw my way: the weather, the bugs and even the wild animals. It was actually my friends who forced me to give up gardening. Have you ever noticed how conversations in the summer eventually swing around to gardening: how many quarts of jam somebody made from their four strawberry plants, how someone else picked fresh peas from their garden on Memorial Day, or how a friend had just unearthed a Green Mountain potato that weighed four pounds! When I finally admitted to myself that I just couldn't compete, I quit. I'm still ashamed about it, but the summers are a lot less stressful.

Summer Weddings

One of the unexpected pleasures of coaching college athletes is the invitation to dozens of weddings. Last summer was a busy one, and it provided the opportunity to make some observations concerning this joyful social custom. In my view, the typical marriage ceremony has undergone significant improvement over the past couple of decades.

Back in the 1970s, when many of my schoolmates tied the knot, the typical wedding ceremony was arranged by and staged for the parents and their friends. The bride and groom were performers, obligated to follow a carefully scripted ritual, produced and directed by the previous generation.

In contrast, the weddings I attended this summer were the creation of the young couples being joined. One was held on a hilltop in the Northeast Kingdom, the perfect setting for two outdoor enthusiasts who met skiing and share a love of the mountains.

Another improvement to the traditional ceremony is replacing the old boilerplate vows — promising to love, honor, and obey — with statements written by the participants themselves. I heard a bride promise to stay in shape so the couple could share their love of the outdoors, and I was impressed by a groom's vow to support his wife in the pursuit of her career. Today's couples ask friends and family members to read poetry or perform musical selections appropriate to the occasion. And it is interesting which selections are meaningful for them: Robert Frost, Bob Dylan, The Velveteen Rabbit and Winnie-the-Pooh.

These days the wedding guests are participants in the ceremony, not simply spectators eager to guzzle champagne. Two of this summer's weddings paused midstream while the assembled guests were instructed to introduce themselves to each other. In one of the ceremonies, the minister made it clear that as participants, we shared an obligation to support the young couple and to help the marriage prosper.

Speaking of ministers, three of the four weddings I attended this summer were performed by women. A generation ago, a female minister would have been rare, although 50 percent of the people being married were women. The recent ceremonies conducted by women ministers had a more personal, less regimented feeling, a big improvement from my perspective.

There were positive changes at the wedding receptions as well. I have never enjoyed the rituals of throwing the bride's bouquet to the unmarried bridesmaids and tossing the bride's garter to the assembled bachelors. Happily, those traditions were dropped from this summer's celebrations.

In my generation, the reception was the parents' party. A band played dance tunes from Guy Lombardo or Benny Goodman. As a concession to the newlyweds, there might have been a mellow rendition of a current Beatles' hit, something equivalent to dancing in molasses. This summer's receptions were youthful parties, and the music was terrific.

One wedding joined a young guy from rural Maine with a sophisticated gal from New York City. They make a wonderful couple, but at the reception his rowdy skiing buddies and her cosmopolitan friends eyed each other suspiciously. Then a lively string band lined everyone up for a Virginia Reel. High heels were kicked off and sleeves rolled up, as dozens of city slickers and country bumpkins danced together for all they were worth.

Another reception featured a dynamite French Canadian band: accordion, guitars, fiddle, and drums. Their music was infectious. They played loud, and they didn't play waltzes. The dance floor was packed, not only by the young married couple and their classmates, but by grandparents as well. At each of these receptions, the newlyweds weren't hustled away on their honeymoon. They danced, they caught up with friends, and they enjoyed themselves.

I think today's marriage ceremonies are more personal and more relevant than those of a generation ago. That may not be a big deal, but on the other hand, if we can improve the survival rate of marriages in this country to more than 50 percent, maybe it is important. I was inspired by the weddings I attended this summer and I look forward to more. If you haven't been to a wedding for a few years, don't pass up the opportunity.

Outward Bound from Tashkent

The four powerful Soviet troop transports roared through the dry Uzbek foothills, trailing a plume of dust a mile long. Above our heads scores of small, agile sokols (kestrels) rode the hot updrafts, scanning the dry grass for a meal. Far below, on the valley floor, a turbulent river raced its way from the western end of the Tien Shan mountains to the Aral Sea, 450 miles away. The trucks were hauling an intriguing payload into the remote Uzbek countryside. Fourteen American combat veterans of the Vietnam War (and two younger American interpreters) had been joined by about twenty Soviet veterans of their recent war in Afghanistan and were headed for a six-day, Outward Bound–type expedition in a beautifully remote and unspoiled part of Soviet Central Asia, never before open to Americans.

The project was the brainchild of an American woman, Diana Glasgow of Earthstewards Network, a non-profit foundation dedicated to promoting world peace through citizen-to-citizen diplomacy. Glasgow knew, through the experiences of close friends, the pain, suffering, guilt, and alienation experienced by many of our Vietnam War veterans and of the recent advancements made in identifying and treating post-traumatic stress disorder (PTSD). She also knew from Soviet acquaintances that the young veterans of their war in Afghanistan were experiencing many of the same symptoms. Diana envisioned a series of exchanges of American Vietnam vets and Soviet Afghan vets to help heal the psychological scars, share advancements in physical technology (such as prosthetic devices and wheelchairs), build a poignant cultural bridge between our divergent political systems, and, finally, call attention, in a unique way, to the futility of war.

The first projects met with tremendous success. Young Soviet veterans, feeling isolated from their countrymen, poured forth their pent-up emotions to American PTSD experts visiting Moscow. American technicians offered state-of-the-art information on the design and construction of modern, lightweight wheelchairs and prosthetics for amputees. American vets reassured their younger Soviet counterparts that much of the public awareness in the States (including the creation of the Vietnam Veterans Memorial in Washington, D.C.), had been the work of dedicated individuals rather than government agencies. A group of Soviet veterans that visited the United States was inspired by the national concern generated by the Vietnam Veterans Memorial, and reassured by living in the homes of Vietnam vets who had put the war behind them and built productive lives for themselves and their families.

The initial exchanges had generated an impressive amount of media coverage in both countries. What should be the next step? There were literally thousands of Afghan war veterans superficially re-assimilated into Soviet society, but privately suffering from the guilt, anger and alienation of PTSD. Diana Glasgow contacted one of America's most experienced crusaders in the field, Bob Rheault (pronounced "row").

Bob had been a career U.S. Army officer, distinguishing himself from his days as a West Point cadet through his command of the Fifth Special Forces in Vietnam. As a colonel in the infantry, he had a reputation for fierce loyalty to the men under his command, and it was this characteristic that brought his military career to a premature conclusion during the Vietnam War. Like many combat veterans, Bob struggled with the adjustment to civilian life, but ultimately found his niche directing the Outward Bound training program at Hurricane Island, Maine. Outward Bound is a highly respected pioneer in experiential outdoor education, dedicated to helping participants discover within themselves the qualities of leadership, self-discipline, teamwork and mutual respect. After a decade of providing the benefits of Outward Bound to everyone from inner city high school dropouts to Fortune Five Hundred CEOs, Bob decided to bring Outward Bound to Veterans' Hospitals. The results were so rewarding that the former colonel stepped down from his director's position at Hurricane Island to devote his full time to working with Vietnam veterans.

Diana Glasgow couldn't have selected a better leader. At sixty-three, Bob was lean and fit, and with only a few phone calls could put together a group of qualified, dedicated Vietnam veterans, many of whom had experience as Outward Bound instructors, who, quite literally, would have followed "The Colonel" anywhere. The plan then, was for up to twenty American Vietnam vets to travel via Moscow to Tashkent in Soviet Central Asia, where they would be joined by the same number of Soviet Afghan war veterans for a six-to eight-day wilderness Outward Bound course. The mission: to demonstrate to the Soviets how wilderness experiences requiring self-discipline, mutual trust, cooperation and courage have an extremely positive effect on the private torture of PTSD.

The trucks rolled on through the parched Uzbek hills. By luck, I had thrown my pack in what turned out to be the lead vehicle, so I sat on the wooden bench, holding firmly to the sideboards, as we jostled through the countryside, obscuring the other trucks in our dust cloud. Our truck held an assortment of Americans and Soviets. The Americans were mostly in their forties, a selection of sizes and shapes wrought by almost twenty years of post-Vietnam civilian life. We looked like a group of middle-aged hikers with only a few subtle references to our military past: a faded, camouflage fatigue hat here, a set of subdued airborne jump wings there, a Vietnam Vets of America patch sewn on a windbreaker.

The Soviets, on the other hand, were kids. I had spent the previous eleven years coaching the men's ski team at Dartmouth College, and these Soviet combat veterans reminded me of my college skiers. Except for their eyes. They didn't have the youthful innocence or playful exuberance I'd taken for granted in my Dartmouth skiers. These Soviet vets, in spite of their youth, transmitted a sense of competence, self-assurance and maturity. They were sizing us up, not with hostility or arrogance, and not with wide-eyed curiosity, but with the eyes of much older men, who had seen a lot, had suffered, survived, and weren't afraid of much anymore. Unlike us, they were dressed in a random assortment of military uniforms. Some wore tan or khaki fatigues, others wore camouflage. Several wore military caps of some type, but the single piece of clothing that seemed to unify them was the distinctive blue and white horizontally striped tee shirt visible under every fatigue shirt or jacket. We would learn that these striped shirts, issued as part of the military uniform for Soviet infantrymen and paratroopers, has become a symbol of honor and unity for the Afghan vets, or "Afghantsi" as they are called.

We rolled along the dirt road deeper into the foothills of the Tien Shan mountains, leaving the city of Tashkent far behind. As the day began to cool in the late afternoon, the trucks turned off the dirt track and stopped in a pasture next to a stream that was to be the site of our first base camp. We unloaded and began to organize our gear. An advance party of Soviets had already started supper and had set up several rectangular three-man tents.

As the daylight faded, Bob called us together for an informational update and pep talk. He expressed a concern and frustration at not getting the type of advance planning information to which he was accustomed in the States. We weren't really sure where we were, had no idea where we were going or how long we would be gone, or what type of terrain we would cover. He asked for our patience, and reminded us of our primary mission. It didn't really matter where we were going or how long we would be on the trail, provided that we earned the trust of our Soviet counterparts and were able to convince them that their combat wounds would heal, that eventually, the nightmares would fade away. Bob wrapped up the meeting by dividing us into three groups of five men each, which would allow us to get to know our Soviet teammates more quickly. After assigning each American to either A, B, or C group, he announced, "Morton, you serve as group A leader (along with your Soviet counterpart); Sachs, group B leader; West, group C leader."

I stood silently in confusion and disbelief. Of the fourteen American vets, I was one of the least qualified to lead. Several on our team were highly decorated combat leaders: Hal Moore, a retired three-star general; Mike Beebe, a Green Beret officer in the Fifth Special Forces; Hugh Brown, combat company commander in the Central Highlands; Mike Heaney, infantry first lieutenant, wounded in action; Rusty Sachs, Marine captain and helicopter pilot, and Bob Rheault himself, West Point graduate, full colonel, commander of the Fifth Special Forces. My Vietnam command responsibilities consisted of leading a five-man Mobile Advisory Team in the Mekong Delta in a futile attempt to "win the hearts and minds of the people." Nine of our fourteen members had worked with Bob as instructors in Outward Bound courses; any one of them had better leadership qualifications than I did. For an instant, I toyed with the idea of declining the responsibility, but a glance at Bob's weathered face eliminated that option. This must be a standard Outward Bound method, I thought: put the least qualified in the leadership position and let them work it all out. I kept my mouth shut and resolved to do the best I could.

As I headed across the campground to meet my Soviet counterpart and his group A members, I considered my American teammates, whom I had known for slightly more than twenty-four hours. Jerry Ross lived in upstate New York and had been a combat medic in Vietnam. Like me, he had served late in the war and spent much of his time in the hamlets and villages trying to improve the health conditions of the Vietnamese. He was an experienced Outward Bound instructor and earned his living by teaching troubled teenagers in his hometown. Tom Olsen had also been a medic, and worked at the Veterans' Hospital in Tacoma, Washington. He had been active in Vietnam Veterans support groups, was an experienced counselor, and was well informed on PTSD. Mike Heaney was a Middlebury graduate, and an ROTC infantry officer. He arrived in Vietnam during the height of the conflict in the late 1960s. After several months of fighting in the Central Highlands, he caught a fragment from an exploding mortar round in the back of his right calf and was sent home. Mike is now an attorney in New Jersey. The final American in group A wasn't an American at all, but a British subject. Fletcher Douglas was a college student, competent (though not fluent) in Russian, who was a last-minute stand-in for a Russian-speaking Vietnam vet who was forced to withdraw from the project.

As I approached the Soviets, I realized my first bit of good fortune. The Soviet with whom I would share group A leadership duties was Villya. We had met that morning at the Tashkent airport. He appeared younger than the other Soviets and with his Oriental eyes, dark hair and high cheekbones, looked more at home in Tashkent than the fair-skinned, stocky Russians. He didn't speak much English. My Russian was limited to a few useless phrases like, "Pardon me, what time do tickets go on sale for the Bolshoi?" We got by pretty well in German. He was a bachelor in his mid-twenties, who had arrived in Afghanistan as an eighteen-year-old infantryman and served two years in combat, eventually as a medic.

Also assigned to our group was Artu, tall, athletic, good looking, quick to smile and laugh. He hiked the entire trip wearing an old beat-up pair of soccer shoes, often carrying a pack weighing at least sixty pounds. Artu didn't talk about Afghanistan. There was Costya, perhaps the most capable Soviet in the group—tough, self-reliant, determined. He wore an AK-47 bayonet in a sheath on his belt. During rest breaks or quiet times around the campfire, Costya's bayonet would be flashing around his body in a combination juggling act and agility drill that was both awesome and terrifying to watch. Vitalic, like Artu, reminded me of an All-American college soccer player, physically fit, alert and energetic. Vitalic had an amateur tattoo on his shoulder (either an Orthodox cathedral or a Moslem mosque, I couldn't be sure which) and right below it a large shiny scar from a Mujahedin ambush that killed the rest of his squad.

Sasha was the only Afghantsi from Moscow. He was serious, self-assured, and remote at the beginning of the trip. He studied martial arts and was often seen at dusk, after an exhausting day of hiking, practicing his positions, balanced on a rock some distance from the campsite. As the trip wore on, he seemed to relax and interact more with the rest of us, but some felt he might have had additional duties on the trip, of which we were not fully aware.

Leosha was Bob Rheault's counterpart, leader of the entire Soviet contingent. As such, he floated from one group to another. As the trip progressed, he spent more time with group A. He was the most emotional of the Soviets and could elicit tears from any one of the others after only a few minutes of his guitar playing and singing at the evening campfire. Leosha commanded the respect of all the Afghantsi. Although they were roughly the same age, they treated him as an older brother or a father. Finally, there was Dima, group A's hard-smoking, hard-drinking, microbiologist interpreter. Dima was not an Afghantsi. He was a scientist, but he was a lover of the mountains and was intensely curious about Americans. As the trip wore on, Dima became more absorbed in our mission, to the point where he often became choked with emotion while translating an especially painful combat memory or the lyrics to one of Leosha's provoking ballads.

The adventure was really about to begin. We were camped somewhere in a remote valley of Uzbekistan between Kyrgyzstan to the south and Kazakhstan to the north, about to set out on a six-day trek through mountains never before open to Americans, guided and accompanied by former soldiers of an army we had been taught to regard as our mortal enemy. As I crawled into my sleeping bag, I realized that the stars were more brilliant than I had ever seen them, the Milky Way a distinct band across the sky. As I often do at home in Vermont, I watched for a satellite and almost immediately saw two. I wondered if they were "ours" or "theirs." Then I noticed Orion and went to sleep trying to remember if he was visible in the Vermont sky at this time of the year.

We awoke the next morning eager to be under way and yet somewhat uneasy, since we still knew very little regarding the route we would take or the difficulty of the terrain. After breakfast it was announced that we would make a day hike to a high lake about 5 kilometers away, a sort of shake-down cruise. The Afghantsi had retained the services of three experienced mountain guides, or "alpinists." They were Sasha, an experienced climber who had traveled considerably and seemed to be in charge; Sergei, a miniature powerhouse on the trail and several times Soviet hang-gliding champion; and Edvard, a darkly tanned, hunched-over man of almost sixty, who routinely carried twice as much weight in his pack as any of the rest of us. These three were clearly trying to evaluate us, so each led a combined Soviet/American group up the valley to the beautiful alpine lake. It was during this hike that I stumbled across my second bit of good luck—so to speak. Before working for Dartmouth, I had lived for ten years in Alaska. On hunting expeditions and camping trips we frequently encountered bear "scat" on the trail. When I almost stepped in a pile of it on the way to the Uzbek mountain lake, I recognized it immediately. From my work with the U.S. Biathlon team, I had become acquainted with the current Soviet champion, Valeriy Medvedtsev, and knew that the first two syllables of his last name meant "bear." As I stepped around the pile in the trail, I pointed at it and casually said over my shoulder to the Soviet following me, "Medvedt!" I don't know what shocked him more: that this middle-aged American knew bear scat when he stepped in it, or that he knew the Russian word for it! The incident did wonders for my rapport with the Soviet members of group A.

The lake was an aquamarine gem high in a hidden pass. The day was hot, the air dry, and the lake so inviting that it didn't take us long to strip down and plunge in. Once we started breathing again, it didn't take us long to flail our way back to the rocky shore — the water temperature was scarcely above freezing. Refreshed by the swim and stimulated by several hours of hiking, we retraced our steps to the base camp by the river in time for supper.

The "alpinists" must have approved of what they saw because the word came down that the following morning we would pack up, load the trucks and drive to the drop off point for our five-day trek. After supper there were toasts to international friendship, toasts to the mountains, and silent toasts to fallen comrades who were with us in our thoughts. Then there were songs around the campfire as the darkness closed in. Matt West slipped away from the dying fire, and from a nearby hillside played "Taps" on his trumpet. The Americans stiffened to attention and the old soldiers, Bob Rheault and Hal Moore, stared with glazed eyes past the fire into the darkness.

The next morning, before we boarded the trucks, we were summoned to a pre-departure formation. A rag-tag outfit loosely lined up in groups A, B and C. There were several short speeches in the warm sun, and Bob signaled to me that it was time to distribute the anoraks.

Earlier in the summer I had asked Bob if there were any plans to provide the trip members with commemorative souvenirs or items to trade with the Soviets (trading is a big part of any international sporting event). He gave the okay to do what I could through my contacts in the ski industry. My first call was to Sally McCoy of The North Face in Berkeley, California. Sally had been a student leader in the Dartmouth Outing Club and, soon after joining The North Face, was a member of a Mt. Everest expedition. She was intrigued by our project and offered fifty bright blue anoraks (pull-on windbreakers).

About the same time, I met several Soviet students on an exchange to Dartmouth for the summer term. One was a talented artist who eagerly designed a meaningful logo to be embroidered on the anoraks. The design featured a vertical rifle used as a flagstaff for a white flag of truce on which was emblazoned the American eagle and the Soviet hammer and sickle. Beneath the flag were the initials USA and CCCP. Bob and I had kept the jackets out of sight until the speeches were over and we were about to climb aboard the trucks. The effect was magical. As the anoraks were handed out, we were transformed from a motley rabble of has-been soldiers to an exuberant group of outdoorsmen with a common destination and a common purpose. We piled aboard the Soviet Army trucks and once again headed across the Uzbek foothills.

The trucks drove on for a couple of hours. More than once, we were forced to detour around washouts or ford wild, mountain streams as we climbed steadily higher toward the rugged peaks. The mountains around us reminded me of the Rockies in Colorado or Utah, with sparse vegetation and sharp ridges and peaks.

The ride was broken up by one other diversion: a visit to a traditional hillside farm where we were welcomed by the aging patriarch into his home and treated to tea, bread, cheese and honey. It was a memorable experience for all of us, but especially meaningful for me, since my role as an advisor in Vietnam required many similar visits to the homes of gracious and generous subsistence farmers. Although thousands of miles and almost twenty years separated me from the Mekong Delta, the uncanny similarities of the scene evoked strong memories.

By midafternoon the trucks had reached a high hillside meadow and could go no farther. We unloaded the packs, took a couple of photos of the spectacular view, and headed up the trail. I was happy to finally be on foot. The planes, buses and trucks had taken us through some interesting country, but from its conception, the project centered on this extended hike and I was relieved to finally be under way. The trail gradually climbed the steep hillside as we worked our way up the valley toward the source of the river that raged far below in the valley floor. The scenery reminded me of Alaska, except here there was much less vegetation.

I trudged along the trail behind Mike Heaney. He was wearing the new Tecnica boots we had been given. Tecnica USA, known primarily for alpine ski boots, had provided each American with a new pair of high-tech, hiking boots (another result of my ski business contacts). Mike had apologetically returned his first pair for a different size, explaining that it was sometimes difficult getting a good fit for his wounded right foot. Although Mike didn't limp, about half of his right calf muscle was gone and the scar ran down his leg into his boot. He'd explained to me earlier that he'd lost some flexibility in the ankle and couldn't feel much with the foot, so crossing streams or walking at night was difficult.

When some of us began to fade, our "alpinist" Sasha called for a rest break. The Soviets instantly produced cigarettes and clearly relished the opportunity to smoke. Younger and stronger than their American teammates, the Afghantsi probably could have hiked non-stop all day, but they needed their cigarette breaks and we needed the rest! International cooperation at its best.

Break over, we shouldered our packs and continued up the valley. I had noticed that although we entered this steep mountain valley high on the hillside and continued roughly following the contour line, as we worked our way into the mountains, the river in the valley grew closer. I estimated that our trail and the river would join in a couple more miles; perhaps that would be the campsite. I was right, and wrong. We did meet the river and we stopped there for an extended break, lunch you could call it, although it was closer to 4 p.m. But it wasn't to be the campsite. Several of us stripped down and swam in the glacial river—instantaneously refreshing.

The Soviets got fires started, boiled water for tea and spread out Uzbek bread, butter and sausage for lunch. A ten-pound wheel of cheese had been part of my assigned load, so I unpacked it and eagerly entreated everyone to eat a lot of cheese. The Afghantsi laughed and it became a ritual joke for the rest of the hike. Every time we stopped for more than a smoke break, I would unpack this huge wheel of cheese and beg everyone to eat some of it.

Before long we were back on the trail with assurance from Sasha that the evening's campsite was only about 5 kilometers further up the valley. I calculated in my mind: a good cross-country skier can cover a kilometer in three minutes, times five equals fifteen minutes! I knew I could run a 10 kilometer race in under thirty-six minutes; half of that would be eighteen minutes! But with sixty-pound packs, steadily climbing over rough terrain, with frequent rest stops, 5 kilometers was going to take hours. And it did! We finally stopped on a rocky bend in the river, not a campsite at all, but the only flat ground in sight. We established camp, and before long Villya called us to supper. Around the blazing campfire with the roaring mountain stream close by, we stuffed ourselves on ploff (rice pilaf), Uzbek bread, sausage and tea. I had been apprehensive about Russian food, remembering stories about severe shortages of meat, vegetables and sugar. But none of us went hungry. In fact, our hosts were so generous and eager to please that we often felt we were disappointing them by turning down second helpings.

As we finished eating, the Soviets lit their cigarettes, and I tried to break the ice on the subject of the war. With Dima translating, I talked a little about Vietnam and the difficulty many of us had adjusting to civilian life when we returned. Tom, Mike and Jerry pitched in, and within minutes the Afghantsi, led by Villya, were pouring out stories of combat, homecoming, confusion and frustration. I listened with amazement and empathy as my young Soviet counterpart told of two years of fierce combat with an invisible enemy, followed by a return to a country that thought he had been planting trees and building schools for twenty-four months. Then I watched with admiration as Mike, Jerry and Tom, all experienced instructors in Outward Bound courses for Vietnam veterans, reassured, encouraged and supported our young Afghantsi teammates.

As the fire died and there was a pause in the conversation, Tom explained that in his vet support groups in Tacoma, they always wrapped up meetings with a group hug. Dima had to translate the word and the concept. Leosha was the first to comprehend and with a broad smile and extended arms he proclaimed in a loud voice, "GRUPA AHH UGH!"

The next day's hike was a long, hard one, covering several thousand feet of vertical. After supper, still standing around the campfire in the darkness, the young Soviets tentatively asked, through Dima, if we would join them in a toast. Speaking for the Americans, I said sure, we would be glad to join them in a small toast, explaining that for personal reasons a couple of our guys didn't drink any alcohol. They nodded understandingly and a bottle of vodka magically appeared. Cups and glasses were filled with vodka (or tea) and the first ceremonial toast was under way. For the Soviets, a toast is an art form, part poetry, part inspiration, part challenge. They never stop at one toast. It almost becomes a contest, not to down the most vodka, but in the toast itself to capture the emotion of the moment, to elicit feelings of pride or accomplishment, and quite simply to bring tears to the eyes. I did my best by toasting our hosts, the beauty of their mountains and to future projects that would bring us all together. Then, as he refilled glasses and cups, Leosha explained through Dima that traditionally the third toast is a silent toast to fallen comrades. We quietly raised our glasses to those Americans and Soviets who would never drink with friends under the stars, but were in our hearts. The clear notes of Matt West's trumpet echoed across the campsite: "Chariots of Fire," "Battle Hymn of the Republic" and "Taps." Leosha called for "GRUPA AHH UGH" around the fire. Then we felt our way through the dark to our sleeping bags.

The next day was beautiful. We were high in the peaks of the Tien Shan mountains and, after a late afternoon decision to make camp early and head for 12,300-foot Nahodka Pass, the highest point of our trip, the next day, we had what amounted to a couple of hours of free time. The group A members were reading, writing in their journals, or sleeping. I spent several minutes looking at the steep wall we would climb with full packs to reach the pass. Although I had never done much technical climbing, both ski training and hunting in Alaska had provided me with more than the normal share of time in the mountains. I asked Bob if I would create problems scouting around a little before the sun went down. He approved, but suggested that I invite a Soviet or two, and tell "Alpinist" Sasha where we were headed. Villya and Uri (from group B) were eager to go, so with Sasha's blessing we headed toward the steep wall below the pass. Costya and Edvard had headed off to our left and had seemed to run into dead ends that forced them back down. I thought I could see a route with only minimum exposure to loose shale and scree, which probably led to the pass. I knew that the steep mountainside would look different once we were on it, so I tried to memorize the terrain features of the route as it appeared from the bottom.

Without packs and with only a couple of "smoke breaks" for my partners, we reached the pass in less than an hour. Sergei, Vitalic and "Moscow" Sasha greeted us with enthusiasm. After Villya explained the decision to camp below for the night and climb the pass the following day, we passed the water bottle around. Sergei stopped mid-sentence as if he had forgotten something. Straightening up, with the water bottle held high, he proposed a toast to "the first American to ever reach Nahodka Pass!"

It was time for us "mountain scouts" to return to camp. Sergei was suffering a severe allergic reaction to the dust or pollen in the air and Vitalic wasn't feeling well. Along with "Moscow" Sasha they elected to head down over the snowfield to the next campsite. They would either climb back up in the morning to help everyone across the snow, or meet us in the evening at the camp. With the sun behind the peaks, we put on our windbreakers for the descent back to our glacier-side campsite. On the way down, we refined our route and marked it every so often with rock cairns.

The next morning, Bob lobbied for an early start. As we broke camp and packed up, Costya casually remarked that wolves had raided in the night and eaten all the remaining sausage. I visualized the silent predators inspecting the campsite in the moonlight, delicately extricating the two-foot-long sausages from a backpack, and smugly trotting off with their prizes. Villya would lead group A to the pass using the route we had explored the previous day. Uri would lead group B, and I was assigned TDY (military lingo for "temporary duty") to lead group C. I knew the route, but there was the underlying tension that, with heavy packs, one slip—a missed step or a rock kicked loose above another group—and we could be in a real jam. With Bob, Hal and Edvard in group C, I didn't want to screw up.

Climbing carefully but steadily we reached the pass in just under an hour and a half. Villya was beaming. He had led group A to the pass in under an hour! There was a celebration on the knife-edge ridge that formed Nahodka Pass. Everyone was taking photos: photos of "grupa Ahh," "grupa B," "grupa C"; photos of Marines; photos of Special Forces and Spetznatz; photos of Outward Bound instructors; and photos for college alumni magazines.

As "Alpinist" Sasha and Edvard secured ropes to ice axes for our descent across the steep snowfield, Fletcher Douglas, the group A translator, made perhaps his most significant contribution of the trip. We had been told that the custom among Soviet alpinists was to leave a note for the next expedition. We agreed to a single message, written both in English and Russian, but had a tough time getting started. In an offhand sort of way, in the excitement of the moment, someone said, "Hey, Fletcher, this is up your alley. Help us compose a note to be left here on the top." So the young academic, who thought he'd be translating road signs and restaurant menus, sat on a rock at 12,300 feet above sea level, and with one foot in Uzbekistan and the other in Kazakhstan, he wrote a brief but moving paragraph, which captured the essence of our mission of peace and understanding. When translated into Russian and read to the assembled group standing in the pass, his words brought tears to our eyes.

We regrouped and headed over easier terrain, to the designated campsite on a second lake further down the valley. As we started to unpack the tents, Leosha intervened, saying, "Only one tent tonight for emergencies. The rest of us will sleep in the road." Dima explained that "sleeping in the road" meant sleeping lined up next to each other. I had planned to sleep off by myself in hopes of getting a good night's rest, but in the interest of team unity, I threw my pad and sleeping bag in line next to Costya's.

With supper under way, Villya and Artu explained through Dima that Vitalic had become very sick. In Afghanistan, he had been stricken with hepatitis and typhus, and the exertion of the hiking the day before had brought on a relapse. Villya had some of Vitalic's medication. He and Artu planned to run the hour and a half to the final campsite, where Vitalic was waiting. They were both clearly concerned about their friend's illness. It would be a tough run down the trail in the dark, after a full day's hiking with heavy packs. We wished them luck and sent our regards to Vitalic as they jogged off into the moonlight.

With supper over, we dragged a large cedar log into the fire (we were back below the tree line) and settled in for some songs and stories. Sasha the alpinist joined our circle, pulled out a vodka bottle and offered a toast to "grupa Ahh: first up the pass, first over the snowfield, and first across the rock face above the lake." He had picked what seemed to be wild cranberries. With our cups half full of vodka and our hands full of berries, we were to down the liquid, and chase it with a mouthful of the tart berries. Of course, to fulfill our diplomatic obligations, we offered a toast to Sasha, who had led us safely up and over the pass, to the beauty of the mountains, to Afghantsi-Vietnamsi friendship, and so on. We ran out of berries before we ran out of vodka.

Leosha and Costya played the guitar and sang while a full moon rose above the jagged mountain peaks. The moonlight sparkled off the surface of the lake as Matt West, from the hillside above the camp, played several selections on his trumpet. As always, he ended with "Taps," but the song that struck me with real significance was, "There's a Place for Us" from West Side Story. I crawled into my bag, one more sardine in a row, between Costya and Mike Heaney, and was soon asleep.

Bob (and Matt) let us sleep late, at least until the sun was up. Only a couple of hours' worth of easy downhill hiking remained to the last campsite, where we would spend a final night before being trucked back to Tashkent. We cooked breakfast, broke camp and packed at a leisurely pace. Villya reported that Vitalic had been very sick, but the medicine they brought had seemed to help.

We followed a well-worn trail along the glacial stream out of the valley. Down in the trees, the towering peaks and hanging glaciers were behind us. A couple of figures appeared on the trail, hiking toward us. It turned out to be Vitalic — looking weak, somewhat tentative, but happy — and Igor, one of the Afghantsi who had organized the trip from Tashkent but had been unable to participate on the hike. There were enthusiastic, warm greetings all around, like brothers reunited after years, rather than days, or in Vitalic's case, hours. We walked the final miles of the trail together, recounting for Igor's benefit the entire adventure in impressive detail.

The trail entered a wide, natural field bordered on the left by the wild mountain river, and on the right by a sparse cedar woods. This was the final campsite. Before we had even dropped our packs, old Edvard was enthusiastically entreating everyone to collect firewood. I assumed that they had another communal banquet planned and needed lots of firewood to cook the huge ploff. Edvard instructed us to bring the wood down by the river, where we found a large pile of rocks with a soot-darkened hole beneath it. This, we learned, was to be our sauna! It was just about noon when Edvard started the fire under the rock pile, which he tended religiously all afternoon, occasionally calling for "more wood!"

It was a real luxury to have some free time in the daylight after several days of hiking with heavy packs until dusk and then setting up camp in the dark. I helped to put up the group A tents, but quietly found myself a soft, flat space under a couple of cedar trees to spread out my sleeping bag. I was determined to get a decent night's sleep at last. Jerry Ross and I found a small pool in the river where it looked like the raging current wouldn't sweep us away, and each took a bath (so to speak). It wasn't a bath in the traditional sense—you splashed yourself with the intensely cold water as long as you could bear it, soaped up on the bank, and then stepped back in the river to rinse off—but after five days of sweating and several layers of Uzbekistan and Kazakhstan dust, it felt magnificent.

The warm, sunny afternoon wore on and by 6:30 Edvard, flushed with excitement, announced that the sauna was ready. Tending the fire all afternoon, Edvard had heated the rock pile until it almost vibrated. With help from Sasha the alpinist, he erected an army wall tent over the rock pile and placed an old park bench on either side of the rocks within the tent. It was old fashioned, it was makeshift, and it was probably the hottest sauna I have ever experienced! As a Nordic skier, I have enjoyed sauna baths in Scandinavia, Central Europe, and all over North America. I enjoyed them enough to dig a pond and build a sauna near my home in Vermont. We usually "fire up" our sauna once a week, summer or winter. I may not be an international authority on saunas, but I certainly have taken a lot of them. Old Edvard's Kazakhstan army tent sauna was one of the best ever! He orchestrated the event like a symphony conductor. The tent could accommodate about twelve sweating bodies at a time, so Edvard, guarding the canvas flap entrance, would admit or release bathers as he saw fit. Once he had a full house, he would enter with a fistful of birch branches. One by one he would drag us off the benches to a space in front of the rock pile, where he would vigorously thrash us, back, chest and legs, with the switches. Surviving this beating, you would resume your seat on the bench until he opened the flap to permit escape to the river. This same glacial stream, which had seemed so painfully cold earlier in the day, felt blissfully refreshing after the stifling heat of the tent. We emerged bright pink and gasping for breath.

For many Soviets and Americans this was enough. But an authentic Scandinavian sauna is three cycles of hot room to cold bath, and I was going to get my money's worth. On my second trip into the tent, I looked around to take attendance. By now the bathers were mostly Soviets, but next to me on the bench, grinning from ear to ear, was Hal Moore, "The General," as the young Afghantsi reverently called him. Hal had served a tour with the NATO forces in Norway and, like me, relished a good hot sauna. He sat up straight, while the rest of us hunched over to avoid the searing heat trapped in the peak of the tent. If the Soviets were impressed with our sixty-seven-year-old infantry officer on the trail, he became legendary in that sauna.

Supper was similar to our first night in the mountains, one large ploff of rice, lamb and vegetables, which fed all thirty of us. We stood shoulder to shoulder around the campfire, one large circle of Americans and Soviets, as first Leosha, then Bob recapped the highlights of the trek. Someone broke out the guitar and the Soviets began to sing. A firm hand on my shoulder pulled me back from the fire and out of the circle. It was "Alpinist" Sasha, and Dima translated for him. He regarded two of us, Tom Olsen and myself, as kindred spirits who truly loved the mountains. He wanted us to join him in toasting the mountains and friendship built on alpinism. As an aside, Dima mentioned that what we were drinking was very special stuff. Our little group also included Sergei and Costya. Sasha produced a short glass bottle about the size of a quart of motor oil. The liquid it contained was clear, so I assumed it was vodka. But there was a new format in this group. Sasha raised the bottle, praised the mountains, alpinism, friendship, and took a drink, chasing it quickly with a gulp of water from a canteen. He passed both bottles to his right and the ritual was repeated. I was halfway around the circle and getting uneasy as the Soviets coughed and tears sprang from their eyes. When the bottles were passed to me, I remember thinking, "It couldn't be any worse than Vietnamese Ba si de." I took a good mouthful and concentrated on swallowing without choking. It went down smoothly, and I had it made until I exhaled. It felt like my sinuses were on fire. The water chaser was too late to put out the blaze behind my eyes and the tears started. The Soviets smiled as I passed the bottles to my right. Finally, mercifully, Sasha's bottle was empty and we were free to rejoin the main group, still singing around the big campfire. Fortunately, they were all shoulder to shoulder, arm in arm, which helped those of us returning from Sasha's circle remain upright. The guitar was passed around the fire, and after several Soviet songs, Andy Padlo, our crackerjack interpreter from California, knocked their socks off with a couple of Country and Western tunes. We were interrupted by Matt West, who for the last time in the mountains, climbed a hillside in the dark and played his trumpet. The fireside singing subsided as we all listened to Matt. First, he played the "Naval Hymn" for the benefit of the American and Soviet Marines in the group. Then, deliberately and clearly, he played "Taps," with special meaning this time, since it was our final night in the mountains. There were lots of damp eyes in the firelight as the final notes echoed up the valley.

Almost as an afterthought, Matt started a melody that the singers around the fire quickly picked up: "Oh, beautiful, for spacious skies, for amber waves of grain ... " As I stood between Villya and Artu, my arms around their shoulders, the tears ran down my cheeks. I was so choked up I couldn't sing the words and the tears kept coming. Villya and Artu broke from the big circle and closed in on me. Tom Olsen joined us and I could tell he was too far gone to sing. The four of us, two Americans and two Soviets, hugged each other tightly, with bowed heads and uncontrollable tears, as Matt played the final verse of "America."

Matt rejoined the group around the fire, the guitar music replaced his trumpet and the four of us returned to the circle. There were pats on the back, a firm grip on the shoulder, or a quick hug as both Soviets and Americans drifted one by one back toward the tents and sleeping bags. About that time, Jack Jones was handed the guitar. I had heard him sing earlier on in the trip, and I knew he loved Country and Western songs. With a smaller group of diehards, there was no stopping him. The songs kept coming out, mostly late '60's, Vietnam-vintage folk songs, many of which the Soviets had heard and could join in. We sang them all—"Puff, the Magic Dragon," "This Land Is Your Land," "We Shall Overcome," "Country Road," and others. Two songs were especially memorable. When we started "Leaving on a Jet Plane," it reminded me of a friend who used to sing it in Vietnam, and I got choked up again. I was standing shoulder to shoulder with Hugh Brown, who had been harmonizing beautifully, so I looked at him assuming that he would carry the tune. When I saw tears in his eyes and heard no words from his mouth, I assumed the song had special meaning for him also. We just swayed, arm on shoulder, humming along the best we could.

Someone suggested "Michael Row the Boat Ashore," and everyone quickly joined in. We followed the chorus with the standard verses about the Jordan River. Jack ad-libbed a verse about the Uzbek Mountains and Soviet friendship. The rest of us responded eagerly with the chorus. Then, to our surprise, Stefan, the Soviet Marine, ad-libbed a verse in Russian! I couldn't translate the words, but the rhyme and meter were perfect, and we all responded again with the chorus. The pattern had been established and it continued for several magical moments; Jack would compose a verse and we would respond with the chorus, then Stefan would sing a verse in Russian, and we would come back with the chorus. I will never hear that song again without thinking of a campsite in remote Kazakhstan surrounded by Soviet and American veterans.

For me, and I suspect for several others, that last night in the mountains was the highlight of our trip, although we were to spend two days with our counterparts in Tashkent, and another three days in Moscow. Both cities were interesting and we were treated as honored guests for the remainder of our stay, but only two events brought the same intensity, or depth of feeling, as our Outward Bound trek in the Tien Shan mountains.

The first took place in Tashkent. When we returned to the city from the mountains, the Americans were distributed among our Soviet hosts. For the next two days, we stayed in their homes, met their families and friends, and enjoyed their hospitality. I was hosted by my "grupa Ahh" counterpart, Villya, who was a bachelor (though engaged to be married) and a law student. All of Villya's spare time was spent on a club he founded for troubled teenagers. The club had an obvious military slant and appeared to be a combination of our Girl/Boy Scouts and college ROTC. Villya was anxious to show several of us the rooms that had been donated to the club: one was decked out as a meeting hall and disco; the other, decorated with posters and flags, would become a museum of artifacts from the Afghanistan war. Leading a group of American vets, Afghantsi, and several curious teenagers, Villya unlocked a storeroom off the future museum. Inside were shelves crammed with Soviet military hardware and clothing. Radios, backpacks, helmets and tents littered the floor. Villya passed around a heavy metal cylinder about the size of a twelve-ounce bottle of Coke. It was a Soviet mortar round. When it was passed to Mike Heaney, he studied it carefully in his hand, and said to no one in particular, "This is exactly what blew the hell out of my leg." Even though many of those present did not speak English, the room was instantly silent as everyone watched Mike. Before anyone could speak, Villya put one arm around Mike's shoulder. He took the mortar round with his other hand, at the same time saying in Russian, "Never again, Misha, never again!"

"Moscow" Sasha accompanied us from Tashkent back to his hometown, and served as our tour guide for the three days we were there. We saw most of the sights and met a few of the Moscow Afghantsi who had participated in an earlier exchange. Around noon on our last full day in the Soviet Union, a Sunday, we boarded a bus for Friendship Park and the monument to those

Soviet soldiers who died fighting in Afghanistan. We had been forewarned that what we would see was no more than a temporary memorial and that a more fitting tribute would be constructed when sufficient funds were raised. We left the bus, bought flowers in an open-air market and walked a couple of blocks to the park. A relatively small stone, not more than three feet high, supported a bronze plaque, which explained that on that site would be constructed a monument to the Soviet soldiers who gave their lives in Afghanistan. The surrounding corner of the park seemed abandoned and neglected. In the distance, Muscovites strolled or pushed baby carriages around a lake, on what appeared to be well-maintained paths. Aside from an older woman in a worn overcoat and a young Asian man, we were the only visitors to the stone.

Following Bob Rheault's lead, one by one, we placed our flowers in front of the plaque. Other visitors seemed to materialize, as about twenty of us, many in the distinctive blue North Face anoraks, paid our respects to the 15,000 young Soviets who died in Afghanistan. Matt West slipped off one last time, and we all came to attention as he played "Taps." A well-dressed woman in her early forties knelt to add her flowers to those in front of the stone and fingered the small American flag we had placed there. When she stood and turned around, tears streamed down her cheeks. Big Tom Dinsmore reached out a strong arm and gently drew the sobbing Soviet mother into a bear hug. There was no need for an interpreter.

Almost 1,800 miles to the southeast, high in the Tien Shan mountains, on the border between Uzbekistan and Kazakhstan, a small American flag and a short written paragraph in English and Russian were evidence that a small group of American veterans and their younger Soviet brothers had spent several challenging days learning, sharing, and working together to achieve world peace.

Sports and Life

The Centennial Boston Marathon

In 490 B.C., a Greek messenger named Phillipides ran the 25 miles from Marathon to Athens with news of victory over the Persians. In 1886, Baron Pierre de Coubertin, the man who revived the Olympic Games, was convinced that a distance race would be a popular addition to the traditional Olympic track and field events. That year, at the first Modern Olympic Games in Athens, the marathon champion was a Greek shepherd who completed the race in just under three hours.

Here in America, on Patriot's Day a century ago, fifteen men lined up in front of Metcalf's Mill in Ashland, Massachusetts, for the first Boston Marathon. The participants in that event were regarded not as highly trained athletes, but as death-defying daredevils. According to legend, Phillipides died moments after delivering his message to the Athenians, and in the late 1800s, it was commonplace on city streets in this country to see horses drop from exhaustion.

Those first marathoners drew crowds of spectators, but most were drawn by a morbid sense of curiosity. The winner of the inaugural Boston Marathon was John J. McDermott, who ran the course in two hours, fifty-five minutes and ten seconds.

How things have changed! On April 15, 1996, more than 38,700 runners filled the streets of Hopkinton, awaiting the start of the centennial edition of the Boston Marathon. Boston is the oldest marathon in America, and the standard by which all other foot races in our nation are measured. Almost everyone who runs was determined to be a part of the 100th birthday party. This created an economic bonanza for Boston as runners from all over the world congregated, filling hotels from Providence, Rhode Island, to Portsmouth, New Hampshire, and eating mountains of pasta.

But it also meant a monumental challenge for the Boston Athletic Association, the organizers of the race. Normally the Boston Marathon attracts around 10,000 runners. How would the organizers get four times that many competitors to the starting line, the morning of the race? How much water and Gatorade do 40,000 runners drink over the course of 26 miles? How do you tabulate accurate results when more than one hundred runners cross the finish line every minute for more than two hours?

My first hint that the '96 Boston Marathon really was a big deal, came when I picked up my start number at the Hines Auditorium. The cavernous hall was mobbed with lean, fit people in T-shirts and windbreakers from all over the world. To be issued an official racing number, each preregistered runner had to show a photo I.D.! Rumors claimed that disappointed runners were offering as much as $2,000 for an official starting number, even though competing under someone else's name was strictly forbidden.

Early Monday morning we joined an orderly line of runners that completely encircled two sides of Boston Common. I chatted with athletes from Finland, Japan, and the Czech Republic. The bus ride to the starting line, normally about an hour, became twice that long, due to the heavy traffic. Runners who had been hydrating since before dawn, could wait no longer. In the gridlock on the outskirts of Hopkinton, hundreds bolted from the buses, and sprinted across muddy corn fields to relieve themselves in the woods beyond.

At the assembly area, there was scarcely time to pin on a race number before loudspeakers instructed us to leave for the starting line. We crammed into roped pens just off Main Street, containing 1,000 runners each. The pungent smell of Ben Gay mingled with the aroma of Polish sausage being grilled on the town square for hungry spectators. The warm spring air was filled with the rhythmic whop... whop... whop... whop of helicopters overhead.

At noon a muffled BOOM from a National Guard canon announced the start, and an army of 38,000 began shuffling toward the line. It was slow going for the first few miles; so many tightly packed runners trying to avoid bumping or tripping one another, as they sought to find a comfortable pace.

Even as the crush spread out and there was room to run, it was more of a social event than a race. There was constant conversation and encouragement among runners. The cheering from the spectators lining the course was deafening. Wellesley College was a tunnel of screaming young women.

I have participated in dozens of marathons through the years, and I hope to run many more, but Boston's centennial birthday party was a celebration worthy of the event. I'm grateful that I was on hand to share the fun.

Sports and Life

Sherman Adams' Long Walk

During the decade I coached the Dartmouth Ski Team, we occasionally held summer workouts at the college's impressive, Ravine Lodge, which was constructed near the base of Mount Moosilauke in 1939. Almost any evening from late spring through foliage season, you can find the rustic dining room filled with enthusiastic hikers and nature lovers. After supper, when the dishes have been cleared, the stories begin: of exhausting treks through the White Mountains, of harrowing encounters with black bears on the Appalachian Trail, and of daring rescue attempts in howling blizzards.

One summer evening, after my skiers had run the 17-mile length of Franconia Ridge, a spry, little, white-haired Dartmouth alum was captivating the undergrads with his account of Outing Club adventures in the 1920s. The storyteller was Sherman Adams, who had gained national attention as President Eisenhower's Chief of Staff, and more recently, as the founder of Loon Mountain Ski Area.

But that night in the Ravine Lodge, the cocky senior citizen was berating my skier's traverse of Franconia Ridge. He told of the Long Walks of the 1920s, an informal contest among Dartmouth students to determine "how far a well-conditioned Outing Clubber could travel in a day."

In the spring of 1919, after failing to reach Springfield, Massachusetts, 75 miles from Hanover, Sherman Adams decided to train for a record-breaking attempt. On Memorial Day, 1920, Adams and William Fowler set out at midnight from the Skyline cabin, 3 miles north of Littleton, New Hampshire. Paced, fed and encouraged by other Outing Club members, they walked trails and back roads until they reached Mount Cube at 4:30 in the afternoon, a distance of 62 miles. By that point Adams is quoted in David Hooke's History of the D.O.C. as saying, "we were pretty far gone, but bound we should make it, and nothing could stop us..."

They did make it, with thirteen minutes to spare. Eighty-three miles in under twenty-four hours! The feisty, white-haired alum had my young skiers totally engrossed with his story, and since we did a lot of training in the White Mountains, they had a sincere respect for his accomplishment.

"You must have jogged some of the gradual downhills and flats?" I asked, remembering several of our ski team hikes. Adams puffed up like a bantam rooster, his face turned red, and he glared at me as if I'd called him a liar. "We WALKED, every step of the way!"

I was embarrassed that one of New Hampshire's most notable public figures had thought my question was intended to undermine his story, and the encounter remained vivid in my mind. Although the record-setting effort in 1920 did not follow the route of today's Appalachian Trail, I kept wondering how I might measure up against those champion hikers.

Since I hadn't trained for a record-setting attempt as the two old Dartmouth men had, I decided to test myself by hiking roughly half the distance in twelve hours. The Appalachian Trail crosses route 25A in Orford, New Hampshire, just north of Mount Cube. From there, the trail winds south to Hanover for 35 miles, including 8,500 feet of climbing.

On a warm, overcast day in July, with my day pack stuffed with food, water bottles and dry socks, I headed into the woods from route 25A, just before seven in the morning. At eight, I enjoyed the panorama of a fog-shrouded Connecticut River Valley from the summit of Mount Cube. By 10:15 I had descended Cube and climbed the gentle shoulder of Smarts Mountain.

I ate my lunch within sight of the Dartmouth Skiway. My optimism was tempered by blisters on my feet, and stiffness in my legs. The climb up Moose Mountain seemed much longer than I had remembered from ski team hikes, and by the time I crossed Three Mile Road in Etna, I was an hour behind schedule. It began to rain, but I was hopeful the shower might discourage the deer flies.

I knew I was nearing Hanover, but I was out of water, it was raining harder, and the blisters on my heels had escalated beyond a minor annoyance. I finally staggered out of the woods at 6:15 and reached Robinson Hall, the home of the Dartmouth Outing Club, with twelve minutes to spare.

Sore and tired after only twelve hours, I had developed a very healthy respect for the two old Dartmouth alums. Sherman Adams and William Fowler's record-setting 83-mile walk in 1920 won't be threatened by me any time soon.

Giving Blood

I hate needles. I always have. It began when I was a kid, back when family doctors still made house calls, and penicillin was the miracle cure for everything. Doc Tadem was a wonderful guy and a terrific role model, frequently riding his bike or paddling his canoe to the hospital long before physical fitness was a national craze. But too often his late-night visits to our house included that dreaded phrase, "Well, I'd better give you a little mosquito bite," as he rummaged through his black bag for the penicillin and a hypodermic needle. Those were the days when syringes were the diameter of fountain pens, and your butt hurt for a week after the shot.

Then there were the polio vaccinations administered by the school nurse and her storm troopers in the gym. I remember the national panic caused by the polio epidemic, and I remember what a hero Jonas Salk was for discovering a vaccine. But the day we started those inoculations is also seared in my memory. Our whole school—students, teachers, everybody— assembled in the gymnasium and formed long lines at tables piled high with syringes. Just the sight of so many needles made me feel light-headed. With hundreds of kids to immunize, the medical staff was all business. You approached the table and one rugged nurse locked you in a bear hug while a second nurse swabbed your shoulder with alcohol, then jabbed in the needle and depressed the plunger. The fainters were simply dragged out of line by the hugging nurse. I dreaded the injection, but I was terrified of passing out and humiliating myself in front of my classmates.

The army provided a whole new level of needle phobia. At Fort Benning, Georgia, home of the Infantry, being macho wasn't just a personality trait, it was the foundation for the entire culture. During in-processing, we were lined up, shirts in one hand, medical records in the other, then marched through a gauntlet of medics armed with pneumatic guns that shot serum into our shoulders. If you flinched, the pressurized medicine sliced your skin like a razor, and the blood flowed freely to your fingertips. And in 1968 it was assumed we were all headed for the Garden Spot of Southeast Asia, so we got dozens of shots, including for plague, cholera, diphtheria, typhoid, and hepatitis.

I know great progress has been made in recent decades with the development of smaller, sharper needles, but it's hard to overcome old fears. After her first year in college, my daughter, Julie, mentioned she had participated in several Red Cross blood drives. I admired her generosity and felt guilty that I always seemed to find some excuse to avoid donating blood.

Then my wife, Mimi, was diagnosed with cancer, and I was confronted with more needles than I had ever imagined existed. She endured routine blood tests, intravenous drips and bone marrow biopsies. For more than two years, she had to give herself two injections a day. Talk about facing your fears: I wouldn't have seen more needles if I had worked in a hospital. But still, I avoided the blood drives, even though my wife received dozens of transfusions during the course of her treatment.

Mimi lost her struggle with cancer on January 21, 1998. One of her best friends noticed there was a Red Cross blood drive a week later, and rallied support among friends and neighbors to donate blood in Mimi's memory. Finally, I was cornered. I couldn't allow dozens of people to donate blood in my wife's honor and not do so myself.

Arriving at the blood drive, the sight of the busy volunteers hefting dark red, plastic pouches made me queasy. I squinted through the medical release forms with blurry vision. When my name was called, I staggered to the vacant position, certain my knees were about to buckle. The friendly nurse seemed oblivious to the fact I was about to pass out from fear. She chatted cheerfully as she found my vein and prepared the site. I scarcely felt the needle. She gave me a rubber ball to squeeze and turned to assist another donor.

Moments later, she glanced back in surprise, "Whoa, easy on that ball, you're done!"

Five minutes, seven at the most, and I had filled the plastic pouch. It was virtually painless, and an important double victory for me. I was part of a very meaningful tribute to my wife that produced nearly one hundred units of blood to help people who desperately needed it. As a bonus, I overcame a fear of needles that had plagued me since childhood. Giving blood doesn't hurt. In fact, giving blood made me feel wonderful.

In the Shadow of Mount Everest

The invitation came out of the blue. A college classmate whom I had seldom seen in the thirty years since graduation, asked if I could join a group of six, middle-aged guys for three weeks of trekking in Nepal. Like most everyone else in America, I had read Into Thin Air, Jon Krakauer's gripping account of the disastrous 1996 Mount Everest expeditions that cost nine climbers their lives. I will never forget the intensely poignant yet ironic image of the expedition leader, Rob Hall, talking to his pregnant wife back home in New Zealand by cellular telephone, as he slowly froze to death near the summit of the world's highest mountain.

So, of course I accepted the invitation, and on September 30th we arrived in Kathmandu, jet-lagged but eager for what lay ahead. We were greeted by Wongchu Sherpa, a short, solid man with a quick smile, whose accented English was delivered machine gun style. Wongchu explained that we had arrived during a Hindu festival, which involved the sacrificial slaughter of cattle, goats and sheep. In parts of Kathmandu, the streets literally flowed with blood. The Sherpas, a small Buddhist minority in Nepal, believed it would rain until the blood was washed away.

Whatever the reason, the rain caused three days of canceled flights to Lukla, the starting point of our trek. But the delay wasn't a total waste. On our second day of lounging in the airport, a member of our group spotted a tall, gray-haired man, waiting to board a plane.

"I think that's Sir Edmund Hillary," one of my trekking partners announced.   My college classmate, Bill McCollom, had the gumption to find out, and after politely approaching the elderly gentleman, was rewarded by a friendly conversation with the most famous mountain climber in history.

Eventually, the weather cleared enough for a white-knuckle flight to the mountain hamlet of Lukla, and our trek began. We quickly settled into a routine: up early for a breakfast of tea and porridge, on the trail by 8:00 a.m., hiking until midafternoon with a break for lunch, and establishing our campsite before a dense blanket of clouds engulfed the deep valleys every afternoon. The days were warm and clear; the scenery, breath-takingly beautiful. In fact, we had precious little breath to spare, since our route led from 9,200 feet above sea level to well over 18,000 feet.

A week into our trek, we approached a tiny outpost called Gorak Shep, the last settlement before the Everest Base Camp. The trail was buzzing with the news that Jon Krakauer was there to dedicate a chorten, or stone monument to those who had perished on Everest in 1996.

We met Krakauer near the new memorial. He was obviously struggling with the emotional turmoil of saying good-bye to the members of his climbing party who would forever remain in Nepal.

The following day as we prepared to leave Gorak Shep, our local guide announced with excitement that Kagi Sherpa was relaxing in a nearby tea house. Kagi was a young, barrel-chested climber, who had publicly proclaimed his intention to establish a new speed record up Mount Everest: eighteen hours, from the base camp to the summit, unassisted and without bottled oxygen. His goal was astounding when compared to a typical Everest expedition, which requires weeks, even months. Several of our group spoke with Kagi, and wished him well in his attempt.

More than a week later, we were enjoying the fragrant warmth of a small bakery in the village of Khumjung. Another group of trekkers joined us. A fit, confident woman sat on the bench beside me. It was evident from her accent that she was from New Zealand. As a conversation developed, I realized she was the widow of Rob Hall, the leader of Krakauer's ill-fated Everest expedition. Jan Hall and members of her family had returned to the Khumbu to visit Rob's memorial, and to reassure their many Sherpa friends that life goes on.

That evening we learned that Kagi Sherpa had made his record-breaking attempt on Everest. Deep snow on the final push to the summit had put his goal of eighteen hours out of reach, but his time of twenty hours and twenty-four minutes was still a new record. It's fitting that the fastest man to the summit of the world's highest mountain is a Sherpa.

Race to Win and Eat Like There's No Tomorrow

Years ago, a training friend established what he called the Fat Boy's Running Club. He got T-shirts printed up with our motto, "Run for fun, race to win, and eat like there's no tomorrow." The group has survived countless mutations through the years, but the motto still rings true. Many of us middle-aged, former athletes continue to exercise not only for the love of sport, but for the freedom to eat what we want. Every experienced marathoner knows you can't run 26 miles without hurting, but carbo-loading on pasta, totally guilt-free, for several days prior to an event, makes that pain all worth it.

Being an athlete has also led me to various places in the world, and therefore, exotic food I might never have experienced otherwise. I'm definitely a meatloaf and mashed potatoes kind of guy, so some of those culinary adventures were well outside my comfort zone.

In 1974, the Soviets hosted the World Biathlon Championships in Minsk, the capital of Belorussia. They spared no expense to impress the visiting athletes and coaches. After the gala opening ceremony, we were guided to a lavish reception, where the vodka flowed like water and mounds of caviar, heaped more than a foot high, filled tables throughout the hall. To be polite, I sampled both the black and the orange, knowing what an expensive delicacy Russian caviar was back in the States. It still tasted like fish eggs to me.

Racing in France or Italy can be a challenge because of the alcohol. Athletes in those countries have wine with lunch, a cocktail before dinner, wine with the evening meal, followed by an aperitif. All this is before they go out on the town for some serious drinking! These customs are especially taxing for biathletes who have enough trouble seeing the targets when they're sober.

While the meals in western Europe can be delicious and even artistic, at the 1969 World Biathlon Championships in Poland, it was quite the opposite. I suspect Zakopane bid for the event in an effort to draw tourists back to their mountainous, winter sport resort, but the Cold War and Soviet domination made living conditions grim in Poland at that time.

During our two weeks in Zakopane, we were served animal parts seldom seen on American tables. One evening, I paused to study the grayish, slimy meat next to the ever-present cabbage and boiled potatoes on my plate. Two starving teammates dug in immediately, but their contorted expressions confirmed my fears; supper was pickled brains.

But my most daring culinary adventures took place during a tour in Vietnam. As a Mobile Advisory Team leader, I often ate with my Vietnamese counterpart. Usually that meant steamed rice with tiny pieces of fish or chicken, and some type of vegetable. But there were notable exceptions. At one local banquet, where we Americans were the guests of honor, we consumed a huge, smoked eel, 4 feet long and as thick as your wrist. This was no modest accomplishment using only chop sticks!

Another time, I was inspecting the perimeter of an outpost when I encountered an old Vietnamese soldier proudly preparing our supper, a rice paddy rat the size of a house cat. That evening's meal probably would have tasted fine, if I hadn't seen it being prepared.

My most memorable meal in Vietnam, however, was one I created myself. Sanitation was a serious problem in the Mekong Delta. The Vietnamese used the canals for everything: drinking water, bathing, fishing, and as a sewer.

Some innovative American scientist developed a variety of catfish that thrived on human waste, and my advisory team was ordered to demonstrate this advancement in sanitation to the residents of our hamlet. We partitioned off a corner of a flooded rice paddy and installed the catfish. Then we constructed a privy on bamboo pilings over the fish pond. For several weeks our latrine became the focal point of the village as the Vietnamese studied our experiment with fascination and amusement.

After weaning the fattened catfish off their normal diet for a couple of weeks, we followed the consultant's directive, and invited the village elders over for a fish fry. In spite of our best efforts to explain the elegant simplicity of this innovative approach to their sanitation problems and their occasional food shortages; the Vietnamese politely declined the opportunity to savor our catfish.

To be totally honest, since that tour in Vietnam, I've never much cared for catfish myself.

92

Terror in the Beauty Salon

The first haircuts I can remember were at the kitchen table with my mother wielding a set of clippers she'd ordered from the Sears catalog. Eventually, I graduated to the local barbershop, where I got pretty much the same buzz cut I'd received at home, but the atmosphere was totally different. In those days, the barber shop was an exciting glimpse into the world of men. There was a casual banter between the barbers and their customers. The shop might contain the chief of police, a local doctor, a farmer, and a businessman, in addition to a couple of us school kids. The conversations were always interesting: politics, sports, speculation about the cause of a recent house fire or the breakup of a marriage. We kids seldom spoke, fearing the grownups would remember we were listening and they would censor their stories.

The haircuts were uncomplicated and predictable. When the barber nodded in your direction, you hopped up into his huge, chrome and leather chair. He snapped the sheet around your neck, and asked, "What'll it be today?" The answer never varied: "The usual." This was pure formality, since our mothers gave the barber explicit instructions when they dropped us off.

Haircuts in college were more entertaining. Two elderly barbers in Middlebury held court in a regal shop of oak and marble, which must have been a showplace at the turn of the previous century. I suppose the popularity of the Beatles and the hippie movement in the 1960s decimated their client base, but those of us in army ROTC kept the two old barbers in business. As an added bonus, the Middlebury barbers had a gregarious parakeet who ranged freely throughout the shop. It was not uncommon for the parakeet to land on your shoulder and peck at your ear. The bird also enjoyed parading up and down the counter, admiring himself in the huge mirrors. More than once I noticed the barber deftly wipe a fresh parakeet poop off the polished marble with the towel he then returned to my shoulder.

These no-frills barber shops are an endangered species. I found one near my home, and was happy for several years, until the two old barbers sold the business to a couple of young women. Fortunately, the new owners didn't renovate the shop, and I've weathered the traumatic transition. Now the conversations are about their kids rather than sports, but the haircuts are just as good and are still reasonably priced.

Then, on a recent Saturday morning I was overcome by panic. I had an important appointment early Monday morning and realized it had been months since my last haircut. I dropped everything and raced into town, only to find my usual barber shop closed for the weekend. Desperately, I walked the streets searching for a haircut.

The only place open on Saturday morning was a very fancy, progressive hairstyling salon. I was frightened just looking through the door at all the chrome, mirrors, and hair-drying contraptions. There were huge posters on the walls of very handsome people, with very dramatic hairstyles. This was not my kind of barber shop, but I was desperate. I summoned all my courage and opened the door.

I was greeted by an attractive and friendly young woman named Lisa. Studying her massive schedule sheet, she asked if I had an appointment.

"Ah ... no. I've never been here before. I just need a regular haircut," I stammered. For some reason, that remark drew the attention of everyone else in the shop, all of them women. Lisa must have taken pity on me, because after studying her schedule again, she announced, "Well, I've just had a cancellation, so I can cut your hair myself."

It wasn't just a haircut. First she gave me a shampoo. Then, back in her chair in front of a huge mirror, Lisa began combing my wet hair in totally new directions — straight back, parted down the middle, not parted at all. Meanwhile, I counted eighteen chrome bottles of hair-care products in front of me: shampoos, rinses, conditioners, mousses, and gels. I never knew there were so many concoctions you could put on your hair.

When she finished cutting, Lisa picked up the blow-dryer, and I cringed. Then, before I could react, she reached for the mousse.

"Hey, Lisa, I don't need any of that stuff." Too late.

"Sure you do, just a little to give it some body."

I willingly handed over twenty-five bucks, eager to make my escape. I thanked Lisa, then stepped out into the street, feeling like a pampered poodle at a dog show. The only problem is that I've had several nice compliments on my new haircut. I just haven't decided whether they are worth another terror-filled visit to the styling salon.

Sports and Life

The Twenty-Seventh U.S. Marine Corps Marathon

I spent four years in army ROTC during college, followed by four more years as an infantry officer. It's an unfortunate reality that esprit de corps and unit pride often foster unhealthy rivalries and even open hostility between the branches of our military. An old army joke asserts that an infantry rifle squad consists of ten soldiers, while the comparable U.S. Marine Corps squad requires eleven. The extra marine is the photographer, who's always first on the beach to ensure that the other marines get maximum publicity. My eight years in the U.S. Army was ample time to develop a healthy disdain for the U.S. Marine Corps.

I avoided the U.S. Marine Corps Marathon for as long as I could, but I finally gave in, participating for the first time in 1991 with the very personal goal of finishing ahead of as many "jarheads" as possible. There was all the patriotic hoopla I had dreaded: formations of marines running in combat boots shouting cadence for 26 miles; bare-chested, muscle-bound marines running with huge flags; and of course, thousands of marines lining the route, encouraging those who were compelled to run.

I had to admit, however, it was an impressive event. From the 105 howitzer used as a starting gun, to the symbolic climb and finish at the Iwo Jima Monument, the U.S. Marine Corps had organized a very successful marathon, and I returned for a second dose in 1993.

At that time in its twenty-seventh year, in the autumn of 2002, drawing nearly twenty thousand participants annually, the U.S. Marine Corps Marathon was widely regarded as one of the best in the world. With a stepdaughter in her senior year at George Washington University, I had planned a family weekend around a return to the marathon. After some quality time with our college student Friday night, followed by a little sightseeing on Saturday, my wife, Kay, and I joined the throng on the Metro early Sunday morning for the short ride to Arlington National Cemetery and the starting line. As I waited to stash my warm-ups in the baggage tent, a line of VPs was led through the crush of runners. I was pleased to see Vermont Senator Patrick Leahy among the dignitaries. He served on the Senate committee that writes the defense budget, and his son was a marine.

Moments before the start, Sergeant Daniel Clark, a Massachusetts state trooper, sang the national anthem. Standing silently with twenty thousand other runners, next to the endless rows of military graves, just down the hill from the Iwo Jima statue, and across the Potomac River from the Lincoln Memorial, was a powerful experience. Then the howitzer boomed, and the crush surged forward across the starting line. Just beyond the first mile we circled the Pentagon, remarkably restored only thirteen months after the terrorist attack.

At mile nine we took the Key Bridge into Georgetown, followed by an excursion on the Rock Creek Parkway before passing the Kennedy Center and the Lincoln Memorial. I spotted my family in the crowd behind the Vietnam Veterans Memorial. Their encouragement carried me past the White House, the Supreme Court and the Capitol Building. Somewhere beyond the Smithsonian, approaching mile twenty, I began to fade. My prerace goals evaporated and psychologically I settled into survival mode. I thought I might be able to jog the final six miles to the finish.

Years ago, on Memorial Day weekend at the Vermont City Marathon, I ran in a singlet with an enlargement of the Vietnam Service Ribbon in honor of all the Vietnam vets who could not run, and as a reminder of my good fortune, that I could. In the early stages of the U.S. Marine Corps Marathon, occasional bystanders recognized the green, red and gold symbol on my shirt and shouted, "That-a-way Vietnam vet."

Moments after I ran out of gas, I reached an aid station where dozens of young marines in combat fatigues shouted encouragement as they held out cups of water. A crusty old sergeant spotted my shirt, snapped to attention, whipped me the most professional salute I have ever seen, and said, "Thank you for serving, Sir." I returned his salute and thanked him, as I ran past. Then it struck me that many of these same marines might soon be fighting and dying in Iraq.

Somewhere, I found a reserve and got back on pace. I pushed hard up the final hill and around the Iwo Jima Monument, finishing a few minutes ahead of my target time. But more importantly, I gained a new appreciation for the elite branch of our military that has defended our freedom with their lives for 227 years. Semper Fi.

Acknowledging My Addiction

In the spring of 1989, my running buddy Dave Faucher discovered a new marathon in Burlington. The first Vermont City Marathon was a blast: excellent organization, plenty of supportive spectators, and a beautiful course featuring impressive vistas across Lake Champlain. As a bonus, Faucher won the 40-to-49 age group, and I was second. The following years, Dave repeated the Masters Champion, while I slipped to fourth and sixth in the age group. But the men's field had grown from 345 finishers to nearly 500 in three years, and I was hooked.

One aspect of the Vermont City Marathon that creates universal appeal is the relay, which gives everyone the chance to participate, regardless of their level of conditioning.

My plan in '92 was to run the opening 3-mile leg for a relay team, then continue on to complete the full marathon. But as anyone who ran that year will remember, the wind blew, and a pelting rain threatened to change to sleet. Moments out of the start, my hamstring seized up and I limped painfully to the first tag zone. Twenty-three more miles that day was out of the question.

May 30, 1993, fell during my college reunion. After two days of celebrating and late night parties, I arose in Middlebury before dawn, determined to be at Battery Park well before the 8:00 a.m. start.

Sometime during the mid-1990s the organizers issued distinctive, blue numbers to the handful of fanatics who had entered every Vermont City Marathon since the beginning. Although it was an honor to wear the colored number, few of the spectators understood its significance. For the past three years, the colored numbers have also carried the words "Hall of Fame," which seem to elicit reactions from awe to pity.

In the spring of 1998, I was offered work in Alaska's Denali National Park. It had been a banner snow year in Alaska, so my training for the marathon was minimal. My buddies John Donovan and Dave Faucher came to the rescue. We talked and joked our way through what—without their entertainment—would have been a very painful 26 miles.

The following year, my daughter graduated from college. Luckily her commencement ceremonies were held the day after the marathon. Julie was grateful that I arrived on time, even though she took a ribbing from classmates who commented, "Your dad walks funny."

1999 was the year that Frank Shorter spoke at the prerace banquet. Early the next morning, before Battery Park overflowed with nervous runners, I was stretching and admiring the view of the Adirondacks when the Olympic marathon champion approached. We had a wonderful conversation about running, the Olympics, and a mutual concern regarding the proliferation of illegal doping. As he turned to go, I asked if he'd autograph my race bib. Now I have a Vermont City Marathon competition number that has significance beyond the designation Hall of Fame.

I'll see you in Burlington on the morning before Memorial Day.

The Heart of an Olympian

It was March 22, 2003, and spring had officially sprung two days earlier. The temperature was several degrees above freezing in Presque Isle, Maine, but 20 inches of snow still covered the ground. I had traveled to northern Maine from my home in Thetford, Vermont, for the Nordic Heritage Spring Series—several days of cross-country ski-racing designed to extend the competitive season and to provide an opportunity for promising youngsters in Aroostook County to race against some of the top skiers in the nation. I hadn't yet fully recovered from a chest cold I'd acquired two weeks earlier during a grueling 50-kilometer race (that's 31 miles, for those not used to metric distances) from Great Glen to Bretton Woods in northern New Hampshire. Nevertheless, I didn't want to miss the chance to wrap up the season in Presque Isle. I'd registered for two events using the classic skiing technique, a straight, forward-and-back gliding motion, in addition to one freestyle event, a technique that's like speed skating on skis.

But moments into the 10-kilometer classic event, I had the distinct sensation that accompanies skiing at high altitude, a constriction at the base of my throat and a tingling in my fingers. But Presque Isle's elevation is only about 500 feet above sea level. Assuming that I was simply feeling the lingering effects of the cold, I throttled back on the tough climbs and managed to finish the race. The 15-kilometer freestyle event the next day was just as frustrating. I decided that staying in Presque Isle for the 30-kilometer classic was pointless, so I packed up early and headed home.

A few days later I was in New Gloucester, Maine, at Pineland Farms—an agricultural, educational, and recreational center recently created on the campus of the state's former mental institution. I had been hired a couple of years earlier to lay out a trail system there, and thanks to the bountiful snows of 2003, I was back to design some extensions. As the Pineland Farms officials and I scouted out locations for the new trails, I happened to mention the name of a local engineer and wetlands expert who had become a friend during some previous trail projects I'd done in that part of Maine. I was stunned to learn that my friend had suffered a heart attack and died while cross-country skiing just a few months earlier. The unusual sensations I had experienced during the races at Presque Isle had attracted my attention, but the news of my friend's fatal heart attack jolted me to action.

When I returned home from Pineland, I called my doctor, who had been one of my Nordic skiers during my coaching days at Dartmouth twenty years earlier. He assured me there was probably nothing to worry about, but just to be certain he scheduled a stress test. Within days, I was jogging on a treadmill at Dartmouth Hitchcock Medical Center, with instructions to sound off if the sensations I had experienced in Presque Isle returned. It was some consolation that it required a reasonably steep grade and a brisk pace on the treadmill to recreate the constricted breathing and the tingling fingers.

The test results were conclusive: there was a 50-percent occlusion of the main artery supplying blood to my heart. That was the bad news. But there was some good news as well. Thanks to my high level of physical activity, the problem had been identified early—probably before the restricted blood flow had damaged my heart. Sadly, many people in our country have become so sedentary that their arteries are 80- or 90-percent restricted before any dramatic symptoms are apparent—and by then their heart is often irreparably damaged. An additional piece of good news was that my recovery should be quick and complete, since I was otherwise fit and healthy.

Even so, it was quite a shock to be diagnosed with heart disease. I'm fifty-seven years old and have never smoked. My most recent blood test had shown an acceptable cholesterol level of 177. And I have been a dedicated (some would even say fanatic) endurance athlete for forty years. I began competing in cross-country skiing in high school and continued in college. My senior year at Middlebury, I missed being the NCAA champion by four seconds in a forty-five-minute race at altitude in Colorado.

I was even able to finagle serving three of the four years of my U.S. Army obligation on skis, assigned to the Winter Biathlon Training Center at Fort Richardson, Alaska. Biathlon—an athletic event with military roots—consists of cross-country skiing combined with rifle marksmanship. At Fort Richardson, we were training on snow by October 1st and had usually logged 1,200 kilometers (almost 750 miles) on skis before our first race every winter.

That experience led to my participation in two Winter Olympics—Sapporo in 1972 and Innsbruck in 1976—plus seven Biathlon World Championships and a couple of military ski championships. After retiring from international competition in 1976, I continued to ski, mostly for the satisfaction of being fit. Through the years, as job and family responsibilities have permitted, I've enjoyed competing in master's cross-country competitions throughout the region. In March of 2000, I joined several friends for a week of classic skiing—444 kilometers—across Finland, from the Russian border to Sweden.

My off-season training for Nordic skiing consists of hiking, cycling, and a lot of running. As a result, I've finished more than fifty marathons, from Maine to Alaska, as well as hundreds of shorter road races and trail runs. In July of 2002, my wife, Kay, and I pedaled 100 miles in the Audrey Prouty Century Ride, an annual event that raises money for research at Dartmouth's Norris Cotton Cancer Center. And last October, I ran the U.S. Marine Corps Marathon in Washington, D.C., and was pleased to finish third in my age group with a time of 3:09:40. So, although I might have worried that I'd someday be a candidate for knee- or hip-replacement surgery, I never for a moment questioned the durability of my heart. If exercise was the key to a healthy heart, I figured mine would still be beating long after the rest of me had collapsed in a heap of worn-out parts.

Anyway, back to last spring: after further consultation with my doctor and a Dartmouth cardiologist, I was scheduled for a catheterization. On April 22, Kay accompanied me to DHMC for what is now a routine procedure—threading a tiny cable, or catheter, from a large blood vessel in the groin up into the heart to quite literally take a look at the obstruction in the artery.

In many cases, the catheter can then be used to perform an angioplasty—a procedure involving the insertion of a tiny, inflatable device at the end of the catheter; this "balloon" expands, forcing the plaque responsible for the obstruction out of the way. Then a tiny mesh stent, or reinforcement, is installed to keep the artery open. The procedure is done under local anesthesia, so you can actually watch on an overhead TV screen as this tiny wire pokes around in your heart.

Soon after the doctor manipulating the catheter pointed out my obstruction, he withdrew the instrument rather than beginning the angioplasty, so I suspected that my situation was more complicated than some. I learned later that the occlusion was too close to a junction of two arteries to be suitable for a stent. But I was assured that a bypass operation would almost certainly enable me to return to my accustomed level of physical activity.

On May 13, Kay and I met with a cardiothoracic surgeon scheduled to perform my bypass. I quickly learned that the surgeon was training for the annual bicycle race up New Hampshire's highest peak, 6,288-foot Mount Washington. Needless to say, we hit it off immediately. I have to admit, however, that he got my attention when he warned me that for half an hour, while he performed the bypass, my heart would be stopped and my blood oxygenated and circulated by a machine. Come to think of it, slicing up and stitching a beating heart would probably be pretty tricky.

My surgeon was even understanding enough to let me participate in the fifteenth annual Vermont City Marathon on May 25. Since Kay was the captain of a women's relay team, and I was one of only nineteen men and women who had run in the race every year since its establishment (out of more than five thousand annual registrants), I hated to miss the event. I agreed to the doctor's reasonable "no running" order and walked the 3.3 miles of the first relay leg before cheering Kay and her teammates on to a fourth-place finish in the women's 40-to-50 age category.

Three days later, on Wednesday, May 28, several family members accompanied me through the pre-op preparations. I felt reasonably relaxed, thanks to the optimism and reassurance provided by several running and skiing buddies who are doctors and medical professionals. After the inevitable delays, the anesthesiologist arrived. He cheerfully coached me through what was about to happen, prepared an injection, then said to Kay, "If you want to give him a kiss he'll remember, now's the time."

He wasn't exaggerating. Several hours later, I came to in the Cardiothoracic Intensive Care Unit and began discussing the joys of pond hockey with a nurse from Newfoundland. I had absolutely no recollection of the fact that several family members and a few friends had all visited me as soon as they were permitted, following the operation. Apparently, I had been coherent enough to reassure them about how I felt and had even managed the appropriate military response, "Carry on," when a fellow veteran saluted on his way out.

By the time Kay returned on Thursday morning, I had been relocated to the Intermediate Cardiac Care Unit and was admiring the view of the New Hampshire hills from the window of my fourth-floor room—eager to begin my first shuffling excursions around the central nursing pod. Later that day, and again on Friday, Kay joined me for "exercise classes," and our walks grew longer.

Having coached skiers for many years, I knew the value of positive thinking and visualization. I kept reminding myself of the optimism the doctors had expressed and of their assurance that I'd have a quick recovery. Two minor incidents challenged that confidence. The day after the operation I was given an incentive spirometer—a plastic contraption that measures the strength of your breathing. I was told to inhale through the device as deeply as possible ten times every hour. The spirometer had a scale from 0 to 4,000, but that first day I could barely get the indicator to move; even 500 seemed out of reach.

"Do patients really get this thing up to 4,000?" I asked a nurse.

"Oh, sure," she answered.

It was discouraging to see how far I had to go before I would be breathing normally again.

The second incident involved pain medication. When I awoke in cardiothoracic intensive care following the operation, I remember feeling as if I were floating blissfully above the bed. Such is the power of morphine. The next day, in the Intermediate Cardiac Care Unit, I was switched to Percocet, administered every four hours. Late that afternoon, enjoying a visit from my daughter, Julie, I failed to notice that my 4:00 p.m. fix of Percocet had not been delivered. By 5:00, I had moved up the scale from mildly uncomfortable to definitely hurting. It was 5:30 before an apologetic nurse brought my medication, but by then I was well behind the pain curve. It was a miserable night until another sympathetic nurse finally sought permission from the doctor to administer a dose of morphine to get me back ahead of the pain. The educational part of the incident was experiencing the intensity of the pain when the drugs wore off, as well as recognizing how effectively modern drugs can mask such pain.

By Saturday morning, after visits from my doctors, I was cleared to go home, pending a couple of out-processing requirements. I had to donate more blood for additional lab work — a procedure that would have brought on a cold sweat and perhaps a fainting spell only a short time before, but was no longer any big deal. I also had to have a chest X-ray to verify that my recovery was progressing normally. Again, no problem. And, finally, I had to defecate. I found it a bit ironic that you can bounce back from having your chest cracked open like a Thanksgiving turkey and your heart stopped for half an hour, but the ultimate requirement for leaving the hospital is to perform one of the most elemental bodily functions. But after two days of round the clock pain killers and a liquid diet, moving your bowels isn't that easy. Fortunately (or unfortunately, depending upon your perspective), the nurses have their time-tested methods, so I was on the way home by noon.

Thus began phase two of my recovery program. I advanced to very slow walks out the driveway to fetch the mail, experimented with the dosage of my pain medication for maximum effectiveness but minimum digestive-tract disruption, and gained weight thanks to wonderful home-cooked meals prepared by Kay and several thoughtful families in our church.

Another aspect of my recovery was participation in cardiac rehab classes. I resisted these classes initially, for a couple of reasons. For starters, the classes were three times a week at DHMC, and since I wasn't allowed to drive for a month following the operation, I'd be inconveniencing Kay or someone else to provide me with transportation.

Secondly, with my coaching and racing background, I figured I knew how to get back in shape as well as anyone. But the fitness experts in DHMC's Cardiac Rehab Center dispelled that misconception pretty quickly. At my first session, I met the seven other members of my class: men and women of various ages, physical states, and occupations who were linked together by heart disease. We learned to abrade specific locations on our chests and apply the electrodes that would send signals to a computer that monitored our vital signs during our exercise regimen. After a four-minute warm-up, we did three ten-minute sessions on each of the machines in the lab: treadmills, stationary bicycles, and rowing ergometers. Since all the class members were recovering from some sort of cardiac incident, the instructors carefully monitored our workloads and heart rates. In spite of the diversity of the class, there was a cheerful, cooperative atmosphere in the sessions — perhaps due to the awareness that we had all been given an early warning or, in some cases, a second chance.

Many of the exercise sessions were followed by lectures on topics related to heart disease. This was another aspect of the program that I initially dreaded, but soon grew to appreciate. The first lecture was about the risk factors that contribute to coronary artery disease: smoking, a diet high in saturated fat, high blood pressure, obesity, stress, lack of exercise, and a family history of heart disease.

On the plus side, I have never smoked, I'm not significantly overweight, and I get plenty of exercise. But I certainly could be more careful about what I eat, I could learn better techniques for dealing with stress, and I realized that I might have a family history of heart disease. It has definitely been helpful to look at these risk factors individually so that I can take steps to minimize the ones susceptible to change.

Probably the area that holds the greatest promise (and challenge) for me is diet. During many years of full-time training for international competition, my dietary goal was simply to consume enough calories to sustain two and often three workouts a day. Those habits are hard to break, especially when the food and restaurant industries are determined to give us "more for our money" every time we sit down to a meal. Those green glass Coca Cola bottles we baby boomers remember from our youth held eight ounces. Today's plastic Coke bottles, which fill convenience-store coolers across the country, hold twenty ounces. Is it any surprise that obesity has become a national health crisis?

A second risk factor that may have contributed to my heart disease is ineffective stress management. Stress is not necessarily a bad thing. In fact, in sports, the judicious application of stress can improve performance. It's how we learn to manage stress that makes the difference. I'm afraid I have a tendency to put too many projects on my to-do list, then focus on what I didn't accomplish in a given day or week. And when something ticks me off, I tend to stew about it rather than blowing off steam at the time. These are not healthy habits in terms of managing stress.

In late June, a month after my operation, Kay and I met again with my cardiothoracic surgeon. He was pleased by the progress of my recovery. I was cleared to resume driving, an amazing privilege that most of us take totally for granted. He also gave me the okay to try cycling, staying on flat terrain at first and being sensitive to any chest pain. He advised holding off on running for a couple more weeks and said it would probably be fall before I'd be ready for hard physical work like using a chainsaw or splitting firewood.

I told him that I had my sights set on a more immediate goal—participating in the 2003 Audrey Prouty Ride. Kay and I had upgraded our old bikes in anticipation of the 2003 event. My surgeon agreed to let me do the 25-mile version, which—after a couple of training rides the week before the event—was a piece of cake.

When I reached the six-week threshold, I asked a technician in the Cardiac Rehab Center if I could crank up the treadmill and really run. I said, "Aside from a sore chest, I feel fine. I've been taking it easy for several months now, and I'm eager to get back in shape."

She agreed, but added a note of caution.

"John, you've made terrific progress," she said, "but we don't want to rush it. After an operation like yours, especially when the heart has been stopped for a period of time, it's not uncommon for the heartbeat to be somewhat irregular for a while. We don't want you pushing so hard that you develop some type of arrhythmia."

"Well," I countered, feeling very confident, "I haven't had any irregular heartbeats working out in here, have I?"

"A few," she responded with a smile.

Since that conversation, I have done exactly what the trainers tell me to do. If I return to my former level of fitness, it will be thanks to the guidance of the many knowledgeable professionals whom I have met since that ski race last March in Presque Isle.

Like many Americans, I complain about the outrageous cost of medical insurance and the shocking profits reported by some pharmaceutical companies. But if I cross the finish line of the Vermont City Marathon on Memorial Day weekend of 2004 in three hours plus a few minutes, it will be thanks to the incredible technological advances of American medicine and the caring, dedicated people who deliver that technology.

And now, if you'll pardon me, I've gotta run . . .

The Moosilauke Triathlon

I recently participated in a unique reunion that stimulated considerable reflection and adjustment of my perspective. But first, a little background. I've finally come to recognize and even accept that I'm a goal-oriented person. As a competitive skier, setting goals was never a problem: earn a spot on the high school team, represent the college team at the winter carnivals, qualify for the NCAA Championships, or ultimately, compete for the U.S. at the Winter Olympics.

As a high school and college ski coach, the goals were equally as clear, although tempered by an awareness that competitive sport is just one facet of young students' busy lives. Still, the character traits developed through competitive sports are so valuable in life, I felt no hesitation instilling in my athletes a strong goal orientation.

During more than a decade of coaching the Nordic men's team at Dartmouth, including dozens of NCAA Championship participants and a handful of Olympians, I noticed that my athletes generally fell into two groups: those who loved to race and trained only because it was essential for good results, and those who loved to train and raced mainly to justify all the training they did. Both groups caused me frustration. The skiers who loved to race were often ambivalent about mid-week workouts, frequently missing practices to finish a paper, study for a test, or to attend an academic extra-help session. Skiers in the second group would never miss a practice, but might be stricken with a mysterious sore throat or cough hours before we were scheduled to depart for a race. But as someone who thrived on racing myself, I had the most difficulty understanding the guys who would train diligently all week, then approach the competitions with trepidation and anxiety. For many of them training became an end in itself, and they were constantly creating ever-more elaborate and innovative workouts.

Every fall, before the incoming freshmen became familiar with the campus, the ski team conducted an orienteering workout, which had pairs of athletes scampering all over Hanover for the entire afternoon. One civic-minded skier cajoled his teammates into roller skiing from the

Canadian border at Derby Line, Vermont, back to Hanover in an effort to raise awareness of OXFAM's efforts to eradicate world hunger.

But the ultimate ski team workout was probably the Moosilauke Triathlon. Mount Moosilauke, with an elevation of 4,810 feet, is the southwestern limit of New Hampshire's White Mountain range. Dartmouth College owns the mountain and a beautiful log lodge, which was built at its base by students before World War II. In the early 1980s, a Dartmouth Nordic skier thought it would be great fun to hike from the Ravine Lodge, over the summit, and south on the Appalachian Trail to Route 25C, something over 12 miles. Then the athletes would switch to roller skis and kick and glide an additional 15 miles to Orford, New Hampshire. Finally, exchanging their ski poles for paddles at the Connecticut River, the skiers would paddle the Ledyard Canoe Club's 30-foot war canoe the final 18 miles to Hanover.

It was no surprise, almost twenty-five years ago, that my eager Nordic skier had no trouble finding a dozen of his Dartmouth teammates who thought the workout would be "awesome." And it was awesome, as well as totally exhausting. What was surprising, however, was when this same enthusiastic skier, now a federal judge in Washington, D.C., began e-mailing former teammates about a re-creation of the workout, he again had no trouble filling the war canoe. They came from as far as San Francisco. They all carved time out from demanding careers and busy schedules. Some brought their families. Their only concession to our advancing years was the substitution of bicycles for roller skis on the middle section.

From my perspective, as their former coach, it was not just like old times, it was better than old times. There was a deep appreciation of our natural surroundings, which we probably took for granted before, and a mutual admiration for what former teammates had accomplished in the past two decades. And finally, for me, a vivid reminder that the journey is at least as important as the destination, a concept that had eluded me, but I suspect some of my skiers understood more than twenty years ago, when they were undergraduates.

Running the Vermont City Marathon

I've run marathons on the coast of Maine and in the wilderness of Alaska. I've gawked at our national monuments during the U.S. Marine Corps Marathon and experienced the cultural diversity of the Big Apple in the New York City Marathon. Just over a year ago, I was one of the privileged 38,000 who good-naturedly jostled each other from Hopkinton to Boston. But for almost a decade, my favorite race has been the Vermont City Marathon.

Since 1988, on the Sunday before Memorial Day, Burlington has hosted what has become Vermont's largest sporting event, and the second biggest marathon in New England. One key to the event's success is the simultaneous running of the certified 26.2 mile marathon, and a five-person relay team competition. With relay distances from 3.3 to 6.6 miles, running enthusiasts of all ages and levels of fitness can be part of the fun.

Early in the morning, the last Sunday in May, you join hundreds of other runners at Battery Park for the start. Although you try to stay calm and conserve your energy for the challenge ahead, the excitement is infectious. As you stretch and pin on your racing number, your gaze repeatedly returns to the deep blue expanse of Lake Champlain and the peaks of the Adirondacks beyond. You sip water, check your shoelaces dozens of times and try to convince yourself that you really don't have to stand in line for the porta potty again.

Shortly before 8:00 a.m. you're engulfed by the sea of runners flowing from the park to the street. You're overcome by the distinctive smells of Ben Gay and suntan lotion as you strain to hear final instructions garbled over a bullhorn. The governor and the mayor may wish you well and offer a few words of advice. As the seconds tick off, the crowd becomes strangely quiet. Hundreds of dedicated runners carefully poise fingers on the start buttons of their digital wrist watches.

The gun goes off, a roar of approval rises from the crowd, and you're swept along in a river of runners through the streets of downtown Burlington. On South Willard Street, sleepy residents, some still in their bathrobes, sit on their front steps clutching coffee mugs. There is joking and banter among the runners. Through the 1-mile and 2-mile markers, runners check their watches and discuss pacing strategy. You glance at the competitors around you, looking for the terry cloth wristbands that identify them as relay team members rather than marathoners.

Church Street is strangely vacant, with only clusters of early morning spectators, but around the corner in Battery Park the crowd is loud and enthusiastic. Heading out of the city on the Northern Connector Highway, which has been closed to traffic, you're daunted by the runners spread out ahead of you, but making the turn near mile 7, you're amazed by how many others are behind you.

As you return to Battery Park and Church Street, more people have gathered: musicians play, you can smell breakfasts cooking, and the spectators finally appear to be awake. South of town, Pine Street seems so long and straight you're convinced you're headed for Middlebury, but eventually a few turns through a residential neighborhood bring you to the shore of Lake Champlain. There may be a refreshing breeze off the water, and after 15 miles, the sparkling blue of the waves is incredibly inviting.

At mile 16 you face one of your stiffest challenges, the climb from the waterfront back up the bluff to Battery Park. But you're urged along by hundreds of enthusiastic spectators and the impressive Taiko Drummers, whose dramatic rhythms inspire you up the hill. The miles add up as you head out North Avenue. By this point you are tired, perhaps in "survival mode," and it's unnerving to be headed away from the finish line. But soon after the 21-mile mark, you leave the road for the Lakeside Bike Path. Your final 4 miles seem like a pastoral, green tunnel through overhanging trees, broken only by spectacular views of Lake Champlain.

In an abrupt but welcome transition, you leave the quiet solitude of the shaded bike path for the wildly cheering throng at Waterfront Park. It is difficult to imagine a better site for the finish line. Joined by your family and friends you stretch out on the grass and soak in the panorama of the lake and the Adirondacks beyond. There is plenty of good food and festive music. It's a state-wide, celebration-picnic. You relax in the warm sun, recounting the challenges of the race and comparing blisters. You feel the satisfaction of having worked very hard to achieve a goal you set for yourself months earlier.

The Vermont City Marathon has become a tradition in our family, as firmly entrenched as cutting a Christmas tree or hiding Easter eggs. I can't imagine what else I'd do on Memorial Day weekend. I'll see you there!

The Solstice Hike

At first glance, John Griesemer of Lyme, New Hampshire, seems an unlikely candidate to be the region's "Pied Piper of Endurance Hikes." His thinning hair, slight build and random assortment of rummage sale exercise clothes do not conjure up images of the fearless mountain guide.

Originally from New Jersey, Griesemer attended the wedding of a friend and fell in love with the Upper Valley. He landed a job writing for the local paper and began performing in community theater. In one of those interesting twists of fate, John played Romeo to my wife Kay's Juliet, long before I knew either of them.

John's talent on stage led to an agent and roles on TV, in movies and in theaters far from his home in Lyme. He resisted the temptation to relocate to New York City because he knew the Upper Valley was a better place to raise his family, and because he couldn't bear the thought of being away from the mountains.

After bagging all forty-eight of the 4,000-foot peaks in New Hampshire's White Mountains, Johnny G. (as he's fondly known among his hiking buddies) began to organize epic treks to lure his friends out onto the trails. His signature creation is the Solstice Hike, an endurance adventure to commemorate the longest day of the year.

There are three keys to Griesemer's success in organizing these annual events: his knowledge of the mountains, his enthusiasm, and email. Sometime early in the spring a long list of men, mostly middle-aged former athletes and outdoor enthusiasts in Lyme and the surrounding towns, receive an e-mail from Griesemer announcing the date of the Solstice Hike and the proposed route. This announcement usually generates dozens of responses: complaints about the severity of the route, complaints about the obscenely early departure time, and good-natured teasing about who's too old or out of shape to complete the hike.

This year's event was a classic traverse of the Presidential Range, ascending Mount Madison from Route 2 in Randolph, New Hampshire, then on to the summits of Mounts Adams, Jefferson and Clay before a break for lunch at the Mount Washington summit station. After lunch it was down the Crawford path to Lake of the Clouds, Mounts Monroe, Franklin, Eisenhower, and Pierce, then the descent to Route 302 in Crawford Notch. The distance covered was just under 20 miles with a total elevation gain of nearly 10,000 vertical feet.

At 3:00 a.m. on June 25, seventeen bleary-eyed, gravelly voiced adventurers gathered in Lyme as Griesemer organized the transportation. It was a diverse group of men, ranging in age from a college sophomore to several others nearly eligible to collect social security. There were a couple of medical doctors, an architect, college professors, a few lawyers, consultants, and a candidate for the U.S. Congress.

By 4:30, our caravan arrived at Crawford Notch, where we left a car.

Then it was on to the base of the Cog Railroad, where we left a second vehicle in the event someone had to abbreviate the entire traverse. As the sky brightened with the dawn, we encountered a deer and several moose on the remote, Jefferson Notch road. Someone joked about spotting a bear to score a wildlife hat trick, and rounding the next turn, a mature black bear paused in the middle of the road before lumbering into the undergrowth.

With temperatures forecast well into the nineties, we were eager to get up onto the ridge. Once above tree line, we were met by a surprisingly strong, warm wind. The summit of Madison provided our first rest stop. As we waited for stragglers, Griesemer clucked around like a mother hen gathering her brood. It was impressive looking down at how far we had come, but a glance through the haze toward the distant bulk of Mount Washington was intimidating, since that was our destination for lunch!

Thanks to a steady pace and enthusiastic conversation with hiking buddies, the miles and summits passed quickly. At noon, we crunched across a swath of cinders and the Cog Railway not far below the Summit Visitor's Center. Again, Johnny G. gathered his flock, first to sample the chili dogs in the cafeteria, then to assemble on the observation platform for a group photo. After a cell phone call to razz the wimps who had opted for the beach instead of the Solstice Hike, it was down the ridge toward Lake of the Clouds and the remaining summits.

Late in the afternoon, with the final peak behind us, we staggered down the Crawford Path on blisters and aching muscles. After nearly 20 miles and 10,000 feet of climbing, a skinny dip into a pristine pool on a mountain stream capped a perfect day.

At the parking lot, Johnny G. took a head count, handed out frosted beverages from the trunk of his car, and reminded everyone of the Independence Day run from the Connecticut River to the summit of Smarts. But that's another story.

Sports and Life

Marathon Flashbacks

With the return of warmer weather and the running of the Vermont City Marathon only weeks, rather than months away, I was reminded of some images from previous races I completed. Although I've run more than sixty marathons in the past thirty-seven years, it began as a way to stay in shape for skiing, so I haven't kept accurate records.

My first marathon was the Equinox, in Fairbanks, Alaska, as a member of the U.S. Biathlon Training Center. In the early 1970s, the Parks Highway had just been completed, cutting the driving distance between Anchorage and Fairbanks to 378 miles. Sven Johansen, our tough old Swedish ski coach, thought it would be great publicity for the team if we ran the new highway, camping along the way, arriving in Fairbanks by mid-September for the marathon.

Rarely did an athlete risk challenging Sven's training plan, but thankfully, on this occasion someone piped up, "Great idea, Sven, then we could swim to Europe this winter for the biathlon races and save all that airfare!"

I believe it was at my second Equinox Marathon, a couple of years later, that I battled for three hours with Spencer Lyman, a tough runner from McGrath, Alaska, who ran track at the University of Oregon. The Fairbanks course had plenty of hills where I could pull away from Lyman, but he'd reel me in on the flats. After 26 miles of running shoulder to shoulder, when the finish line finally appeared across several athletic fields, Spencer said, "Well, it's been great, but I gotta go." He put on a sprint that left me a hundred yards behind in just a few seconds.

After four years in the Army, I taught high school English and coached skiing and running in Anchorage. The Mayor's Midnight Sun Marathon was established in the mid 1970s, incorporating several miles of tank trails on Fort Richardson before traversing the city on beautiful new bike paths. Several of my high school students were in terrific shape and determined to run. On workouts together prior to the race, I shared with them the wisdom of experienced marathoners: "Remember, the halfway point of a marathon is 20 miles."

On race day, they bubbled with enthusiasm, and during the first few miles, chomped impatiently at the bit. By 10 miles they had all succumbed to the temptation and left me in the dust. By 20 miles, I had passed each of them back, offering encouragement as I plodded along. All of my students finished, some with impressive times for a first marathon, but they all paid dearly for running too fast, too early in the race.

Soon after returning to Vermont in 1978, my former army buddy, Terry Aldrich, suggested we run the Green Mountain Marathon on Grand Isle, to qualify for Boston. The course on Grand Isle was relatively flat and fast, with much of the route on shaded dirt roads. In those days, we needed a 2:50 to qualify for Boston, which would take careful pacing.

We were right on schedule for most of the race but began to fade in the final miles. Terry was stronger, so he ran ahead, while I frantically checked my watch as the minutes and seconds piled up. Crossing the finish line, my watch displayed 2:50:01. Could it be possible that I had run for almost 3 hours only to miss qualifying for Boston by one second?

Fortunately, before I had the opportunity to become too despondent, they posted the unofficial times, and mine was listed as 2:49:59. I've never known if I was slow with my wristwatch or if some sympathetic race official shaved a couple of seconds for me.

The big events, like Boston, the U.S. Marine Corps, or New York City, have a special type of excitement. During the mid 1980s I ran the New York City Marathon twice. The second time, I was in shape and on pace to go under 2:40 — until the Queensboro Bridge seemed like mountain and I realized that the unseasonable heat was putting me under. I hobbled on for a while, then slowed to a walk. Almost immediately a strong, sweaty arm wrapped my shoulders, and I looked into the smiling face of a muscular black man. "Come on, now," he said. "You doan' wanna be walkin' here, white boy, you in Harlem."

A glance around confirmed the location, and I did find the energy to keep running. In retrospect, I'm sure he was joking, but I owe that friendly runner my best finish at New York.

Eight Old Guys Paddle North

I 'd heard about the Geriatric Adventure Society for years, mostly through Willem Lange's entertaining commentaries on Vermont Public Radio. Decades ago, Will and a fellow Outward Bound instructor selected that name for a group of young, adventurous outdoor enthusiasts, who relished expeditions a little wilder and more remote than the standard Outward Bound fare they provided to their students.

Through the decades, members of that informal club have gathered for backcountry skiing, hikes, and paddling expeditions in northern Canada. Several years ago I was invited to join them for a ski trek on the Haute Route, high in the Alps, from Chamonix, France, to Zermatt, Switzerland. Family obligations at the time prevented me from participating, and I've regretted it ever since, fearing I had passed up the opportunity to join a very special fraternity. Thankfully, last summer I had a second chance.

Members of the Geriatric Adventure Society had planned an ambitious canoe trip, 235 miles down the George River, which flows north into Ungava Bay near the Quebec/Labrador border. Probably the duration of the trip (three weeks), and the expense (airfare and excess baggage fees were significant), scared away some of the regular participants, but when I was invited to fill a vacancy, I jumped at the chance.

I had plenty of misgivings. Although I've spent some time in a canoe, I had no experience in whitewater. I was also aware that members of the Geriatric Adventure Society had been dragging each other out of tight spots in the wilderness for decades. One of the most colorful and enthusiastic members of the group, Dr. Dudley Weider, who had died suddenly while skiing a few months earlier, would be sorely missed. I would definitely be the rookie on the trip.

In addition, we were headed into world-class fly-fishing territory, and my fishing skills hadn't advanced much beyond the worm on the hook stage. But I greatly admired the men I knew who were signed on, and it was safe to assume that the others would be just as capable and resourceful in the outdoors.

It's fascinating how the mind works. Glancing through the notes I jotted down during the expedition, I see there are recurring themes. Although I was in reasonably good shape, the paddling was tough. The first 70 miles consisted of a long, narrow lake where we encountered headwinds and a significant chop on the water. When finally we felt the powerful current of the river pulling us, the sense of relief was soon replaced by anxiety caused by the impending rapids. There were almost daily references in my notes to rain squalls, persistent headwinds, white-knuckle attempts to thread the fragile canoes through seemingly endless rapids, and whenever the wind abated, clouds of insects. There were descriptions of stumbling chest deep through slippery boulders in the powerful current as we lined the boats around treacherous rapids, and images of all eight of us huddled under the cook tarp, sipping soup in a squall. More than once, we were forced by fierce winds and whitecaps to remain on shore all day, hoping the weather would moderate enough by dusk to paddle a few miles further before dark.

All that is in my journal of the adventure, but that's not the way I remember it. I can still feel the awesome power of the river, the phenomenal volume of water: sometimes perfectly smooth and inky black, other times a deafening, raging torrent of white foam, lined for miles by walls of boulders the size of cars, which the current had pushed out of its way.

I remember climbing to the summit of a windswept hill above a campsite and seeing a landscape scoured by the glacier, bare rock, pothole ponds and pockets of birch and spruce valiantly hanging on in a very inhospitable environment.

I remember the fish, and the unbridled joy and excitement grown men derive from casting a line, feeling the strike and skillfully landing a magnificent, wild trout. But more than anything else, I have fond memories of my fellow paddlers. The group's name, Geriatric Adventure Society, is not so much an ironic joke any more. Among the eight participants there were four artificial knees, one artificial hip, and a couple of cardiac bypass survivors. But the physical challenges only intensified the appreciation for the out of doors and for capable, experienced friends with whom to share it.

Wildlife on the Trails

I've had the good fortune to spend much of my working life in the woods. One of the great joys of being in the forest is a wildlife encounter. Occasionally, this is also a source of anxiety. Through the years, I've had my share of memorable meetings with Mother Nature's critters.

Alaska is noted for moose and bear, and during my ten years there I had encounters with both. Moose were common in the hills above Anchorage, and we saw them frequently at the biathlon training site at Fort Richardson. Since moose don't have particularly good eyesight, the accepted procedure when an animal blocked the trail was to shout and wave your arms to get their attention. Usually, that was enough to get them to saunter off into the alders.

Once, during a time trial in a blizzard, we skied the same 2.5-kilometer loop several times. Some of my teammates, while taking position on the shooting range, shouted warnings about a large cow moose near the trail. On my final loop, nearly blinded by the falling snow, I smelled her before I saw the wall of dark hair racing, hooves flying, down a hill beside me. I could have put out a hand and pushed off her flank to open a little space between us. Thankfully, she veered off the trail and we avoided a collision, which certainly would have been much worse for me than for her.

More recently, working on a trail in northern New Hampshire, I was concentrating on hanging flagging and following the natural contour of the land when I heard a loud snort. I looked up to see a young bull moose glaring at me, the hair on his neck bristling. I struggled to talk calmly, as I slowly backed away. Thankfully, he didn't consider me a threat and never charged.

While designing trails at the Nordic Heritage Center in Presque Isle, Maine, I spooked a cow moose and her yearling calf almost every day for a couple of weeks. I talked to them as well, and by the time I finished flagging the trails there, both moose virtually ignored me.

On another job not far from Presque Isle, in Madawaska, I had quite a surprise. During several days of exploring the woods while reconfiguring their trail system, I had seen fresh moose sign. I was confident I'd stumble across an animal before I finished the trail. On my final day, while double-checking what I had flagged, I heard a thrashing in nearby bushes. "I've finally spooked that moose," I thought, eagerly moving ahead for a look. What I saw was a spruce tree bending under the weight of two black bear cubs, clambering over each other to reach the top. Instantly, my mind jumped from the anticipation of seeing a moose to the sickening recognition that mother bear could not be far away. I spotted her through the undergrowth, snapping her jaws as she advanced toward me. Trying to sound calm and reassuring, I talked to her while backing away from her cubs.

Some of my other wildlife encounters haven't stimulated so much adrenaline, but have also been memorable. A few autumns ago, I designed a trail for a church camp in central Wisconsin. The property consisted of overgrown fields and oak forest. Finishing up about sunset one afternoon, I was drawn into an abandoned cornfield by a baffling racket, loud, raucous, and unlike anything I had heard before. I got close enough in the fading light to see about a dozen Sand Hill cranes prancing, flapping their wings, and sounding a lot like a college fraternity after a football victory on homecoming weekend.

No matter how many times I flush a ruffed grouse, their explosive takeoff makes my heart stop. More than once I've paused to study the terrain or look at my map and had the sensation that I was being watched. A quick scan of overhead limbs often reveals a hawk or an owl sitting motionless, but very attentive.

One exception, a few years ago, was a northern goshawk who didn't want me in its territory and wasn't shy about letting me know it. After repeated loud cries, it dropped from its branch and kept swooping at me until I retreated. It was an appropriate reminder that the forest is the home of wildlife and when we visit, we are guests in their home.

Thoughts about Chrysler

The headlines regarding Chrysler's bankruptcy, sale to Fiat, and the probable loss of thousands of American jobs reminded me of a unique and memorable connection I had with the company.

In 1988, I was Team Leader for the U.S. biathletes at the Calgary Winter Olympics. The Nordic skiing events were held more than an hour west of Calgary in the beautiful mountain village of Canmore. Gloria Chadwick, a feisty, former Alpine racer, was the U.S. Olympic Committee's top official in Canmore, responsible for the U.S. cross-country skiers and biathletes, as well as their coaches, trainers, team doctors and waxing technicians.

Several days after the Opening Ceremony, as the competitive events in Canmore were getting underway, Gloria cornered me with a dilemma. The Jeep Dealers of America were having their annual conference at Lake Louise, more than an hour northwest of Canmore, and they wanted some U.S. Olympians to attend. Jeep, Chrysler Corporation's most popular brand, had contributed more than a million dollars, in addition to dozens of four-wheel-drive Jeep Cherokees for the team's use at the Games. The U.S. Olympic Committee was determined to honor the company's request. Gloria had been directed to assemble a group of athletes, dressed in their most patriotic Olympic outfits, and drive them to Lake Louise for the big banquet.

Only a couple of athletes were interested in the expedition, so we recruited a few coaches and wax technicians to fill out the delegation, piled into Gloria's Jeep and headed west. Almost immediately it began to snow. Within minutes, we were engulfed in a full-blown, Rocky Mountain blizzard. When a tractor-trailer began to jack-knife immediately ahead of us, Gloria slammed the Jeep into low range and burst through the snowbank on the right shoulder. As her panicked passengers braced for the worst, Gloria calmly plowed through the drifts until we were beyond the truck, then powered her way back onto the road.

"That's the great thing about these Jeeps," she remarked casually, "that four-wheel-drive is there when you need it."

Arriving at the magnificent Lake Louise hotel, we were hustled into a huge dining room, filled with hundreds of boisterous Jeep dealers and their families. As we followed our host to the long head table, accompanied by the enthusiastic applause of the crowd, he asked, "Now which one of you will be introducing Mr. Iacocca?" Baffled glances were exchanged among the Olympians, then Gloria recovered and blurted, "Oh… John will do that."

Before I could protest, I was guided to a seat at the head table not far from the famous auto executive who had been responsible for the creation of the Mustang, before leaving Ford to rescue Chrysler with the development of the minivan. Along the way, Iacocca had added to his national prominence by assuming responsibility for the restoration of the Statue of Liberty, which he accomplished in time for the nation's bicentennial.

I was seated between two executives of the Jeep Division, who spent most of dinner explaining how proud they were to be supporting the Olympic Team. As our plates were being cleared, I learned the specifics of my assignment. After welcoming the dealers and their families, the head of the Jeep Division would introduce me. Then I would acknowledge the other Olympians, before introducing Mr. Iacocca to the gathering.

Fortunately, the entire experience had evolved so quickly, even sitting at a head table in a vast dining room a few seats away from Lee Iacocca, I hadn't had time to panic. When it came my turn to speak, I began by simply relating our close call in the snowstorm, emphasizing the excellent off-road performance of our Jeep. That drew a standing ovation from the partisan crowd. After presenting the other Olympians, I introduced Mr. Iacocca by acknowledging his impact on the auto industry but emphasizing the contribution he had made to all of us by rescuing the Statue of Liberty. That hit the right note. The assembled dealers stood and cheered as if their team had just won the Super Bowl!

Lee Iacocca built upon that enthusiasm and gave his dealers a pep talk worthy of any successful NFL coach's halftime locker room appeal. I've always felt grateful that a coincidental set of circumstances gave me the opportunity to see a gifted leader, in action, at the top of his game.

Cold Feet about the Cruise

My wife, Kay, and I are fans of Garrison Keillor's variety show, A Prairie Home Companion, and listen to it on Vermont Public Radio whenever we can. A number of summers ago, Garrison and several members of the A Prairie Home Companion cast performed at Meadowbrook in Guilford, New Hampshire, so Kay and I braved the traffic and the summer heat to see the show in person. We weren't disappointed.

So, when I heard about a cruise from Copenhagen, up the west coast of Norway with Garrison Keillor and the cast of A Prairie Home Companion, I couldn't resist. But as our departure date approached, I had some misgivings. For starters, I'm not a cruise ship kind of guy. Friends of ours who have raved about cruise ship vacations always talk about the gourmet meals and the excitement of gambling in the casinos. I certainly don't need to gain any more weight, and I lost my interest in gambling in eighth grade when some high school kids taught me to play poker then cleaned me out of several weeks' worth of after-school earnings.

But I guess what really had me worried was a vivid memory from over forty years ago, when I spent the summer hitch-hiking around Europe. I had been exploring Norway for a couple of weeks and headed back to Germany to meet a friend. In the Norwegian port of Kristiansand I boarded the huge, ocean-going ferry, the Crown Prince Harold for the half-day hop across the Skagerrak, to Hirtshals, Denmark. Loaded with hundreds of cars and trucks below deck, the giant ship rumbled out of the Norwegian harbor in the pre-dawn darkness. I found a locker for my backpack, then wandered the ship in search of some breakfast.

The dining room was high on the forward part of the ship. By the time I found it, the tables were filled with business travelers and families on vacation. Almost as soon as I found a seat, I noticed the panoramic windows surrounding the dining room rhythmically changed from a dark, slate gray to light, turquoise, green. It took me a while to comprehend that the giant ship was plowing through waves that were sending, not just white foam, but green water several decks above the water line. Just then, a young father at the table next to me turned deathly pale and projectile vomited orange juice all over his wife and two kids. I decided to skip breakfast and try to find some fresh air.

A couple of decks higher and back toward the stern, I discovered a dozen passengers out on deck in the stiff breeze. From their apparent concentration on the ocean, I assumed that someone must have spotted another ship, or perhaps a whale, so I maneuvered toward the railing to see what was so interesting. It wasn't until I had found a spot, downwind, at the end of the line that I was sprayed with wind-blown vomit and I realized there was nothing to see in the ocean: these folks were all barfing their guts out over the side.

I rushed to the stern almost frantic to escape other passengers. I found a spacious sun deck, arranged with dozens of lounge chairs in semicircular rows. Most of the chairs were taken by passengers who were wrapped snugly in heavy woolen blankets. As I searched for a vacant lounge chair, a passenger threw off his blanket and retched into a bowl he held on his lap. From the other side of the sun deck, another passenger did the same thing, followed by another. The arching rows of lounge chairs gave the impression of an orchestra, and I imagined some invisible conductor standing in front of these seasick musicians, who on cue, threw back their blankets and performed their gut-wrenching solos.

I spent the remainder of the voyage trying to avoid other passengers, all of whom seemed to be deathly sick. It was a challenge, since no corner of the huge ship seemed to be spared the evidence of sea sickness. It was close, but thankfully, I held it together until we approached the harbor in Denmark. It was not until later that I learned that the Skagerrak, where the winds and currents of Baltic Sea and the North Sea meet, has a reputation for being the most consistently rough water on earth.

Of course, I haven't mentioned a word of this to Kay. No doubt, the Crown Prince Harold, even though an impressive ship years ago, wasn't equipped with all the stabilizers and gyros that keep today's liners cruising smooth and steady. I mean, today's travelers wouldn't be bragging about gourmet meals and gambling if they were seasick all the time and their poker chips were getting tossed across the felt-covered tables, right? I don't suppose this could all be some elaborate prank designed to provide Garrison Keillor with new material for next year's "News from Lake Wobegon?" Actually, I'm beginning to feel a little queasy…

Four Old Ski-Shooters Return to Alaska

Prior to the 1960 Winter Olympics in Squaw Valley, California, where biathlon was reintroduced after a thirty-six-year hiatus, the U.S. Army established a training center for the sport at Fort Richardson, on the outskirts of Anchorage, Alaska. For fifteen years, during the Vietnam era, promising skiers in the military sought an assignment to "The Unit" to train for, and compete in, the challenging sport of winter biathlon. Most of these athletes had competed on collegiate or university ski teams before being drafted into the service or fulfilling an ROTC active-duty commitment.

For the majority of soldiers assigned to Fort Rich, many from the Deep South or urban areas throughout the "Lower 48," Alaska seemed to be a hostile planet: months of alarmingly brief days and endless nights, unbelievably cold temperatures and howling winds, all surrounded by vast stretches of wilderness inhabited by fearsome wild animals.

Aside from their arduous and constant physical training, the biathletes, in contrast, regarded Alaska as a smorgasbord of outdoor adventure. There were countless peaks to climb and rivers to paddle, as well as hunting and fishing opportunities widely regarded as the best in the world. Of the several hundred athletes who cycled through the training center between 1958 and 1973, many would remain in Alaska to make their homes and establish careers, while most of the others returned to Alaska sporadically, to reunite with friends and get their fix of The Great Outdoors.

Pete, a member of the '72 Sapporo Olympic Team and veteran of the training center, had the foresight decades ago to purchase an abandoned fish cannery site on Raspberry Strait, not far from Kodiak. In the years since, he has spent a couple of months every summer cleaning up the debris from the cannery, building a comfortable cabin and exploring the nearby bays and streams with his fishing gear and camera. Earlier this summer, Pete hosted three of his former biathlon buddies, Terry, David and myself, to a week of the best Alaska had to offer.

From Kodiak's no-frills airport, Pete drove us to the harbor, packed with all types of craft from modest, open skiffs to the massive, commercial fishing vessels made famous on television's popular The Deadliest Catch.

After stocking up with groceries and adult beverages, we loaded Pete's 26-foot aluminum fishing cruiser for the ninety-minute sprint to his cabin. The Alaskan scenery was breathtaking: snow-covered peaks in the distance, forested hillsides descending to the shore, and the icy, dark water dotted with countless, comical sea otters, floating casually on their backs as we roared past.

We spent the next week fishing for halibut, cod and rock fish off Pete's boat. For variety, we rowed an inflatable Zodiac to shore and fly-fished for the red salmon that were working their way upstream to spawn. The fly-fishing was especially exciting considering the massive bear tracks evident in the beaten trails along the streams. Terry took the fishing honors by landing a 150-pound halibut, while David succumbed to Pete's traditional prank of secretly attaching a five-gallon pail of bricks to the rookie's line. After Terry's monster, Pete's pail trick was very convincing until David reeled it to the surface.

After a full day of fishing, we would stop to pull Pete's crab pot, which several times provided a delicious tanner crab dinner for the four of us. To take a break from fishing, we spent a morning helping Pete repair a sea wall that had been damaged by a winter storm and the afternoon hiking the impressive hill behind the old cannery site. The panoramic view from the summit was unforgettable, the snowcapped Alaska Range and Shelikof Strait to the northwest, Raspberry Strait and Kodiak Island to the south.

There was only one somewhat sobering aspect to this otherwise spectacular Alaskan reunion. As we began comparing notes of the forty years since we were stationed at Fort Rich together, it became apparent that we'd all experienced some close calls and near misses. Three of us had survived serious heart issues, one had endured a recent brush with cancer and we'd all had our share of "wake-up calls." In fact, two other buddies were unable to attend, due to knee replacement surgery and cancer treatment.

I guess the message here is, even highly trained, Olympic athletes are not immune to the challenges of the advancing years, and the corollary might be, if you've always wanted to experience Alaska, go now.

Occupational Hazards

Many outdoor enthusiasts who know me enviously assert that I have the ideal job. I can't disagree with them. As a trail designer, I spend much of my time "at work" walking through the woods exploring possible routes for proposed trail systems. Usually, I'm by myself, trying to notice natural features in the landscape, suitable potential stream crossings, and which stand of trees would add to the scenic beauty of the finished trail. Pretty good duty if you love being outdoors.

However, like any occupation, trail design work does have a few drawbacks. This past summer, a frequent irritation was the rain. If you are walking out the driveway to get the paper in a downpour, you simply put on your raingear and get going. If, however you are planning to spend eight hours exploring a wooded site for a proposed trail, you can count on being soaked to the skin for most of the day. I think Gore-Tex is a valiant effort, a fabric intended to keep the rain out while allowing an active body to "breathe," but I can testify that it doesn't work for a full day of trashing through the pucker brush. An added detriment to rainy days in the woods is that everything—fallen logs, roots, leaves and rocks—becomes very slippery. Early last summer, my feet went out from under me and I hit a flat rock so hard I saw stars. By the time I arrived home that evening, the side of my leg was an unbelievable purple from my waist to my knee. What almost compensated for the pain and stiffness was the disbelief and sympathy it engendered in my wife.

I suppose one of the unintended consequences of our mobile society and global climate change is the migration of ticks north. I spent much of my childhood in the woods, and never remember finding a tick, but times have changed. Although their prevalence seems to vary year to year, both deer ticks and the larger wood ticks are now common throughout most of the northeast. The good news is that they seem to take their time, up to three hours, attaching themselves to a new host. I make a habit of showering immediately after a day in the woods where I suspect a heavy infestation of ticks. My personal record is thirteen ticks discovered during one shower.

Another reality of summertime bushwhacking is finding spider webs with your face. In the mornings when they are covered with dew, it is often possible to see the spider webs, but later in the day, with the dappled sunshine partially blocked by the forest canopy, the spider webs are invisible. I've developed a sort of nervous wave while walking in the woods, which discourages black flies and mosquitoes as well as sweeps the remnants of webs and spiders off my face.

As you might expect, I've had a few adrenaline-producing encounters with moose and black bears. One young bull moose made a half-hearted false charge, and a sow black bear gave me a convincing growl after she cuffed her cubs up a fir tree. In each instance, I tried to speak reassuringly as I backed away. After hours of walking alone in the woods, nothing gets your pulse up like a steaming pile of bear scat or the racket of branches and saplings snapping in the path of a running moose.

Birds are rarely an issue, but last summer I encountered a pair of nesting goshawks who were definitely upset that I was in their neighborhood. These birds are relatively rare and extremely territorial. Initially, they voiced their displeasure with a raucous chorus but then advanced to swooping through the trees just over my head. I recalled an incident in Anchorage, Alaska, where a trail runner was attacked by a great horned owl, resulting in eighty stitches to repair the lacerations in his scalp. I routed the trail I was designing well away from the goshawks' nest.

Not long ago, I landed a trail project in New York's Hudson River Valley. The site is honeycombed with caves, mines and kilns, the remnants of a thriving cement business back in the 1800s. Although I rarely worry about snakes in northern New England, the limestone cliffs and rock outcroppings seemed like ideal habitat. I asked the site manager if he'd encountered any copperheads. "Sure," he responded, "all the time. I'm surprised you haven't stumbled across any yet. And the caves are full of bats and spiders. It's really fascinating!"

I can hardly wait.

Marathon Memories

For just the second time in twenty-one years, I won't be in Burlington on Memorial Day weekend for the Vermont City Marathon. Both absences resulted from unavoidable conflicts with weddings. There had been a few tight squeezes during those two decades. In '93, I slipped out early from the Saturday night festivities of my twenty-fifth college reunion so that I could leave campus before dawn and make the 8:00 a.m. start.

A few years later, I couldn't pass up the opportunity to spend the month of May helping the owners of Camp Denali in Alaska's magnificent National Park prepare their wilderness lodge for the summer season. With two feet of snow on the ground and plenty of work, there was little time for running. I returned to Vermont just in time for the marathon, but my lack of training turned it into the proverbial "death march."

In 1999, my daughter graduated from Bates College in Lewiston, Maine. Although the commencement ceremonies were on Monday, Julie wanted me to attend a reception Sunday evening. So, I finished the Vermont City Marathon, limped to the car and drove four hours to Lewiston. I made it to the reception on time, but generated a lot of unnecessary concern because I was so stiff that I could barely walk.

It occurred to me recently that I may have run my last marathon. I love to compete, but for the past several years I've had a hard time being consistent about training. It might be possible to sign up for a 5-kilometer, or even a 10-kilometer race with minimal training, and still have an enjoyable experience, but nobody enjoys a marathon without investing considerable time preparing for it. Of course, one of the tremendous innovations of modern events like the Vermont City Marathon is the inclusion of relay teams, allowing everyone to be part of the celebration, regardless of athletic ability or available training time.

Although I never kept accurate count, I suspect I've run fifty or sixty marathons, which have provided some vivid and entertaining memories. Among my first was the celebrated Equinox Marathon in Fairbanks, Alaska, rated as the second toughest in the U.S. That race became part of the annual training schedule for the athletes assigned to the Army's

Biathlon Training Center at Fort Richardson, just outside of Anchorage. Because of its very hilly route, the early Equinox events were dominated by members of the biathlon team.

A few years later, I survived the inaugural Resurrection Trail Marathon, which began in the isolated village of Hope, Alaska, followed a wilderness trail thirteen miles to East Creek, then returned to Hope. East Creek was where Anchorage high school student Scott McGinnis was seriously mauled by a grizzly bear, and his hiking buddy, Tim Moerlein, scared the bear away, then ran thirteen miles to Hope for help. That marathon never really caught on.

I've run Boston, the grand daddy of all marathons, six times, including the centennial in 1996. It's impossible to describe the feeling of being swept along with more than 30,000 other runners, cheered every step of the way by millions of enthusiastic spectators.

Having spent four years in the U.S. Army, I was able to maintain the obligatory distain for the U.S. Marines until participating in the 1990 Marine Corps Marathon in Washington, D.C. Everything about the event was carefully organized and flawlessly executed. Twelve years later, I returned to a race, which had taken on profound significance. Soon after the start we ran past the scorched scar on the side of the Pentagon, and among the thousands of young marines supporting the event, most would soon be headed for combat in Afghanistan.

Maybe I have a couple more twenty-six milers left in me, but if not, I have no complaints. Besides, I can always pull together a few old buddies for a relay team.

Rain

I learned a long time ago not to complain about the weather. For starters, there is nothing we can do about it. Secondly, the meteorological offering some of us might find objectionable might be exactly what someone else may need. As a Nordic skier, I'm especially sensitive to this phenomenon as I listen to neighbors curse a predicted snowstorm while I gleefully hope we get buried. And of course, living in the northeast, we all recognized long ago the truth in the old adage, "If you don't like New England weather, wait a minute."

In spite of all that, the past two summers have started off pretty wet. I know, I know, the fields are verdant, the ponds are full and the brooks are babbling. Less apparent to the casual observer however, the ground is so saturated that farmers can't cut their hay without creating deep ruts in the fields, while loggers struggle to get timber out of the woods on skid roads that have become quagmires. In the Berkshires, for the past month, folks who have bought lawn tickets for the concerts at Tanglewood have gone home soaked, while in Camden, Maine, the famous schooners have rarely ventured out of the picturesque harbor.

One approach that usually works for me in situations like this is the old, "Well, it could be worse" attitude. With today's instant news coverage from around the globe, it doesn't take long to find a natural disaster that makes our rainy weather seem inconsequential. I imagine we'll all have images of Hurricane Katrina's wind, rain and flooding etched into our memories for a long time to come. Another technique that works for me is to remember pervious situations, which helps keep current conditions in perspective.

In August 1970, I arrived in South Vietnam toward the end of the annual monsoon season. I vividly remember during the intense heat of the day, towering thunderheads building ominously then, in the late afternoon, releasing an unbelievable amount of water in torrential downpours. The driving rain on the metal roof of our hooch made conversation impossible, while footpaths and roads became brown rivers.

Several years later, I had the opportunity to help finish a house on Douglas Island, a residential neighborhood of Juneau, Alaska. Annual rainfall in Juneau ranges from 55 inches to as much as 90 inches. I was part of a construction crew that worked for almost a month in a steady drizzle. Once, when the persistent rain let up, the clouds parted, and the sun broke through, everyone dropped their tools and bolted for the harbor. The unwritten rule in Juneau is that whenever the sun comes out, folks take the day off and go fishing.

Along with fishing, the other cultural imperative in Alaska is hunting. Many Alaskan families fill their freezers every autumn with moose or caribou meat, supplemented, perhaps, with duck, goose and grouse. One of my most memorable hunts began in the pouring rain, with two buddies hiking into the Chugach Mountains. Several hours into a five-day hunt, we encountered a swollen stream, which under normal conditions would have required simply taking off our boots and wading across. After fruitlessly trudging up and downstream in search of a manageable crossing, we cinched our heavy packs, held our rifles overhead and waded into the torrent. My buddies made it, but my foot slipped on a greasy rock and I was swept downstream. I managed to scramble out, still clutching my rifle, but everything in my backpack was soaked. The rain continued for the remaining days of our hunt, so nothing I had, including my sleeping bag, ever dried out.

More recently, I was invited to join Will Lange and some of his "Geriatric Adventurers" on a two-week canoe trip down the George River in Northern Quebec to Ungava Bay. It was a terrific expedition on an impressive river through wild country, but it rained a lot. I remember days paddling for hours, into the wind, with a cold rain pelting my face. Our lunch consisted of huddling around a Coleman stove in the driving rain, eagerly anticipating a cup of hot soup. Evening brought valiant attempts to erect tents in the storm, gathering firewood to cook supper, then crawling, exhausted, into damp sleeping bags. Of course, all that rain kept the black flies and mosquitoes at bay.

Which reminds me of that old expression attributed to the Vikings, "Anything that doesn't actually kill you, will make you stronger." I suppose a variation of that philosophy might be, all this rain we've been experiencing will make us really appreciate the sunshine.

Two Hikes that Made the Summer

This past summer began very wet. It seemed to rain for weeks, with few breaks of blue sky for outdoor recreation. Adding to the scheduling challenge was my wife's summer academic load. After years of fantasizing about pursuing an advanced degree, Kay had immersed herself in a master's program at Dartmouth and was struggling to stay afloat in a sea of reading assignments, written reports and classroom lectures. In addition, my business was booming. Perhaps some of the economic stimulus money was trickling down through the highway paving projects to community recreation trails? Whatever the reason, I had trail projects underway from Millinocket, Maine, to Pomeroy, Ohio, leaving precious little time for traditional summer fun.

Willem Lange saved the day. We had met years earlier at a Vermont Public Radio event that involved climbing Mt. Mansfield. After hiking together for an hour, Will apologized for being slow, confessing that he was a few weeks out from replacement knee surgery. I was astounded. Most folks with artificial knees consider a stroll through the mall a vigorous outing, and this guy was grousing about being slow up Vermont's highest peak.

Through the years we bumped into each other at various events and I looked forward to his weekly newspaper column. Will is an inspiration because he dispels the stereotype of the "dumb jock." Here is a guy who can easily hold his own intellectually with most college professors yet thought it was great fun to ski several hundred miles of the famous Iditarod Trail in the Alaskan bush.

I was thrilled, three years ago, when I was invited to join Will's infamous Geriatric Adventure Society for a three-week canoe expedition down the remote George River to Ungava Bay on the edge of the Canadian Arctic. Since then, Kay and I had enjoyed some of Will's shows for New Hampshire Public Television featuring outdoor activities in the Granite State.

Early in September Will called to see if Kay and I could join him for a hike up Tuckerman's Ravine on Mount Washington, with an overnight at the famous Lake of the Clouds hut. At the appointed time we met Will and the three members of the film crew at the Appalachian Mountain Club's base in Pinkham Notch, New Hampshire. Hiking one of the most challenging trails in the White Mountains with Will and the crew was entertaining and inspiring. After eight major orthopedic surgeries, Will is slower, but amazingly steady, regardless of the severity of the climb. Our arrival at Lake of the Clouds was like traveling with a rock star. It seemed that everyone spending the last night of the season on Mount Washington was a devoted fan of Willem Lange. It was a treat for Kay and me to be part of the celebration.

A week later, I was at a comfortable sporting camp on a remote island, in a scenic lake not far from Jackman, Maine. I had been invited to join a group of men who have been gathering in the Maine wilderness one weekend a year for the past two decades. Among the recreational options was a short motorboat trip across the lake to a hiking trail that led to the summit of Sally Mountain, with an impressive, 360-degree vista. Nearly a dozen participants opted for the hike, although it was quickly evident that several had allowed the stress of their careers to jeopardize their physical condition. One executive from Texas who confessed to a fondness for barbeque and a dread of exercise was struggling to keep up with the group.

Moments after I suggested we let the others go ahead and follow at our own pace, I heard branches snapping in the forest to our left.

I turned to the Texan. "Larry, I think there's a big animal through those trees, right there!"

As he was protesting, "Naw, not way up here on this mountain…" a magnificent, full-grown bull moose, with a rack that seemed to stretch to Canada, burst through the brush and trotted purposefully toward us. As Larry fumbled for his camera, I shouted, "Not now…look for the biggest tree you can find and get behind it quick!"

After a few strides in our direction, the bull plowed off into the brush, and our pulses began to recede below 200. For the Texan, it was an encounter he will recount to impressed listeners for years; for me it was one of two hikes that saved the summer.

A Wildlife Bonanza

One of the constant pleasures of my work designing trails is the thrill of observing wildlife. Here in the northeast, the flash of a white-tailed deer bounding off through the underbrush or the heart-stopping thunder of a ruffed grouse taking wing from almost underfoot is nearly a daily occurrence. Somewhat less frequent, and therefore more exciting, are encounters with hawks, owls, wild turkeys, and occasionally, moose. Although I sometimes see evidence of bear and coyote, I intentionally make plenty of noise in the woods when I'm working, so I've rarely stumbled across those animals in the wild.

Not long ago, however, my wife, Kay, and I enjoyed a wildlife bonanza. Pete Karns, a former biathlon teammate of mine from forty years ago and his wife Jeanine invited Kay and me to join them at their cabin on Raspberry Strait, which carves a channel between Kodiak and Afognak Islands, about 250 miles southwest of Anchorage, Alaska. Kodiak Island is noted as the site of the nation's largest Coast Guard station, the epicenter of some of the world's best fishing, and the home of the impressive, Kodiak brown bear. Kodiak bears are a variety of grizzlies that, thanks to an abundant food supply, grow to frightening proportions. Although I had lived in Alaska for a decade years ago, I had never made it out to Kodiak, so Kay and I were both thrilled to accept the Karns' invitation.

Pete and Jeanine met us at the Kodiak airport for the short drive to the municipal boat harbor. Although there were a few pleasure boats tied to the docks, most of the slips accommodated commercial fishing boats, even a couple of the crabbers made famous in the television series, "The Deadliest Catch." Pete and Jeanine's boat was a 30-foot, twin-hulled, aluminum cabin cruiser designed for fishing. It was powered by twin diesels that could skim the boat over calm water like a hydroplane, or make a manageable, if bone-jarring, two-hour trip through the chop from Kodiak harbor back to their cabin on Raspberry Strait.

Peter Karns was the best American biathlete of his era. In addition to several national championships, he finished fourteenth in the individual event at the Sapporo Olympics, and was key to the relay team's impressive sixth place result. Even when we served in Alaska together, Pete was as successful at fishing as he was in biathlon. If anything, his passion for fishing had intensified through the years. The morning after our arrival, we were on the boat, headed into the Shelikof Strait in search of silver salmon.

The abundance of wildlife was inspiring. As we motored to one of Pete's fishing spots, he diverted close to an outcropping of rock, nearly obscured by noisy sea lions. Some slid into the water as we approached, but the belligerent bulls held their ground and barked defiantly. Moments later, shiny backs broke the surface not far from the boat. We had been discovered by a pod of Dall's porpoises. Looking like smaller versions of Orcas with distinctive, white and black markings, they frolicked in the bow wake of the boat.

Later, adrift in a large bay surrounded on three sides by rugged hills, some still displaying remnants of last winter's snow, while fishing the bottom for halibut, we were surprised by a loud, "whoosh," perhaps 50 meters from the boat. A couple of finback whales casually arced through the surface, spouting as they entered the bay from the Shelikof Strait.

After a few days of fishing, Pete announced it was time to look for bears. With the pink salmon run just ending and the silvers about to arrive, every beach or rocky shoreline where a stream poured into the surf was a possible bear viewing site. Using Pete's small, inflatable dingy from the anchored fishing boat, we explored a couple of ominous locations littered with salmon remnants, huge patches of matted grass, and impressive piles of bear scat.

Finally, cruising beyond the surf we spotted a Kodiak grizzly ambling down a beach. By the time we anchored and deployed the dingy the bear had wandered out of sight behind the dunes, according to Pete, headed for the hills after detecting our presence. Since the dingy was too small for all four of us, Pete was going to drop me on the beach before returning for our wives. As we struggled to negotiate the surf at the mouth of a stream, the bear came plunging, like a freight train from behind the dune, straight toward us. I was sure we were goners, but Pete smiled calmly as the bear pounced on a salmon less than 50 yards from us. It was all part of his Alaskan, wildlife experience.

The Over-the-Hill Gang Survives the Allagash

In November of 1968, I was delighted to be facing an exhausting trip from Fort Benning, Georgia, to Alaska, because most of my classmates from the Infantry Officer's Basic Course were headed to Ranger School, followed by a couple of months in Fort Polk, Louisiana, then to a combat tour in Vietnam. I had finagled an assignment to the Modern Winter Biathlon Training Center at Fort Richardson, just outside of Anchorage. There I joined fewer than twenty other former college skiers who had been selected to train for the Military Ski Championships, the Biathlon World Championships, and the Winter Olympics.

Although we were all grateful to be in Alaska rather than Southeast Asia, it was not a cushy assignment. The training was intense, often involving three exhausting workouts a day, and the competition was fierce. Although on one level we were all friends and teammates, it was never forgotten that only six of us would earn a trip to the World Championships or the Olympics. As a result, we competed at everything: how many kilometers we skied in training, who won the weekly time trails, even who was first in the chow line.

After our military service, many of us remained friends and stayed in contact while others fell out of touch, although a love of the outdoors, especially Nordic skiing, remained a common interest. Last fall, Terry, who had recently retired from a career as a college ski coach, e-mailed proposing an adventure: six of us old biathletes would reunite for a week-long paddle the length of Maine's famous, nearly one-hundred-mile Allagash Wilderness Waterway. In addition to Terry and me from Vermont, Dan and Dennis would represent Minnesota. George, after an academic career in Montana, had relocated to New Hampshire; and David, as a long-time Maine resident, would fill the role of "local guide."

The weeks sped by and before long I was rummaging through mildewed camping gear and untangling ancient fishing line in a last minute panic to get ready. Five of us descended on David's house in Maine to pack for the trip, catch up with buddies we hadn't seen (in some cases) for decades, feast on lobsters and steamed clams, and swap stories about our adventures in Alaska almost fifty years ago. It is truly remarkable how individuals experiencing the same event, years ago, can have completely different memories of what actually happened.

The drive from the central coast to the start of our canoe trip just northwest of Baxter State Park was illuminating in terms of just how big Maine is and how much of the interior is undeveloped forest land. We loaded our gear and launched the canoes soon after noon at the southern end of Chamberlain Lake. After weeks of anticipation and the long drive, it was great to finally be on the water, at least for the first few minutes until we paddled into the open lake and into a stiff headwind. In spite of the decades, the old competitive instincts kicked in and the heavily loaded canoes struggled against the wind and the choppy water for three hours. Although none of us had called "Uncle," there were no complaints when David paddled toward the Gravel Beach campsite. My shoulders were so sore I doubted I could get my backpack out of the boat. Dan was so stiff he tripped getting out of the canoe and ended up in the water. We struggled to set up camp before an approaching squall. Terry restored our positive attitudes with a terrific venison stew and French bread. Stories and joking flew around the campfire until the black flies attacked with a vengeance. We agreed to call it a day and stumbled into our tents. It was 7:30 p.m.

From that first evening, the trip kept getting better. Even Terry and I capsizing in the Chase Rapids had a positive outcome since we emerged wet and cold but otherwise unscathed, and it provided the other four plenty of fodder for ridicule for the duration of the trip.

Our third night on the river, Terry presented a bottle of adult beverage that he had skillfully concealed in his pack. As he poured into our camping mugs he proposed a toast to the five former teammates we had lost the past year. This got everyone's attention, since few of us had been aware of all five. We reminisced about our teammates, acknowledged how fast the years have flown, and expressed gratitude for the outdoor experiences and friendships we have enjoyed.

FAMILY

150

Memories of a Rookie Coach

My daughter graduates from high school this spring. It doesn't seem possible that it's really happening. Not that she hasn't studied hard or doesn't deserve her diploma; it's just that, I remember the day, nearly eighteen years ago, when she was born, as clearly as if it were yesterday.

I had been out of the U.S. Army for a few years and was teaching and coaching at a high school. My wife, Mimi, and I agreed it was time to start a family. If I'm not mistaken, the very day she learned that she was pregnant, she enrolled us both in Lamaze classes. I was not especially enthusiastic about this idea, until I learned that the husband's role in the Lamaze method of childbirth is that of a coach. Coaching was my career. I loved coaching. I was determined to be the best coach that ever entered a delivery room.

I remember feeling awkward and out of place at the Lamaze classes. Our portly athletes gossiped about midnight cravings for strange foods and boutiques that featured great maternity clothes. Meanwhile we "coaches" learned how to pant and gasp at different levels of intensity. I gained valuable points with Mimi, however, by stoically suffering through the film on caesarean sections while most of my coaching colleagues bolted for the men's room or the parking lot.

As luck would have it, Mimi's obstetrician was an avid skier. On our second visit to the clinic, he distracted her with a video on breast-feeding, then dragged me into his office to talk skiing, coach-to-coach, so to speak. As the weeks slipped by, the doctor and I became good friends, and Mimi's prenatal checkups actually became ski trip planning sessions.

Well before dawn, nearly a week before her due date, Mimi woke me and confidently announced that it was time to leave for the hospital. Having paid close attention during the Lamaze classes, I knew we were probably facing from twelve to twenty-four hours of labor, so I suggested going for my normal morning run, grabbing a little breakfast, and then heading to the hospital. Not a good idea!

As a high school coach, I was accustomed to having the athletes follow my recommendations, but this time around I felt like a freshman team manager. We were at the hospital, registered and settled into the maternity ward long before sunrise.

After breakfast, my ski-buddy doctor checked on our progress. He confirmed that Mimi would deliver that day, but suggested that a pause that had developed in her labor might be stimulated by walking. Here was an opportunity for some actual coaching! I guided Mimi and pushed her rolling I.V. stand up and down the hospital corridors until a crusty old nurse intervened.

"But I'm her coach," I pleaded, "and the doctor told us to walk."

"He didn't mean she had to complete a marathon before she gives birth," the nurse growled as she led Mimi back to her bed.

During the afternoon, the labor pains became more predictable, and Mimi progressed through the various levels of breathing that we had learned in class. I was right there by her side, feeling a little inadequate in terms of coaching experience, but trying to cheer her on as I would an exhausted athlete, struggling toward the finish line. Her eyes glazed over as she panted frantically through the pain, and I shouted encouragement, "That-a-girl... You can do it... Looking good... Keep it up... Way to go!"

During a pause between contractions, her face strained and dripping with sweat, she turned to me, her coach, and said calmly, "Would you... just... shut... up?"

I was crushed. But the same tough old nurse put a reassuring hand on my shoulder and said, "Don't take it personally, they all get like this."

Just then the doctor breezed in, nodded to the nurses, and said, "Well folks, let's go catch this baby."

I followed him into a locker room where we changed into hospital scrubs and he chatted about great ski runs. We arrived in the delivery room just as Mimi was wheeled in.

The rest is still a blur. I hugged my straining, sweating athlete as she pushed with all her might. Before I could comprehend what had happened, the doctor tossed me a small, blanketed bundle, and announced, "Congratulations, coach, meet your new daughter."

Thankfully, that was one pass I didn't fumble.

Monster Trout

I've never been much of a fisherman, but a dozen years ago we decided to put in a pond near our home, and I jumped at the opportunity to stock it with trout. The pond was perfect for swimming and skating, but I was afraid it might be too shallow for fish. As an experiment, I bought fifty, six-inch rainbow trout and a large bag of floating fish food. I enjoyed wandering down to the pond in the evening, tossing a fistful of pellets on the water, and watching the surface boil as the eager little rainbows feasted.

I wasn't optimistic that they would make it through the winter, but when the ice went out in the spring, the iridescent silver shapes flashed through the water just as they had the previous summer. Encouraged, I ordered more rainbows and more fish food. This went on for a couple of years before the word got out that we had trout in our pond.

Since our fish were so well fed, they weren't especially easy to catch. The romantic notion of a couple of lazy casts across the pond at dusk producing a fat trout on the grill for supper, was pretty much fantasy. So, when a couple of neighborhood kids asked permission to fish, I answered, "Sure, how about a limit of two fish each, but if you can, catch a couple more for our supper."

This arrangement worked well; the kids always asked permission, they experienced the joys of fishing, and we got an occasional trout for dinner.

One hot summer day, several years after we had begun stocking the pond, I was helping a crew of carpenters build an addition on our house. There were five of us framing the roof, when Jimmy, a boy who lived nearby, walked through the yard with a fishing pole. He spotted me in the rafters, and asked if he could fish the pond.

"Sure," I responded, and as Jimmy headed down the hill, the conversation on the roof turned to fishing.

The fish stories were flowing thick and fast, when Jimmy reappeared, looking frightened and upset. Apparently, he had borrowed his father's valuable fly rod, without asking first, and had hooked a trout that hit with such violence, the rod had been pulled out of his hands and disappeared into the depths of the pond. He was almost in tears as he told the story, while the carpenters struggled to contain their laughter. I reassured

Jimmy I'd get my bathing suit and a diving mask at lunchtime, and recover his dad's pole. After all, it was a small pond.

Noon hour promised to be so entertaining the entire construction crew carried their lunch pails down to the pond, and sat casually on the bank while I bobbed repeatedly below the surface in search of the expensive fly rod. Eventually I found it, much to Jimmy's relief.

As we headed back to work, the carpenters offered Jimmy several good-natured suggestions about tying the fishing rod to his hands and strapping himself to a tree. He was clearly embarrassed, but so relieved to have his dad's pole back that the teasing didn't seem to bother him too much.

Pounding nails high in the rafters more than an hour later, I had completely forgotten our noontime activities. Then one of the builders shouted, "SUNAOFAGUN!"

We all looked up, afraid a worker had fallen to the ground or nailed his thumb to the roof.

"Will you get a look at that fish!" he continued. Jimmy grinned as he approached the house, his dad's fly rod in one hand, and a huge trout hanging from the other. Without a word, a second carpenter lunged for the ladder and slid to the ground, never touching a rung.

"Lemme see that fish," he commanded. A tape measure magically appeared in his hand. Jimmy proudly hoisted the beautiful fish. The carpenter measured it, as the rest of us stood on the roof in silent awe.

"Twenty-three and five-eighths," the carpenter announced, studying his tape in disbelief.

Jimmy smiled, thanked me again for retrieving the fishing rod, then headed off through the woods. Just before he disappeared through the trees, a third builder shouted from the roof, "Hey Jimmy, was that the monster that stole your fishing pole?"

"Nope," Jimmy called back, "this one hadn't been hooked before. The big one's still in there."

It took us several weeks to finish the renovations on the house, and occasionally our dog would growl and bark at odd hours during the night. It never bothered me too much though. I just figured a couple of hard-working carpenters were relaxing a little, down at the pond.

The Shrine Game

I'm not much of a football fan. I don't look back on my four years of high school football with many fond memories. As a ski coach, first for high school and then for college athletes, I was often frustrated because the fortunes of the football team seemed to dictate the budget and enrollment decisions for the entire athletic department.

Then, as the father of a daughter, I noticed the continuing inequity of school sports programs, where money, coaching expertise and public support is lavished on football, while no comparable opportunity exists for girls. I have serious concerns about the violence of the game, and severe misgivings about a sport that requires a promising high school player to gain fifty pounds simply to survive at the college level.

Although I have lived a few minutes north of Hanover, New Hampshire, for almost twenty years, I had never attended the Shrine Maple Sugar Bowl Football Game; that is until this year, when my godson was named to the Vermont team as a defensive end. I knew the forty-two-year-old twin state football rivalry had been dominated by New Hampshire for more than a decade, so I decided to add my support to the underdogs.

Coincidentally, my father-in-law had played defensive end for the Nebraska Corn Huskers and a year with the Green Bay Packers before World War II. What a great way to bridge the generation gap, I thought: high school all-star meets veteran of the leather-helmet days to swap stories of sacking quarterbacks, sixty years apart.

The game had all the color and pageantry you'd expect from a championship. I loved the way the teams were introduced. Two players, one representing each state, ran from opposite end zones to center field, where they shook hands. The game even got off to a great start from my perspective as a Vermonter; the Green Mountain Boys surprised New Hampshire by scoring first. The Granite State responded with two touchdowns, while a passing shower drenched us in the stands. With barely a minute remaining in the first half, Vermont fought back with an exciting touchdown pass, then tied the score with a gutsy two-point conversion.

This was not the usual lopsided mismatch, but a tightly fought battle. With a handful of seconds remaining in the first half, New Hampshire returned the Vermont kickoff 93 yards for a touchdown. Halftime score: New Hampshire 21, Vermont 14.

While the teams refined their strategies in the locker rooms, the hosting Shriners reminded the thousands in the stadium of the purpose behind the annual contest. Proceeds from the event, totaling more than three and a half million dollars in the game's forty-two-year history, help to support the Shriners' twenty-two children's hospitals and burn centers throughout the country, where a needy child is never turned away. The storm clouds dissolved, the sun reappeared, and the teams returned to the field.

The second half was as exciting as the first, with Vermont tying the score at 21 after intercepting a New Hampshire pass. But the Granite State finally pulled ahead to win 27–21. I suspect most fans went home impressed by two teams that had fought hard, but more importantly had raised almost $200,000 for sick and burned children.

I was pleased because my godson had played well, stopping more than his share of New Hampshire advances, and because my father-in-law had enjoyed reconnecting with the rough-and-tumble glory of his youth. But our day wasn't quite over. The stiff, injured knees that cut short the old ball player's career at Green Bay, failed him again. He stumbled and fell on the stadium stairs. The paramedics, who thankfully had been idle during the game, were quick to respond, and in minutes the veteran defensive end was headed for the hospital.

In the emergency room, as doctors and nurses cleaned and stitched a couple of cuts on his arm, it was easy to imagine the tough old ballplayer sixty years earlier pleading, "Hell, this is just a scratch, stitch it up and put me back in the game."

I still have grave misgivings about football. But my memories of the 1995 Shrine Maple Sugar Bowl Game are of talented athletes, both young and old, of big-hearted men in unusual hats, who donate their energy to a very worthy cause, and of the capable folks in our hospitals, who dedicate their lives to helping us when we get hurt. It was much more than just a football game.

Bird Watching

My wife, Mimi, and I had been happily married for twenty-seven years, but at a certain point, she heard that middle-aged couples sometimes drift apart because of divergent interests. The question came up at the dinner table, "So what are the activities we really enjoy doing together?" I was blind-sided by the question and didn't get my answer out quickly enough. So, Mimi took immediate action. Not a day later she announced, "I've signed us up for bird-watching classes. You love being out in the woods, so this is something we can both enjoy!"

I wasn't so sure. Bird watching had always seemed to me about as exciting as watching paint dry, but in the interest of family harmony, I agreed to attend the classes.

The first three evening sessions were held at the home of our instructor, a neighbor named Bill. Rarely have I seen a teacher more enthusiastic about his subject. It was spring, flocks of birds would soon be returning to Vermont from the south, and Bill was more excited than a six-year-old at Christmas. There were eight of us in his class, and it was soon evident that all the others knew a lot more than I did about birds.

Patiently, Bill reviewed the basics especially for my benefit, "Is it the size of a chickadee, the size of a robin, or the size of a crow?"

Now, you can't live in Vermont without picking up a little knowledge about birds. I love to hear the geese as they head south in October, and we have barred owls in our woods that often hoot to each other in the evenings. But there are dozens of L. B. J.'s, those little brown jobbers, that all look the same to me, and to be totally honest, are pretty boring compared to a red-tailed hawk or a great blue heron.

Of course, it was these little brown birds — sparrows, thrushes, and warblers — that captured the interest of the experienced birders. We studied photos and we listened to tape recordings of their songs. We took notes on habitat and memorized distinctive field markings. We were threatened with quizzes and a final exam. Bill was preparing us for three field trips, and he wanted us to be ready. Mimi, who has an amazing memory for details was thriving in the class. I was in way over my head.

Abruptly one evening, Bill looked at his watch. "It's 7:45, follow me, I have a treat for you!" In the lingering dusk of the spring night, he led us out into his yard, to a split rail fence that bordered the road. In whispers, he described the elaborate mating ritual of the male woodcock: the clear, methodical "peeting" from an abandoned hay field, the predictable, spiraling flight high into the evening sky, and the soft, whistling free fall back to the grass, only to begin the entire cycle again.

As he finished his explanation, he turned to the field, and, as if on cue, the woodcock began its routine. It was a fascinating performance, one that occurs every spring, perhaps even within sight of my house, but one that I had never seen before.

The following Saturday the alarm went off at 4:00 a.m. It was pitch-dark and pouring rain. "This is dumb," I said to Mimi as we fumbled into our clothes and bolted down some cereal. Although it was still raining at 7:00, when we reached the large marsh in West Rutland, Bill's enthusiasm was contagious. We stepped out of the cars into a symphony of tweeting, chirping and quacking. Armed with binoculars and bird books, we witnessed more takeoffs and landings in an hour than Boston's Logan Airport sees in a year. According to Bill, several cloudy, rainy days had forced the migrating birds to wait for better weather, so the marsh was alive with song and flight.

Later he took us to a stand of mixed hardwoods. As his admiring students gathered around, Bill closed his eyes and smiled like a conductor entranced by his orchestra. Suddenly he pointed high in the trees behind him. "Hear that," he whispered, "Sweet, sweet, sweeter'n SWEET? That's your chestnut-sided warbler. And that! Teacher, teacher, teacher! That will be your ovenbird. And over there," he pointed off to his right, "Witchity, witchity, which is it. That would be the common yellowthroat." We saw or heard sixty species of birds that one morning in West Rutland!

I doubt I'll ever develop the skill to accurately identify all those little brown jobbers, but I'm certainly more aware of the amazing complexity of our natural world, which is so easy to take for granted. And I practiced. We heard the familiar, "Caw...caw...caw " and I announced with authority, "That would be the American crow." Then, dozens of times a day we heard, "Chick-a-dee-dee-dee," and I assured Mimi, "There's your black-capped chickadee." She might have had second thoughts about bird watching.

Summer Vacation

My wife, Mimi, was sobbing on the living room couch. Our daughter's fourteenth birthday was approaching, and suddenly it was apparent that she was growing up.

"In two years Julie will have her license, she'll be off to college, then she'll be on her own. She'll be too busy to spend time with us anymore. Why didn't we go on more family trips when we had the chance?" Tears flowed as the sobbing resumed.

"Hey, she's only thirteen." I tried to sound reassuring. "I bet we have time for several more family adventures before she's too embarrassed to be seen with us."

Coincidentally, a friend had invited us to his wedding in San Francisco. July might not be the ideal time to see Northern California, Nevada, and Utah, but I had accumulated enough frequent flyer miles to get us out there. Maybe we could have a family vacation in the Wild West without refinancing the house?

San Francisco was great. We stayed with college friends Mimi and I hadn't seen since graduation. Julie was fascinated by their teenage son, primarily because his room was knee deep in dirty clothes, school books, and sports equipment.

"I never want to hear complaints about my room being messy again," Julie announced, as we headed to the wedding in Marin County.

I think the father of the bride owned Northern California! Never before had I seen more luxury cars, more gourmet food, and more glamorous people, all in one place. At the reception, there was a gigantic bowl of avocado dip, which probably cost more than our entire vacation! I felt uneasy when I noticed Mimi and Julie taking notes, talking to the bridesmaids about their dresses, and asking the chef for recipes.

From California we headed east to Nevada. In Reno we stayed at a small hotel next door to the Silver Bells Wedding Parlor and across the street from Cupid's Chapel of Love. After an all-you-can-eat buffet in one of the casinos, I figured I'd teach my family a little lesson about gambling.

"You never win at these games," I announced with authority, "it's just a question of how long it takes you to lose your money." We each put four quarters into a slot machine. It took me thirty seconds to dispose of mine, Mimi stretched her quarters out for a minute or so; but on Julie's final pull, bells rang, lights flashed, and quarters cascaded to the floor. It wasn't exactly the message I was trying to instill.

From Reno we headed southeast. For years I had heard about Moab, Utah, and the Slickrock Trail, a Mecca for mountain bike enthusiasts. With an average daily temperature of 110 degrees in the shade, there were plenty of motel rooms available. The next morning, I was at the local bike shop when it opened at 7:00. I peddled the rented bike 8 miles up to the plateau where the famous Slickrock Trail began, then eagerly headed out on the 10-mile loop. Although I knew enough to bring plenty of water, by mid-morning, with the temperature over 100, I was pretty well whipped. Hours later, when I staggered back to the bike shop, I learned that even the "hard corps" cyclists drive to the trailhead, avoiding the 8-mile climb to the plateau.

To culminate our family vacation, I splurged on a raft trip down the Colorado River. Unlike the photos in the travel brochures, which show raging white water rapids and deep green pools, the Colorado River at Moab in July is a sluggish, muddy brown. But the water was cool, and we spent the day blissfully floating downstream in our life jackets. Since Mimi had a deep-seated fear of snakes, she stayed close to the raft, constantly scanning the riverbank for rattlers.

Back in the motel that evening, we caught the local TV news. Apparently, a wildlife park in Grand Junction, Colorado, had been vandalized and several animals had escaped. A number of crocodiles had been tracked to the banks of the Colorado River. People downstream were being asked to keep an eye out. The color drained from Mimi's face as stared at the TV as if in a trance.

She made a complete recovery after we'd been home for a couple of weeks, but it was safe to say there wouldn't be more family rafting trips out west. When we took any time off that summer, it was for a few day hikes, right here in the Green Mountains.

The Prom Dress

Well, we've survived another prom season. When my daughter, Julie, was a high school junior, I scarcely realized there was a prom season, and I had no idea it was anything to get anxious about. That all changed one beautiful Sunday morning while I was hiking in the mountains, and Julie casually mentioned to her mother that she had been invited to the high school prom. By the time I returned home, a crisis was brewing over the fact that our daughter had no prom dress.

Of course, the phone had been in constant use in my absence, and a solution to the emergency was on the horizon. One of Julie's classmates was also in need of a prom outfit, and a third friend had already found "the perfect dress" in Burlington. In a moment of weakness, I agreed to drive the three teenage girls to Burlington, if they could be ready to leave in fifteen minutes. Mimi shook her head in disbelief.

It's astounding how fast adolescents can get organized when they're motivated. I was in the car with the three girls and headed north by 1:30 p.m. I figured if the stores stayed open until 5:00, we'd have nearly two hours to shop. I might have been a trifle optimistic, considering we were shopping for two prom dresses.

As we headed up Interstate 89, the girls chatted enthusiastically. The conversation centered on fashion, style and dress designs. Since no one asked for my opinion, I concentrated on driving. Soon the discussion shifted to underwear, slips, and strapless bras. The girls were so engrossed, it was clear they had forgotten I was in the car. I didn't know whether to make some observation about strapless bras, just to remind them I was there, or to remain invisible. Thankfully, the topic then shifted to boys, so I kept quiet and listened.

We arrived in Burlington and parked downtown. The classmate who had already found her prom dress, and was therefore an expert, led the expedition. In a couple of the national chain stores that target youthful customers, my three girls admired designer jeans and tank tops. I had to remind them we were looking for prom dresses, and we had just over an hour to find two of them! I suggested they focus on dresses while I scouted the rest of downtown Burlington for stores that might offer additional possibilities.

In twenty minutes of sprinting from one women's store to another, I learned the location of three that might carry dresses appropriate for a formal dance. When I rendezvoused with the girls, I was relieved to find that Julie's classmate had found a dress that she liked. It was actually a sun dress, but it fit well and looked great on her. I certainly didn't feel qualified to judge whether or not she could wear a sun dress to a prom. The clerk wouldn't let her sign for the dress on her dad's credit card, so I came to the rescue with mine.

Then we sprinted off to the three shops I had discovered. We struck out at the first two. Nothing but "poodle dresses," the girls grumbled in disgust. We were running out of time! Our last chance was a small boutique with a French name, which loosely translated, meant "EXPENSIVE." The three girls were "oooing" and "ahhhing" before the door closed behind us. Within minutes, Julie had selected a very simple (should I say, elegant) plum-colored dress. Her friends gushed their praises. The salesgirl, clad in combat boots, cutoff jeans, and a camouflage T-shirt, and who appeared to be even younger than my daughter—this salesgirl—pronounced the selection "perfect."

Finally, Julie stood in front of me for my evaluation. The dress appeared to be a very nice slip, and I was tempted to ask what she planned to wear over it. Actually, I was speechless. It was only then that I realized what a beautiful young woman my teenage daughter had become.

The plum, slip-prom dress was $90.00. I chickened out on making the final decision. The camouflaged salesgirl agreed to mail us the dress if Mimi thought it sounded okay. That night, after a brief family conference at home, we all agreed it was a good choice.

Of course, you can't wear the same $90.00 prom dress two years in a row, so I braced for a renewed bout of prom dress anxiety the next spring. But as any parent knows, kids will keep you guessing. After a couple of futile shopping trips with her friends, our high school senior paid $15.00 for a pair of platform shoes at a sidewalk sale, found a vintage 1920's flapper dress (which she loved) in a friend's barn, and had a wonderful time at the prom.

I suppose the next major dress search we'll face, a few years down the road, will focus on wedding dresses. No telling which direction that one will take.

Sports and Life

The Long Trail, Part 1

The Long Trail is a rugged footpath that stretches 268 miles along the spine of Vermont's Green Mountains, from Canada to Massachusetts. It was the first long-distance hiking trail in the nation, conceived by James Taylor in 1909. When my daughter, Julie, announced that she wanted to hike the Long Trail before heading off to college, it was impossible for me to resist.

I suggested we try a couple of overnights in July to test our equipment and to get a sense of how far we could comfortably hike in a day. Privately, I thought a couple of evenings deep in the woods with the mosquitoes and the rain might temper Julie's enthusiasm for spending the month of August on the trail.

So, on a warm morning in July, we threw our gear into the car and headed south. My wife, Mimi, had agreed to drop us off in Williamstown, Massachusetts, spend the night at a bed and breakfast, then pick us up the following afternoon where the Long Trail crosses Route 9, a few miles east of Bennington, Vermont.

It was a hot summer day. By the time we arrived at the trailhead, we were already sweating, tired and hungry. As Julie and I pushed into the lush vegetation on the trail to Pine Cobble, a two-thousand-foot knoll overlooking Williamstown, Mimi waved goodbye and headed off in search of an air-conditioned restaurant.

Soon after reaching the summit, we joined the Appalachian Trail. It was the modest junction of two footpaths in the woods, marked by a humble wooden sign, but it was a memorable moment. We were about to hike on a trail that spans 2,144 miles, from Georgia to Maine.

By 2:30 we had reached the Vermont state line, also the beginning of the Long Trail. Finally, we were officially underway. A gentle rain began to patter through the broad leaves of the maples and beeches. As I encouraged Julie to smile for a photo in front of the trail sign, she grumbled, "You mean to tell me, those last three and a half miles of climb don't even count?" Talk about being goal-oriented!

At 4:30 we reached the Seth Warner Shelter. Since we were on a shake-down cruise, I wanted to use our old tent rather than stay in the Green

Mountain Club's lean-to. There were no other hikers in the tenting area, so I carefully inspected each of the campsites, checking for level ground and the location of roots and rocks. Once I had selected the best site, I shook the folds of faded nylon, aluminum poles, and plastic stakes out of our tent's stuff sack. Within minutes, Julie and I had the tent up and our sleeping bags arranged inside.

It was not until after supper that we noticed, for the first time, a huge branch, lodged precariously in the fork of a maple tree, directly over our tent.

Julie asked, "Do you think we should move?"

The branch was a widow-maker if I'd ever seen one, but ours was the most comfortable tent site, it would be a major hassle relocating in the dark, and the branch didn't appear ready to fall.

"I think we'll be okay. It would be different if the wind was howling and the trees swaying all over the place."

Julie agreed. We tumbled into our tent and were soon asleep. Sometime later, I was awakened by the rumble of thunder and the flash of lightening. In the strobe-like brightness, I could see my daughter staring at the peak of the tent. "Are you okay?" I asked.

"Is that branch going to fall on us?"

"Naw, it sounds like the storm will blow by to the north. I imagine we'll get some thunder and lightning, but that's about it."

We lay still as the thunder rumbled closer, and the lightning bolts illuminated the forest. As I was about to suggest that we get up and relocate, we heard what sounded like an approaching freight train. We were slammed by a ferocious blast of wind that seemed to tear the leaves from their branches. Then the rain struck like an advancing waterfall. All the time the thunder crashed around us, and the lightening flashed. You could actually smell it. We were surrounded by raging natural forces as violent as any I had ever experienced. Somehow, leaving the tent was unthinkable.

Eventually, the storm passed. We weren't squashed by the massive branch. Over breakfast, Julie admitted that she had really wondered if we were going to die. I confessed that the same thought had crossed my mind. But we survived the storm unscathed, we were full of oatmeal, and were eager to get back on the trail.

Julie set a surprisingly brisk pace. We hiked hard all day and covered more than 11 miles with reasonably heavy packs. Tired, dirty, and drenched with sweat, we met Mimi within five minutes of the prearranged time. Julie was exuberant in her description of the adventure, especially the thunderstorm. We had been scared out of our wits, but hiking the Long Trail was no longer a fantasy. We were hooked.

Sports and Life

The Long Trail, Part 2

I had assumed the wind, rain, thunder and lightning of our first night on the Long Trail would dampen my daughter's enthusiasm for hiking the length of Vermont. I was wrong. So, a week later, Mimi dropped us off just east of Bennington, where the trail crosses Route 9, for the second phase of our adventure. Before long we had climbed out of the valley and were cruising the tree-covered ridges.

At an overlook with an impressive view to the east, we stopped for lunch. Soon, an Appalachian Trail through-hiker joined us. We learned that all the through-hikers adopt trail names, and his was The Maine Moose. He was from Auburn, Maine, had started from Georgia in April, and hoped to reach Mount Katahdin by early September.

Two others stopped to share the viewpoint for lunch. Tahoma was from Seattle and was between jobs in the computer industry. He had been hiking on and off for several weeks with Doc, a professor of aeronautical engineering from Monterey, California. I watched with interest as Tahoma prepared his lunch. He rummaged around in his pack and emerged with a Snickers bar and a jar of peanut butter. He plunged the Snickers deep into the peanut butter, then eagerly chomped the end of the candy bar. His entire lunch took less than three minutes to prepare and consume, providing a whole new definition for the phrase "quick energy."

Julie and I left the A.T. hikers and continued north to the Goddard Shelter, not far from the summit of Glastenbury Mountain. As we cooked our supper, Doc, Tahoma and Moose appeared around the corner of the shelter. While they settled in, we were joined by Echo and Trail Junkie, a young couple from Ohio who were using six months of stress and hardship on the Appalachian Trail to determine whether they were suited to spend the rest of their lives together.

The conversation drifted to the colorful characters who were part of the A.T. community that summer. As darkness closed in and rain dripped off the eaves, we heard about Strider, Flipper, T. Rex, Care Bear, Passalong, and Cat Fish. We learned that Leap Frog was a fifteen-year-old boy who was hiking the 2,144 miles from Georgia to Maine by himself. There were good-natured warnings about infamous hikers who snored loudly, or whose boots could smell up an entire shelter.

The north-bounders had questions about New Hampshire's White Mountains, an imposing barrier so near their final destination in Maine. Meanwhile, the south-bounders heard harrowing accounts of stepping on rattlesnakes in Pennsylvania, and the oppressive heat of Virginia.

The next morning we had breakfast early, packed quickly and were headed north by 7:45. It seemed that most of the through-hikers were so fit, they walked fast while they were hiking, but relaxed in camp, often stopping early in the afternoon, and seldom hitting the trail at the crack of dawn.

Of course, there were exceptions. Several through-hikers we met had mentioned a mysterious north-bounder known as Josh. No one had actually seen him, but his entries could be found in the logbooks along the route. Josh was intriguing because he had started from Georgia later than everyone else, appeared to be averaging an astounding 25 miles a day, and had slipped through most of the through-hikers unnoticed. Tahoma suggested that JOSH actually stood for Jet-Operated Super Hiker: not a real person at all, but instead, an elaborate, well-planned hoax.

The next afternoon, Mimi met us at Kelly Stand as we had arranged. Although we were tired and sweaty, Julie's account of the overnight with the through-hikers was enthusiastic.

But it was Mimi who supplied the excitement following our second excursion on the Long Trail. She did our grocery shopping at the Hanover Co-op, which happens to be right on the A.T. During the summer, it's not unusual to see suntanned through-hikers stuffing their Co-op purchases directly into their towering backpacks.

Julie and I had been home a couple of days when Mimi returned from grocery shopping, and casually mentioned, "I talked with a through-hiker at the Co-op today."

Julie's face lit up, "Oh yeah, what'd he look like?"

"Like they all do, great physical shape, tanned, seemed to be a college kid. He was sitting on a bench outside the store, drinking a carton of orange juice."

"Did you ask his trail name?"

"I did. Said he couldn't think of a good trail name, so he just uses his real name... Josh."

The Long Trail, Part 3

Two tough weekends of hiking only intensified my daughter's determination to walk Vermont's Long Trail, end to end; so early in August we embarked on our first extended expedition. Our plan was to resume our trek where we had left off on the southern shoulder of Stratton Mountain and push north for five days. After a resupply of food, and a night at the Inn where the trail crosses Route 4, we would continue on to Lincoln Gap.

At first, the weather simply wouldn't cooperate; we had hot, humid days and the peaks were shrouded in clouds, robbing us of several hard-earned vistas. The first night we had the Douglas Shelter to ourselves, except for the resident mice and squirrels. The next morning, after a breakfast of oatmeal, we were back on the trail and soon settled into a comfortable routine. Julie led, and set the pace, while I carried the map and checked our progress in the guidebook. The only drawback to this arrangement was that I was the one who got stung. Adding an element of excitement to the Long Trail in August are the yellow jackets, nesting in the ground, sometimes near the path. By late summer they're feisty. The first hiker riles up the nest, anyone following stands a good chance of being stung.

The thunder rolled in and the rain began, but we decided to keep hiking. I was beginning to think we were really foolhardy, stumbling down a mountain in the summer storm, but then we encountered a Green Mountain Club trail crew. They were drenched and coated with mud, but still wrestling with boulders and hacking at stumps in the pouring rain. It was a good reminder that the Long Trail isn't about comfort as much as it's about challenge. We thanked the volunteers for their efforts and pushed on.

That night we had Peru Peak Shelter to ourselves, except for the mice of course. This time, the little varmints found their way into our hanging food sack but couldn't get back out. Two mice in a plastic bag of oatmeal at midnight can make a heck of a racket.

The following night provided a dramatic contrast. After hiking through another late afternoon downpour, we straggled into the Greenwall Shelter to find it filled with Appalachian Trail through-hikers. Scotty was traveling by himself, going fast and light, videotaping much of what he saw. Stepping Wolf and Sir Renity combined a relaxed attitude in camp with a ferocious pace on the trail.

In the shelter that night, there were stories of the many legendary characters who had become part of the trail's mythology. The logbook recorded dozens of colorful trail names adopted by those walking from Georgia to Maine: Country Bob, Lucky Laurel, Passalong, T. Rex, Gypsy Bones, and Strider.

Another two days brought us to our Route 4 rendezvous right on schedule. There's nothing like a week of mud and sweat to make you deeply grateful for a hot shower and a laundromat. After a sound night's sleep in clean sheets, we repacked for the next stage of our journey.

The Long Trail and the Appalachian Trail, which share the same path and shelters north from the Massachusetts border, split just beyond Route 4. The A.T. leads east through New Hampshire to Maine while the Long Trail continues along the spine of the Green Mountains to Canada. We would miss the energy and inspiration of the A.T. through-hikers. Although the Long Trail wound through beautiful hardwoods for several miles beyond the junction, we walked in silence, feeling a little lonely.

The weather improved and we made good progress. Our second night north of Route 4 brought some unanticipated excitement. We shared the Sunrise Shelter, near Brandon Gap, with Jim and Alan, who had hiked the A.T. together years earlier. The two former hiking buddies were introducing Jim's wife, Nancy, a lawyer from Philadelphia, to the joys of the wilderness.

After supper, we hung our food sacks from the rafters, exchanged a few stories by candlelight, then nestled into our sleeping bags. Julie and I had become accustomed to the rustlings of rodents in the dark, but I doubt Nancy got much sleep.

Julie and I woke early, made our breakfast and were about to hit the trail when a scream pierced the morning silence. Nancy had discovered a dead mouse in her sleeping bag. Apparently, she had rolled over during the night and crushed the poor thing. Judging from her reaction, that was probably Nancy's first and last camping trip. But if Jim ever convinces her to tackle the A. T., she already has her trail name... "Mouse Slayer."

Sports and Life

Take a Gopher to Dinner

My father-in-law is almost eighty. Playing football for Nebraska and the Green Bay Packers back in the days of leather helmets took a toll on his knees. Flying B-25s in the Pacific during World War II destroyed his hearing. He's never without a baseball cap. Three decades after the disappearance of his hair, he still can't accept that it's gone. Another trademark is the assortment of sweatshirts, sweaters, and jackets he wears, regardless of the season. In spite of the bad knees, he still loves to ski, but folks who recognize his distinctive outfits give him plenty of room on the slopes.

He's determined not to give up his driver's license, even though driving has caused him some embarrassment lately. After a recent visit to our house, he missed his exit on the interstate and didn't notice the oversight until hours later, when he reached the Canadian border. Another time, he went in for the mail at his local post office, and couldn't find his car when he came back out. He had neglected to set the parking brake. The car rolled down an embankment into the river while he was in buying stamps.

It's not exaggerating to say that George has become a local celebrity. When his wife died of cancer a few months ago, friends pitched in to help him through the readjustment. Neighbors appeared unannounced to mow his lawn or stack firewood. Others visit regularly to ease the loneliness. But since he's not much of a cook, the offer of greatest support came from a local restaurant, where he was invited to join them for supper every evening. He has become a regular there, sitting at the counter in his baseball cap and parka, joking with the waitresses and the cooks.

Not long ago he arrived for dinner in a state of agitation. Fumbling with the zipper of his bulky ski jacket, he told his friends that his cat, Bingo, had frightened a gopher up his pant leg and under his coat. The bewildered staff watched as he tugged at the bulky jacket, and tried to peek down the sleeves.

"George, we don't have gophers around here," the cook gently reminded him. "Why don't you sit down and have some supper."

"Hell, I don't know what it was then, but Bingo scared something right into my coat, " George insisted, still struggling with the zipper.

Then the waitress arrived with his supper, so he gave up on the stubborn zipper and concentrated on his meal. Another customer sat next to George at the counter and ordered. They spoke briefly, but George was concentrating on his food, and conversation was difficult since he had forgotten his hearing aids. Then the newcomer noticed the lump moving between George's shoulder blades.

His curiosity became unbearable. "What's that you got moving across your back?" he asked.

"Pardon?"

"You got something crawling around under your coat," the other customer shouted.

After straining to decipher the statement, George answered, "Oh, my cat scared a gopher into my coat. Can't get the damn zipper open to let him out."

By that time both men had finished their meals, and the shouted conversation had attracted other patrons, who also noticed the moving lump under George's coat. Finally, the cook emerged from the kitchen, took George by the arm, and led him to the door.

"Let's see who you've got in that coat with you," he said as they headed for the parking lot, followed by most of the people in the restaurant.

The cook worked for a moment with the jammed zipper, but soon had it free and hoisted the jacket up off George's shoulders. For an instant, the cook stared at a pair of frightened eyes, then the small animal launched itself into the bushes bordering the parking lot. The cook ducked. The crowd gasped in amazement.

"Hell, George," said the cook, "you had a red squirrel in your coat, the whole time you were eating your supper!"

"I'll be damned, I thought it was a gopher," George responded as he fumbled with the zipper and headed for his car.

A Concert for Strings and Canoe

It had been one of those magnificent, late summer days; a brilliant clear sky, warm sun, but no humidity; a day that gets your attention because for the first time, there's a hint of autumn in the air.

In spite of the inspiring weather, my wife, Mimi, was having a rough time. For starters, our only daughter was headed off to college in a week. Both Mimi and I were still adjusting to the concept of kicking our fledgling out of the nest, and more than once during recent days, I had observed my partner brush the tears away as she folded blue jeans and T-shirts, the uniform of the college student.

Then there was the matter of Mimi's birthday. She had just turned forty-nine. Neither of us has ever been particularly sensitive about our age, but coming face-to-face with fifty is kind of a shock. Even the most optimistic among us can't deny that we've passed the halfway point. It is certainly nothing to get all morose about, but it does make you stop and think.

And then there's her dad, seventy-nine years old and living in a nearby retirement community. He had always been a powerful, even at times domineering, force in her life, but lately he had been struggling. On impulse recently, she had fetched him out to our house, made a delicious lunch and served it on the deck, capitalizing on the nice weather and beautiful view.

The conversation was disjointed and hard to follow. Moments after we finished eating, he fell asleep in the sun. Eventually, he woke up ready to return to his residence. He had to get back to feed his cat. When we dropped him off, it seemed to take him forever to shuffle down the hall to his room.

Mimi's tears flowed freely as we drove away from the retirement community. We stopped in town for a quiet supper, both of us filled with thoughts of growing up, heading off to college, and all too soon, old age. It was a pensive meal. We drove home into a spectacular orange sunset. As we pulled into the yard I was inspired.

"Quick, help me get the canoe onto the car, then get a sweatshirt and the dog. We're going for a paddle before it gets dark." She glanced at the softening pastels in the western sky and shook her head in bewilderment, but she helped me wrestle the canoe from its rack in the garage to the roof of the car.

Moments later we were unloading at Lake Fairlee, a few miles away. The sun had been down for a while, but the sky was still surprisingly bright as we paddled from shore. A couple of motorboats passed us as they returned to the launching ramp.

Soon we had the lake to ourselves. Even the summer camps, which had bustled with activity for the past three months, were silent. The soft pink and purple of the sky above the pines was reflected in the glassy water. We tried to dip our paddles without breaking the silence.

We have friends who own a home on the lake, so we headed across to where they live. Their lights were on. I stayed in the canoe with the dog, while Mimi ran up to their house. Moments later they returned to the shore, and the four of us talked quietly as the light faded and the stars began to appear.

When we finally said good night to our friends, it was dark. Our route back across the lake was illuminated by a few cabin lights at the water's edge and a blanket of stars overhead. Seldom had the Milky Way seemed so brilliant. I had only a vague idea of where to find the boat ramp and our car. As we paddled in silence, I scanned the dark shore for a clue and was drawn to golden light pouring from a small cottage near the water's edge. We paddled closer and classical music began to pour across the calm water. I imagined someone sitting by a radio, but as we floated closer I was amazed to see bows flashing and silver heads bobbing with the music. We had drifted upon a string quartet playing with a confidence and precision that made us feel as though we should have bought tickets. We were surrounded by beautiful music, rocking gently on the calm water, and staring at the endless canopy of constellations above us.

When the music ended, we heard the artists congratulate each other. We were tempted to add our applause but hesitated to break the spell.

Instead, a barred owl, not far from the modest concert hall, broke the silence with her traditional greeting, "Whooo cooks for yooou..." We smiled at each other in the starlight. Then, from the far side of the lake, amplified over the water came a faint response, "Whoooo."

A New Perspective on Illness

During a competitive and coaching career that spanned thirty years, I developed a serious dread of illness. As a member of the U.S. Biathlon Team, I trained nearly a decade for the Winter Olympics, only to have one of those precious competitive opportunities snatched away by a virulent stomach flu. More recently as a coach, I have seen dozens of dedicated skiers fail to make a team, or fall short of their goals in major events, due to sickness. I am nervous around doctors, and I avoid hospitals. Like most endurance athletes, from high school runners to Olympians, I fear the common cold.

My anxiety about illness resulted in two types of behavior. First, I ignored or had little sympathy for people who were sick. Second, on those rare occasions when I succumbed to a cold or the flu, I gave up, convinced that training or competing when sick was pointless.

Three people have helped me revise my view of illness, and I'm grateful to them. Some time ago, my father-in-law moved into a nearby retirement home. Soon thereafter, he was diagnosed with Alzheimer's disease. Before World War II, this fellow had played football for the Nebraska Corn huskers and then the Green Bay Packers. He continued to lift weights and swim three times a week well into his seventies, until the ravages of the disease made the fitness machines too confusing, and the combination for the lock on the pool door, impossible to remember.

But somehow, he retained his sense of humor. He constantly teased other residents and the staff of his retirement community. In spite of football knees so stiff he couldn't rise from a chair without help, he rarely complained about his health.

The other day I had lunch with a college friend. Although we raced against each other on rival teams every winter weekend for four years, through a shared love of the sport we became buddies. After graduation he coached the U.S. Ski Team for a few years, went on to law school, and married a wonderful woman. Just when he seemed to be hitting his stride, he was diagnosed with multiple sclerosis. Aside from occasional letters, we drifted out of touch. I think I was afraid to reconnect with my old rival, reluctant to see what the disease had done to the powerful college skier I remembered, and perhaps on a deeper level, aware that I am every bit as vulnerable to a disease like M.S. as he was.

It turned out to be a wonderful reunion, and I regret I waited so long to get back in touch. He walks slowly now with the aid of crutches, and his speech is sometimes difficult to understand. But the boundless enthusiasm and the broad grin are still there. We suffered through some grueling competitions in college: demanding race courses, freezing temperatures, and difficult snow conditions. But nothing we faced as Nordic skiers compared with the challenges my old buddy now confronted each day, with grit and a remarkable sense of humor.

Then, my wife, Mimi, was diagnosed with cancer. After struggling through the predictable responses of terror, dread, and resignation, she began a course of chemotherapy, augmented with alternative treatments, including acupuncture, massage and Chinese herbs. In addition, she received overwhelming emotional support from friends, relatives and members of our community.

Twelve months after the diagnosis, Mimi was doing well. She was off the chemotherapy and had more energy than she'd had for years. But the most noticeable improvement was in her attitude. She had rekindled a long dormant interest in drawing and painting. She surrounded herself with good music. She loved visiting with friends, especially those who made her laugh. And she had become deeply aware of the natural beauty that surrounds us: the flaming autumn leaves, a brilliant harvest moon, an early winter snowfall.

These three friends helped me to understand that life is not as simple as being either healthy or sick. An old man, whose body is wearing out and whose mind is slipping away, can still make people laugh. A former national team Nordic skier shows as much determination shuffling into a restaurant as he did two decades ago flying over the snow for 50 kilometers. And a beautiful woman with cancer fills her days with

moments of joy and natural wonder.

I may have been a reluctant student, but I'm thankful for what they've taught me about seeing illness from a different perspective.

Up, Up and Away

There are still a few private airplanes tied down next to the grass landing strip, but over the past few years the airfield in Post Mills, Vermont, has become a center for hot air ballooning. Since our home in Thetford is only 6 miles downwind, we often see the impressive airships early in the morning or just before sunset. After years of watching these colorful giants, my curiosity prompted me to visit the Post Mills flight center.

Brian Boland (who sadly passed away recently) had been ballooning for a quarter of a century. In 1970 as a student at Pratt Institute, he designed and constructed a balloon as an art project. At that time there were 150 balloonists worldwide, with about one-third of them in America. Today the sport claims at least 6,000 active balloon pilots.

The required equipment includes the balloon itself, a huge envelope sewn from panels of ripstop nylon. A typical envelope can contain 77,000 cubic feet of hot air. Below the envelope is suspended a wicker basket or gondola, in which the pilot and passengers ride. The basket also carries a canister of liquid propane, fuel for a burner that hangs in the opening of the envelope, just above the basket. Finally, the balloonist needs a pair of inflator fans to deploy the envelope on the ground before the burners are ignited.

After giving me a tour of his facility and patiently explaining the basics of ballooning, Brian had me hooked. I scheduled a flight as a surprise for my wife, Mimi, and our daughter, Julie, whose birthdays are a week apart. On the appointed morning, I roused my family at dawn. We reached the airport before six, with only minor grumbling.

Brian put us to work restraining the envelope as the inflator fans did their job. After a few impressive blasts from the burner, the huge nylon envelope rose gracefully from the grass and gently tugged at the wicker basket. Brian invited us to climb aboard and gave a short safety briefing, reminding us not to leave the basket until the balloon returned to earth. Balloonists don't carry parachutes.

A long, powerful roar from the burner provided the necessary lift, and we were airborne. A warm breeze drew us over deep green forests, brighter green pastures, and the brilliant ribbons of fog that marked the river valleys. As we rose above Lake Fairlee, our reflection drifted silently across the still, dark surface. Ducks flew low and fast, just above the water.

We continued rising to Brian's normal cruising altitude of 1,000 feet, from which we saw our town from an entirely new perspective. There were homes, fields, and ponds we never knew existed because they weren't visible from the roads we usually traveled. We could see how the glacier had scoured the hill tops and carved the river valleys. We looked down on beautiful fields of corn, the meticulously straight rows resembling fabric. As we drifted over the dark water of the Connecticut River, a tiny, pale figure swam from Vermont to New Hampshire.

Brian radioed to his wife, Louise, who followed on the ground in a minivan. As the flight drew to a close, Brian used the radio to inform Louise of his intended landing site, and she raced ahead to seek permission from the landowner. Trees, fences and power lines can be dangerous, so balloonists favor dry pastures or meadows, preferably free from livestock and easily accessible to the van.

What adds excitement to a balloon landing is that winds often blow in different directions at different altitudes. This is where Brian's 5,500 hours of piloting experience comes in handy. As he evaluated the constantly changing options, he alternately fired the burner or pulled a cord that released hot air from the top of the envelope. These maneuvers intensified the drama since there was a fifteen-second delay before the huge balloon reacted to any correction. More than once I was certain we were headed for the trees, when at the last instant, the balloon responded to an earlier blast of flame and rose gracefully over the branches.

When Brian pointed to the corner of a field behind a farmhouse, it appeared to me we would drift well past the target. But as we descended, an air current pulled us back over the pasture, and we touched down precisely where our pilot had predicted.

It was a birthday present that I know Mimi and Julie will remember. For me, it was a convincing demonstration of how everyday surroundings can seem totally different from a new perspective.

Attacking the Montshire Museum

Not long ago, my wife's younger brother and his family arrived for a visit. He has a wonderful wife and two very active boys, ages six and eight. I have one daughter and have always wondered what it would be like to have sons, so I jumped at the chance to whisk my two spirited nephews away for the afternoon. I squeezed Mick and Corey into the cab of my pickup and headed for the Montshire Museum of Science in Norwich.

That was my first mistake. Put a father and his daughter in the front of a pickup truck, and the most excitement you're likely to generate is a disagreement over radio stations. Strap two healthy preteen boys into adjacent seat belts, and you've got an instant brawl. I was trying to win points in the "favorite uncle contest," so I let them wrestle until the resale value of my truck was in jeopardy. Fortunately, we arrived at the museum before they tore an arm rest from the door or the sun visor from the ceiling.

The Montshire Museum is a treasure, a collection of interesting and educational displays designed especially for children. Many of the exhibits require the kids to participate; they crank, or they crawl, they spin, or they lift. The only problem is, young boys of six and eight have absolutely no interest in reading directions.

They sprinted from one station to the next, instantly locating the moving parts, then cranking, spinning, or twisting for all they were worth. There was little interest in the fish tanks or the turtle shells; after a quick glance they raced off to find something that moved.

There was a large vat of soapy water and household items that could be used to make interesting bubbles. Mick quickly discovered that the hula hoop would sustain a slippery film of bubble soap that he could douse over his brother's head.

Then it was on to Andy's Place, an indoor tree house and bear den designed for kids under five. Ignoring the age restrictions, my nephews bolted through the gate. They climbed and jumped and crawled, soon insisting that I join them in the bear's den. Under the disapproving scowls of other parents, I followed the boys into a realistic cave, complete with a hibernating black bear. I scored big points for squirming into the tiny den, but since it was designed for five-year-olds, there were some tense moments as I struggled back out.

On the second floor we quickly scanned the observation beehive and the leaf cutter ant display. A helpful staff member asked if the boys had any questions.

"Naw," answered Corey, "we studied these ants in school."

But moments later, mesmerized by a huge boa constrictor in a glass enclosure, Corey shouted back to the museum employee, "Hey, can you let this snake out?" Panic etched the faces of several nearby parents until the staff member answered, "Sorry, but the snake only comes out when the Naturalist is here."

"We studied snakes in school. I could hold him," Corey persisted.

The two boys slowed their pace only twice during the afternoon. The first time was when they discovered the vending machines. "Look Corey, a Coke only costs 60 cents!" This announcement was accompanied by an endearing glance toward their "favorite" uncle.

"Your mom doesn't mind if you have soda?" I asked. What a stupid question.

"Heck no, she buys us soda all the time. And look, here's a candy machine! Wow, it's even got Lucky Charms!"

After inhaling the soda and candy, my nephews were refueled for a renewed attack on the museum. By this time the Montshire had called for reinforcements and several staff members stood guard at the important exhibits.

Finally, the boys paused for the second time. I caught up to them, transfixed in front of a color computer monitor titled "The Adam and Eve Display." A studious junior high school boy was operating the keyboard. On the color monitor was a detailed illustration of a naked man. With a touch of the keyboard, the older boy zoomed in on the man's torso. Another touch, and the entire screen was filled by a closeup of the man's genitals.

"Wow!" shouted Corey.

"Can you do that with the woman?" asked Mick.

"Time to head home boys! Your folks must be missing you," I said as I dragged them toward the exit.

I learned later that my nephews had enjoyed the afternoon, and that I had even moved up a few places on the "Ranking List of Favorite Uncles." That came as a nice bonus, since, to be honest, I was happy to have just survived the afternoon.

Sports and Life

College Reunion

I had to overcome three deterrents to attend my thirtieth college reunion. Decades earlier, as an idealistic sixteen-year-old, I was invited to a lavish college reunion at a prestigious Ivy League university. From my adolescent perspective, the returning alums seemed determined to impress each other with their successful careers, their luxury cars, and their glamorous wives. I also had the sense that the entire schedule of events was fueled by alcohol.

A few years later, as a student at Middlebury College, I worked in the dining hall during reunion. Middlebury's gathering was casual compared to the ostentatious Ivy League celebration, but I remember thinking those loyal alums were truly ancient, and totally preoccupied with the past.

My third misgiving was the strongest. I met my wife, Mimi, at Middlebury. We would have been married twenty-nine years, just fourteen days before the reunion, but she lost a long struggle with cancer in January. I was afraid that returning to campus would release an uncontrollable flood of emotions.

Five years earlier, with significant anxiety, Mimi and I attended our twenty-fifth reunion together, but it wasn't the competitive show-and-tell I had dreaded. We graduated from college on June 10, 1968: five days after Bobby Kennedy was shot, a few short weeks after a sniper gunned down Martin Luther King, and only four months after the Tet Offensive changed the course of the war in southeast Asia. Within weeks of receiving our diplomas, the Los Angeles suburb of Watts erupted in flames, and the Chicago police brutally crushed demonstrations at the Democratic National Convention.

At our reunion, twenty-five years later, we shared thoughts of how those events had changed our lives. Classmates who fought in Vietnam heard from those who had remained home, enduring the agonizing helplessness of waiting for loved ones to return from combat. For the first time, we who had served in the military listened to our classmates who had protested against the war, who had demonstrated at our ROTC drill sessions, and who had burned their draft cards. With the wisdom of hindsight, we finally understood their side of the story, and we made peace with each other.

Our twenty-fifth reunion, though gut wrenching, had been therapeutic, so with a whole new set of misgivings, I returned to Middlebury for my thirtieth. If anything, the campus was more beautiful than I remembered. There was construction everywhere: a new swimming pool, a new art center, a new hockey rink. And talk about feeling ancient, the college is building a massive new science center to replace the one that opened the year I graduated!

They've made progress in the dorms as well. I was assigned to a brand-new housing unit that bore little resemblance to the noisy, drafty dorms I remembered from my undergraduate days. Thirty years can bring about interesting social changes as well. Back in the sixties, the men lived on one side of the campus, women on the other, and formalized visiting hours were strictly enforced. But the new housing units are not only co-ed, today's male and female students actually share the same bathrooms. That's good training for married life, I suppose.

The greatest changes, however, were not in the college itself, but in my classmates. Guys I remembered as wild party animals had become responsible parents, successful businessmen, and celebrated civic leaders. A nerdish math major, who by his own account was nearly invisible as an undergraduate, flew to the reunion in his own corporate jet after establishing several software companies in the Silicon Valley.

Painfully shy women, whose college experience had consisted of attending classes, living in the library and earning straight A's, returned as confident, self-assured adults, having successfully balanced family and career for thirty years.

But the past three decades weren't all roses. Most of us have scars and bruises from what life has served up. There have been painful broken marriages, unanticipated career changes, and the inevitable loss of loved ones. I had dreaded attending the reunion because I didn't want to spend the weekend wallowing in grief, but I discovered that since graduation, we've all experienced heartbreak. My former classmates knew just how I felt, but they didn't dwell on it.

Three decades after graduation, waistlines are thicker, hair is streaked with silver, and the creases are deeper when we smile. But in my view, that just adds character.

Sports and Life

A Firsthand Look at the Generation Gap

I recently turned fifty-two. My daughter will be twenty-one at the end of the summer. Even though we have a great relationship, and she's one of my best friends, there are areas where our views differ significantly.

Since junior high school, Julie has been a vegetarian. At first, I think it was simply a cool thing to do, a way for her express her individuality. Later, she would explain to anyone who would listen how cruelly some animals are treated before they end up on our dinner tables. Over the years, she has collected a convincing assortment of articles that suggest that the animal fat in our diet contributes to heart disease, high blood pressure and stroke. Though impressive, this evidence has not been easy for me to swallow: a guy who grew up on burgers, bacon and roast beef.

Then there's the issue of clothing. I understand that college students have their traditional, everyday uniform consisting of T-shirts and blue jeans, but I'm talking about more formal occasions. What's appropriate these days to wear to a job interview, or the neighbor's wedding reception?

Julie and I have been miles apart on this topic. I get most of my clothes from the L.L.Bean sale catalog, while she searches for outrageous paisleys and floral prints at the Salvation Army thrift shop. If I question the frayed cuffs of her corduroy pants that drag on the floor, she patiently reminds me that my favorite tie went out of style decades ago. But I try to go easy on the issue of personal appearance, since, so far, she hasn't dyed her hair blue, or pierced various sensitive parts of her body.

Julie and I cheerfully agree to disagree about food and clothing, but another subject that still stimulates a lively discussion is music. I have come to realize that popular music is a cornerstone of youth culture. I remember watching Elvis Presley and the Beatles on The Ed Sullivan Show. During the Vietnam War, I listened to Simon and Garfunkel; Peter, Paul and Mary; and Bob Dylan. But for me, it was just entertainment, little more than pleasing background noise.

Today's kids are musical experts. Their favorite performers help to define our kids' identities among their peers. And music is one area where Julie hasn't yet given up on me. During our road trips to and from her college, I've had heavy doses of her favorites: the Indigo Girls, Ani DiFranco, Dar Williams, and Sweet Honey in the Rock.

So, when I noticed that the Indigo Girls would be performing nearby, I earned major points by bringing home a pair of tickets. As the big day approached, Julie tried to prepare me for what she knew would be a shock.

"It's gonna be crowded dad, I mean, really mobbed! And the music will be VERY loud. Some people even wear ear plugs!"

"Really?" I answered. "Wearing ear plugs to a concert? Kind of like going to an art museum blindfolded, I suppose?"

Julie just groaned.

She was right, of course. The basketball arena was packed. There were hundreds of high school and college kids in blue jeans. The boys wore T-shirts or plaid flannel, the girls wore tight cotton tank tops with sweaters tied around their waists. I had the impression the concert was simply an excuse for these nubile young women to promenade in some type of modern, mating ritual.

It had cost me 28 bucks apiece for our seats, but nobody in the arena was sitting. The entire audience stood throughout the concert, swaying and singing, clapping and dancing. And LOUD! It was astounding how two normal-looking women with guitars could produce such deafening volume. Julie explained that part of the attraction of a live concert is actually "feeling" the music. I didn't understand a single lyric the entire evening, but I certainly felt the music.

What Julie failed to prepare me for was the light show! Banks of intense spotlights bathed the performers and the audience in a constantly changing sea of color. A technician coordinated the lights with the music, adding visual chaos to the deafening sound. The whole scene was reminiscent of an aircraft carrier under attack.

Fortunately, I had enjoyed the Indigo Girls on our car stereo, and it was interesting to see them in person. But I probably won't be attending any more rock concerts right away. At least, not until my ears stop ringing from the last one.

Recycling

Years ago, my daughter introduced me to a new sport, but it wasn't until the local landfill closed that I really honed my skills. Like many of her idealistic classmates, Julie was concerned about our environment. She wrote a short essay on the benefits of recycling, which was published in the local newspaper. In those days, I thought we were recycling if we used the same pickle jars more than one season, or if I saved newspapers to start the fire in the woodstove.

Then the town's landfill in Post Mills was shut down because contaminants appeared to be seeping into the nearby Ompompanoosuc River. Overnight, the fee for disposing household rubbish went from pocket change to big money, and recycling became a matter of financial necessity. Thanks to a few dedicated visionaries, we now have a clean, well-organized recycling center, which has become a community meeting place on Saturday mornings.

Like any other sport, there are rules, but once you've walked through a couple of scrimmages, you get the hang of it. Paper is easy: you've got a dumpster for newsprint, another for glossy magazines and catalogs, and a third for flattened cardboard, like cereal boxes. You want to be careful not to delay your neighbors by loitering at the openings of the dumpsters, but nobody seems to mind if you retrieve a magazine that catches your interest. I couldn't believe someone actually threw away a Victoria's Secret catalog!

Glass is more fun than paper. I've always had a complicated fascination with breaking glass. I know there's something inherently wrong with smashing a bottle on a rock, or hitting a baseball through a window. Broken glass can be dangerous, people get cut. And yet, I occasionally I have this irresistible urge to smash a Coke bottle just to see it shatter into a thousand pieces.

At recycling, you are encouraged to smash your bottles in the metal bins, since the broken glass is more compact than the bottles. Nothing too complicated here: it's either clear glass like mayonnaise jars, or colored, like prune juice bottles. Of course, you'll want to separate out any returnables on which you paid a deposit.

This brings up a word of caution, however. If you live in a small town like I do, remember you're going to see almost everyone you know Saturday morning, and news travels fast. If you had a bunch of buddies over for a few beers, you might not want to recycle all the bottles on the same Saturday, or word might get around that you've developed a drinking problem. Or if you recycle that huge cardboard carton your new wide-screen, high-resolution home entertainment center was packed in, you can be pretty sure you'll have lots of company for the playoff games and the Super Bowl.

Aluminum and tin are pretty straight forward, although I sometimes have difficulty spotting the deposit information stamped into the top of aluminum soda cans.

The station where you can really distinguish the recycling pros from the rookies, is at plastics. The rules for plastics are tricky, and they tend to change without warning. Basically, you've got your number 1 clear plastic: cranberry juice bottles, for example. Of course, ginger ale often comes in light green bottles, but that's still number 1 plastic.

Then you've got your number 2 plastic: laundry detergent containers, milk bottles, and even maple syrup jugs. Color's no clue with these, you've got to look at the tiny code on the bottom of the bottle. But for heaven's sake, sort through your plastics at home; nothing will damage your reputation faster than agonizing over an empty catsup container in front of the plastics bin, or even worse, tossing it in with the Clorox bottles and cider jugs.

Don't be misled into thinking that as you get better at recycling, you'll do it faster. Recycling is like golf, it's primarily a social sport, and catching up on the local news is all part of the game. You should be aware that this aspect of the sport becomes really burdensome during political campaigns, since everyone running for office will be there with a petition to sign or a brochure they want you to read.

I doubt I'll ever make the big leagues in recycling, but I was motivated enough to invest in half a dozen plastic bins so my stuff is pretty well-sorted before I even leave home. It's a good feeling to roll into the recycling center organized, familiar with the rules, and ready to play, so to speak. But it's even better to know that all that trash will be reused somehow, rather than burying our country with landfills.

Sports and Life

What a Deal!

Not long ago, a major airline was promoting a remarkably low, coast to coast airfare, and I snapped at their bait. Two hundred and thirteen dollars round trip to California seemed too good to pass up. My fiancée and her son hadn't visited their relatives in San Francisco for a while, so I moved quickly and snagged three of those bargain tickets before they were sold out. Of course, as soon as the airline representative had my credit card number, she offered to transfer me to their rental car partner for an equally good deal on ground transportation.

We did, in fact, need a rental car, so I stayed on the line for yet another great deal. Before I hung up, I had a brand-new car at a discounted weekly rate, with the possibility of a two-category upgrade when we arrived in California (depending upon availability, of course). My gal's thirteen-year-old thought the upgrade was cool, since it meant the possibility of a Ford Mustang instead of a lowly Escort.

I should know by now that bargains seldom turn out to be as great as they first appear. For openers, although we arrived at the airport in plenty of time, a major snowstorm was roaring in from the mid-west, disrupting schedules across the country. Remembering that our low-budget return from California would have us arriving late at night, I opted for the covered parking garage, instead of a remote lot, which would soon be buried under wind-blown snow drifts. The weekly rate for the parking garage was definitely not a bargain at something over a hundred bucks.

Then we sat in the terminal and waited... and waited... and waited.

Several hours after our scheduled departure, they did get a couple of planes out, and we were finally headed to sunny California. Well, not exactly. Cincinnati was snowed in, so we were diverted to Columbus, Ohio. It soon became obvious that there wouldn't be any departures from Columbus that night. I'm probably getting spoiled in my old age, but spending the night in a departure lounge, listening to the endless recorded warning that "unattended vehicles will be towed at the owner's expense," is no longer my idea of an enjoyable evening, so I scrambled to find a hotel near the airport. Of course, the hotel was a hundred bucks, while supper and breakfast burned up the best part of another hundred.

But the following morning, after a good night's sleep, we flew from Columbus to Cincinnati, and on to San Francisco. Upon arrival, we took the courtesy bus to the rental car office to pick up our four-door compact (or if available, a two-class upgrade). They actually had a Mustang convertible, which looked great, but had the trunk space of a woman's pocketbook, so we upgraded only one class to a boring sedan. At least, that was the opinion of the thirteen-year-old.

We had a great time in California, in spite of the cold, rainy weather. We reconnected with relatives, saw the sights, and ate some delicious food. But, at the end of our stay, when I returned the rental car, I was in for yet another financial surprise. The bill was considerably more than what had been quoted when I made the reservation. A patient woman at the customer service desk explained that the original price was a special, weekly rate, but since I was returning the car after only five days (thanks to our overnight in Ohio), she had to charge me the daily rate. I asked if it was their company's new drive less, pay more plan! She wasn't amused.

So, I have vowed to steer clear of special deals. The other day, however, when I needed a quick lunch, I pulled into the drive-through at a popular burger joint. I wasn't hungry enough for the Super Value Package, which included a jumbo burger, large fries and a gigantic soda for a remarkable $3.95, so I ordered a normal burger and a medium-sized Coke from the metallic speakerphone, before proceeding to the first window as instructed.

"That will be $5.10, sir," the perky teenager with the electronic headgear announced, as she handed me my lunch.

"Let me get this straight," I asked, "I can get a jumbo burger, large fries, and a gigantic drink for $3.95, but if I don't want any fries, and a regular-sized burger and drink is enough, I've got to pay $1.15 more?"

She looked totally bewildered, then mumbled, "Whatever..."

I know communism self-destructed as an economic system a decade ago with the collapse of the Soviet Union, but sometimes, it seems to me, capitalism isn't in such great shape either.

Bike Down a Volcano!

My wife, Kay, and I had been unable to take a honeymoon following our wedding, so we escaped for two weeks the next July. Since Kay had never been to Hawaii, we planned a relaxing getaway on the island of Maui. As we waited for our baggage in the Kahului Airport, jet-lagged but happy, Kay gathered a fistful of colorful tourist brochures. There were sunset dinner cruises, snorkeling on nearby reefs, traditional Hawaiian luaus, even sightseeing trips by helicopter and submarine.

But the brochure that caught our attention proclaimed, Maui's Most Thrilling Experience, Bike Down a Volcano. There were photos of happy families in motorcycle helmets and matching wind suits, blissfully coasting down the access road of Haleakala volcano. Rival companies boasted about their dedication to safety and bragged about celebrities who had descended the mountain with them. Let's be honest here, would you pick the outfit favored by Tom Hanks and Gene Hackman, or the rival company that guided Dan Quail?

Rising majestically out of the ocean to just over 10,000 feet (more than twice the elevation of Mt. Mansfield), Haleakala makes its own weather. The summit is often clear in the morning, but as the trade winds cross the sun-drenched foothills, clouds form, and by afternoon the mountain is shrouded in a dense blanket of moisture. The best opportunity for breathtaking vistas is on the sunrise tour.

What the brochure fails to mention is that departure for the sunrise tour is at 2:15 a.m. What follows is a two-hour traffic jam of vans pulling trailers of bicycles up 38 miles of endless switchbacks and hairpin turns. It was still pitch-dark when we piled out of the van, just below the summit, into a steady wind that made the predawn air feel well below freezing. Around 5:00 a.m., the eastern sky brightened, and several hundred shivering tourists elbowed each other for a place at the railing to photograph the sunrise over Haleakala's eroded crater.

Moments later, tour guides lined up one group after another and headed down the access road. We were given explicit instructions on the space to maintain between cyclists, arm signals for slowing down, and warnings about the fresh cow flaps we would encounter in the ranchland far below.

Was it worth it? You bet. For the experienced cyclist, it's a little discouraging to be paced by the slowest member of the group. We were saddled with a cautious mom from California who must have worn out a set of brakes. But the modest pace permitted a full appreciation of the fantastic scenery as we descended from the barren alpine zone, through shrubland, down into magnificent stands of aromatic eucalyptus trees, followed by the broad pastures of cattle ranches, and finally the pineapple plantations and sugarcane fields along the coast.

If you plan to visit our fiftieth state, don't miss the bike ride down Haleakala. Just remember to bring your parka and ski hat if you choose the sunrise tour.

Exercising for a Worthy Cause

It was a perfect July morning, warm and clear. After an early breakfast, I put our bikes in the back of the pickup truck and my wife, Kay, and I headed into nearby, Hanover, New Hampshire. We were participating in the thirty-third Prouty, an annual fund-raising event for the Norris Cotton Cancer Center. In 1982, four nurses rode their bicycles 100 miles to honor one of their patients, Audrey Prouty. Their effort raised $4,000 for cancer research.

More than three decades later the event has expanded dramatically to include walking, rowing on the Connecticut River, and golfing in addition to cycling routes of various distances. The number of participants has grown to nearly 6,000, with more than 1,000 volunteers supporting the event. This year's contribution to the Norris Cotton Cancer Center will be close to $3 million.

The athletic field of the Richmond Middle School just north of Hanover was a kaleidoscope of colorful cycling jerseys, food tents, bicycle racks and porta potties. The excitement and enthusiasm was tempered only by the hundreds of yellow ribbons fluttering from the start/finish fence with the names of loved ones who had succumbed to cancer.

We are accustomed to seeing occasional cyclists on the rural byways of New England, but thousands of bicyclists sharing the road is an impressive sight. Kay and I observed the entire spectrum of two-wheeled transport, from ultra-fit racers who resembled Tour de France riders, to teenaged couch potatoes plodding along on their BMX bikes. There was an inspiring number of parents pulling their young kids in tag-a-long attachments. One brave fellow struggled up a hill on an antique high-wheel bike that was devoid of gears while his companion kept up an impressive pace on a unicycle.

The SAG stops along the route are a chance to rest your butt, get something to eat and drink and use the porta potty. But it soon becomes apparent that the SAG stops are social events, riders greeting each other, volunteers encouraging the participants and the riders thanking the volunteers for their support.

On a perfect day (weather-wise) as we had this year, riding the roads of the Upper Connecticut River Valley is a complete joy. While we may take our beautiful, rural scenery for granted when speeding down the interstate in a car, riding a bike provides the opportunity to really drink it in. Before long we were back at the Richmond School, standing our bikes in one of the multitude of racks provided and heading for the food tents.

While many are justifiably proud of the growth of the Prouty through the years, and the total of more than $20 million raised for cancer research, the statistics nationally are even more impressive. According to a recent article in Runner's World, road races in the U.S. generated $1.2 billion for charities in 2012. The New York City Marathon recognizes 317 organizations as nonprofit partners while the U.S. Marine Corps Marathon added 30 in 2104, bringing its total to 131.

Since the Leukemia & Lymphoma Society established Team In Training back in 1988, as of 2015, its runners raised $875 million for the charity. Team In Training has about 39,000 runners participating in 200 events across the nation.

But the gold standard of athletic fundraising events is the Pan-Mass Challenge, a two-day trek the length of Massachusetts, from Stockbridge to Provincetown, created by Billy Starr in 1980. The event annually draws 5,500 cyclists from thirty-six states and eight countries. Its fundraising goal for 2015 is $40 million, which is more than half of Dana-Farber's highly successful Jimmy Fund. As of 2014, the Pan-Mass has contributed more than $414 million for cancer research.

In spite of all the conflict and animosity in the news lately, it's gratifying to recognize that there are still plenty of generous people out there working hard to help others. I'm especially impressed that athletes, from legitimate champions to weekend wanna-bes, are contributing more than a billion dollars annually as they participate in their events. Of course, those of us who have run or cycled to raise money for cancer research or a similar worthy cause, realize that the contribution isn't all one way. It's a wonderful feeling to be a part of an effort that is making a difference.

Just Being on the Water

It was still pitch dark when my wife and I stumbled out of bed. Even though it was early summer, Kay and I dressed in warm clothes, jeans, flannel shirts, fleece vests, raincoats. Without much conversation, we poured coffee and headed to the car. On the 11-mile drive to Hanover, New Hampshire, we had the road to ourselves.

Arriving at the Dartmouth College Boathouse on the Connecticut River at 4:50 a.m., I was afraid I'd made a mistake. For decades, I've enjoyed seeing the delicate rowing shells, gliding silently through the early morning fog, and I've admired the dedication and athletic ability of the rowers whom I've known.

Recently, I ran into Fred Cressman, a Thetford neighbor who, after years of coaching collegiate rowing in New York state, returned to Vermont and was quickly recruited to help manage the exploding interest in the sport in the Upper Connecticut River Valley.

Perhaps it's more than just coincidence that in the Dresden School District, encompassing both Hanover, New Hampshire, and Norwich, Vermont, but divided down the middle by the Connecticut River, rowing has become the most popular high school sport, drawing 123 student participants. Fred had invited Kay and me to join him in his launch to observe a workout. Since the high school team shares the Dartmouth crew facilities, they begin their workouts at 5:10 a.m. to be finished and off the dock before the college rowers arrive for their morning workout. I figured it would be worth the trip simply to witness more than one hundred high school students who voluntarily arise each weekday morning at 4:00 a.m.

But sitting in the vacant parking lot in the predawn stillness, I was afraid we had arrived on the wrong day. Then, like magic, headlights appeared. Coaches wearing foul-weather gear or floatable survival suits hopped out of trucks, clipboards in hand. Groggy students piled out of SUVs and carpool vans from Norwich, Hanover, Lyme, Thetford and Strafford.

Although many appeared to be sleepwalking, the students silently took their places alongside the needle-like, 58-foot-long, carbon-fiber shells, some costing as much as $35,000. At the confident command of their coxswain, the athletes hoisted the boat off its storage rack, and marched it down to the dock.

Other students hauled armloads of the long oars down to the river. These oars represent a wonderful Vermont connection, since, for decades the majority of competitive oars, worldwide, have been produced by Concept II in Morrisville, Vermont.

Parents of the rowers volunteer on a rotating schedule to help the eight coaches prepare the outboard-powered launches that shadow the thirteen crews as they stroke their way up and down the river. In a matter of minutes, the athletes were in their boats, the coaches were in the launches, and the workout was underway.

During the years I coached Nordic skiing at Dartmouth, a few of my athletes also rowed in the fall and spring, so I knew that the two sports were compatible in several ways. Peak physical conditioning is essential in both rowing and Nordic skiing, and thanks to the sliding seats, leg strength is every bit as important as back, shoulder and arm strength. It quickly became apparent that proper technique is even more essential in rowing than in cross-country skiing. If you ignore the finer points of technique in skiing, you simply go slower, while poor technique in an eight-person shell can easily result in everyone going for a swim.

There is also a similarity in the two sports regarding stride rate and stride length. In skiing it has long been known that the victory doesn't often go to the athlete with the quickest tempo (stride rate), but instead to the athlete whose strength, balance and poise on skis, produces the longest strides. The same principle appears to be true with rowing as well: long, powerful strokes produce more victories than a fast tempo.

For much of the workout Fred mentioned technical observations to his two novice boats through a large, conical megaphone, a nostalgic holdover from the pre-electronic bullhorn era. Then he instructed the coxswains to position the boats side by side for a timed exercise.

Stopwatch in hand, Fred gave a countdown through the megaphone, and the 58-foot needles, each powered by roughly 1,200 pounds of high school freshmen, surged through the water. It was almost 7:00 a.m., the sky was brightened by gilt-edged clouds reflected on the surface of the river. The two delicate boats raced upstream leaving symmetrical patterns in the water where oar blades and keel had been an instant earlier. Even these novice boys, rowing together for only a few weeks, when synchronized and pulling for all they were worth, made the effort seem more like art than sport.

When asked after the workout what drew them to rowing, several of the students mentioned being part of a closely knit team. One gal explained that there were no stars in rowing, individual efforts became an indistinguishable part of the team result, and she liked that aspect of the sport. But all the students seemed to agree that a major draw was simply being on the water with their coaches and teammates, experiencing the sunrise while most everyone else is still in bed.

Off to College

Not long ago, we experienced one of those family milestones, our youngest was headed off to college. Ever since his sister moved to San Francisco, my stepson, Blair, has been fascinated with California. Last spring, he was accepted at his first choice, the University of Redlands, located just east of Los Angeles. We scheduled a visit to the school before he made his final decision.

Kay was taken by the gardens full of blooming roses in April, while I was drawn to the 8,000-foot, snowcapped peaks that provided a breathtaking backdrop.

Blair was clearly relieved that what he had seen on the school's website was even more spectacular in person. So, on the last day of August, we loaded the car and headed to the Burlington, Vermont, airport. Kay was teary at the prospect of her youngest heading off across the continent, while Blair did his best to conceal a mixture of anxiety and impatience.

During the drive through the pre-dawn darkness, I reminded Blair of a couple of family agreements.

"Remember to e-mail your mom at least once a week," I requested.

"Okay."

"You're going to see lot of crazy behavior in college, including alcohol and drug abuse. Just don't get into a car if the driver has been drinking."

"Okay."

It might have been the early hour, or perhaps Blair's anxiety, but I could not ignite a conversation. I kept my thoughts to myself, but what I wanted to say was this: Blair, you are about to begin the most stimulating, demanding and enjoyable four years of your life. Never again will you be surrounded by so many bright, entertaining, and enthusiastic people your own age. Some of your dearest, lifelong friends you'll meet on the campus during the next four years. In fact, many married couples first met at college.

Find out from returning students which professors are the dynamic teachers. It doesn't matter what subjects they teach. A gifted professor may open a window into an exciting world you never knew existed. Take advantage of the off-campus programs and internships. There is nothing like immersing yourself in a foreign-language and culture during a semester abroad. Volunteering in a hospital is a great way to see if you really want to apply to medical school. Find that delicate balance between studying hard and having fun. With the mountains just minutes from campus and the Pacific Ocean an hour to the west, it should be easy to get a change of scenery.

Blair, the next four years will be challenging and rewarding. Find what energizes you, then pursue it. Discover what brings you joy and cultivate it. Give it your best shot.

Blair was home for the recent holidays. His first semester grades were solid, he's made new friends and he signed up for a spring term in Peru. Must have been mental telepathy…

Simple Pleasures

I'm fascinated by big sporting events. I've had the good fortune to have participated in seven Winter Olympic Games, in several different capacities. There are few experiences in life that can match the thrill of marching into the stadium for the Opening Ceremony, surrounded by Olympians and nearly deafened by the cheering from the grandstands.

I participated in the 1974 Biathlon World Championships in Minsk, Belorussia, the first time the Soviet Union had hosted the event, during an era when their athletes dominated the sport. The ski trails were lined with enthusiastic spectators, six or eight deep, for the entire length of the course. During the team relay, the final event of the Championship, it was estimated that 120,000 spectators packed the hillside to watch the action on the shooting range. No matter where you were on the ski course, you could tell how the Russian athletes were shooting by the roar or groans of the crowd.

I've been squeezed by almost 30,000 sweaty, anxious runners in Hopkinton, Massachusetts, at the start of the centennial edition of the Boston Marathon. I remember concentrating intently, for the first several miles, on not getting tripped or catching an elbow in the face. Around mile twelve, I heard the high-pitched squealing, then ran the narrow gauntlet created by the women of Wellesley College. Nearly four hours after the start, swept along in a river of exhausted runners that followed the blue line painted on the pavement, around the corner of Hereford Street onto Boylston, I glanced up and saw the finish line, three blocks ahead. Some runners had the strength to sprint the final straightaway, while others, within sight of their goal, seized up with muscle cramps and hobbled painfully to the line.

A few years ago, a friend offered my wife, Kay, and me a special sports experience. The Ryder Cup, the exclusive golf tournament pitting a team of the best Americans against their European rivals, was hosted in Brookline, Massachusetts. On a perfect summer day, Kay and I joined our friends (and several thousand other golf enthusiasts), to marvel at the skill and poise of the world's best golfers. We watched Tiger Woods outdistance the others in his foursome down the fairway, only to put his approach shot well over the green and into the gallery. Once the course marshals had pushed the stunned spectators back, and the other three players watched smugly from their positions close to the pin, Tiger studied his shot, took a couple of practice swings, and chipped the ball into the cup!

Although I enjoy the excitement and exhilaration of these sports extravaganzas, I recently experienced an important reminder. Kay had been enduring a nagging pain in her foot, which could be resolved only by surgery. The operation went well, but she had been instructed to stay off her feet for a couple of weeks (a challenging directive for an active person). Soon she was going stir crazy, especially during a string of beautiful, warm, late summer days. Running, hiking and biking were all impossible because of the recovering foot. Then I remembered our old canoe, waiting patiently under the eaves of the garage. As I loaded the canoe on the car, Kay made a picnic lunch and we headed to Grafton Pond in nearby, Enfield, New Hampshire. One characteristic that makes Grafton Pond enjoyable is the convoluted shoreline and scattering of small islands. After exploring for a while, we found a sunny point that provided an ideal spot for our picnic. Lunchtime entertainment was provided by a resident family of loons.

A few days later, we coordinated a visit with our youngest, Blair, who began his sophomore year at Johnson State College a couple of weeks earlier. After the predictable questions and answers about classes, professors, classmates, campus life and new friends, Blair suggested a round of disc golf. Someone, somewhere discovered it was fun to throw Frisbees toward a metal basket on a pole and recently disc golf courses are popping up in parks all over the country. Although Kay was still limping, she was eager to give it a try. Much of the Johnson State course is among majestic, mature pines, a setting that is inspiring as well as challenging. Midway through our round of twelve holes, we were joined by a student from California. He could cover impressive distances with his throws, but a lack of accuracy kept him from dominating the game.

A relaxing paddle on a nearby pond and a low key game of disc golf on a beautiful college campus; in some ways, sport doesn't get any better than that. But best of all it was a wonderful way to celebrate Kay's mom' s birthday.

Take Me Out to the Ball Game

Like most everyone else, I get too much e-mail. It was dumb luck that I hesitated for a second before mindlessly trashing a message from the Vermont Mountaineers. I assumed the Vermont Mountaineers were a group of climbing enthusiasts, probably trying to hit me up for a contribution. I hesitated long enough to open the e-mail and discover that I was being invited to a short ceremony prior to a baseball game in Montpelier at which some of Vermont's former Olympic athletes would be recognized.

Years ago, I had heard about the Vermont Expos, a minor league team in Burlington, affiliated with the Montreal Expos. I'm embarrassed to admit I had heard nothing about the Vermont Mountaineers. The date of the event was July second. My wife, Kay, and I thought that attending at least part of the game with her folks, followed by a dinner in one of Montpelier's restaurants would be a nice way to celebrate her mom's birthday. Turns out, it was a lot better than that.

For starters, Montpelier Recreation Field is a gem of a facility combining a terrific baseball stadium, several tennis courts and a large public swimming pool. On the warm, sunny evening of July second the place was buzzing with healthy activity, reminiscent of how summer evenings should be in small town America. In how many other state capitals can residents leave the windows of their cars rolled down and their cars unlocked while cooling off in the municipal pool?

The Vermont Mountaineers were established in 2003 as part of the New England Collegiate Baseball League. The NECBL is comprised of twelve teams made up of promising collegiate players who aspire to play in the major leagues. Since the players come from NCAA college teams, they are not compensated financially, but they participate in a comprehensive schedule of games throughout June and July, they receive excellent coaching, and their games are routinely attended by professional scouts. The Vermont Mountaineers have won the past two NECBL Championships, and sixteen former Mountaineers are now playing professional baseball. An added bonus is the enthusiasm of the fans and the antics of Skip, the team's woodchuck mascot.

A second aspect of the evening, which became a special treat, was the opportunity to visit with some of Vermont's Olympians. For a small state, Vermont has had impressive representation at the Olympic Games. It is understandable that many would be unable to attend a recognition ceremony like the one hosted by the Mountaineers, but it was a thrill to see those who did show up.

Vermont's first family of Alpine skiing, the Cochran's of Richmond, was well represented. Barbara Ann Cochran was a two-time National Champion in giant slalom and the slalom gold medalist at the 1972 Sapporo Olympics. Dr. Bob Cochran, now a family practitioner in southwestern New Hampshire, was U.S. Alpine Combined National Champion and finished eighth in the Sapporo Olympic downhill. Marilyn Cochran Brown was the overall World Cup Giant Slalom Champion in 1969, the bronze medalist in the 1970 World Championship Alpine Combined, a member of the 1972 Olympic Team and three-time U.S. National Champion. Lindy Cochran Kelley was the top American finisher at the 1976 Olympics in slalom and giant slalom, as well as U.S. National Champion in slalom in 1973 and giant slalom in 1976.

In addition to the Cochrans, Alpine skiing was represented by Doug Lewis, who was a member of the 1984 and 1988 Olympic Teams. Doug was the bronze medalist in the downhill at the 1985 World Championships, and U.S. National Champion twice.

Carlie Geer was named to two Summer Olympic Teams in rowing. She and her sister, Judy were robbed of their first Olympic opportunity by the 1980 Moscow boycott, but Carlie went on to win a silver medal four years later in Los Angeles.

Nordic skiing was well represented by the legendary Larry Damon, who raced cross-country for the U.S. in four Olympics: Cortina, Squaw Valley, Innsbruck and Grenoble. Laura Wilson-Todd made the switch from Alpine to Nordic skiing while an undergraduate at UVM and, as a result, earned spots on both the 1994 and 1998 U.S. Olympic Teams. Marc Gilbertson, a middle school teacher and coach at Lamoille Union High

School in Hyde Park, Vermont, won a 30-kilometer freestyle tryout race in Lake Placid to earn a place on the U.S. Cross-Country Team to Nagano, Japan, in 1998.

What a great summer evening, watching some future major league ball players and reconnecting with some of Vermont's Olympians. As they say, "It doesn't get much better than that."

Sports and Life

Unstructured Play

Sometimes, usually on the spur of the moment, if Mark Breen is forecasting a "scorcher," my wife and I make the three-hour pilgrimage to a beach on the coast of Maine. Recently, as we walked on the fine sand, the surf surging over our ankles, I noticed families enjoying the idyllic, summer day. Many of the adults were sitting in beach chairs reading or chatting, while the kids concentrated on sand castles, some with elaborate turrets and moats. Other children were simply digging holes or describing elaborate patterns in the sand with sticks. They seemed totally engrossed in their projects, breaking only to race into the surf to wash off or to retrieve a bucket of water to resupply a moat.

As I observed variations of the same scene repeated dozens of times along the beach, what struck me was that the children all appeared completely engaged in what they were doing with virtually no adult supervision. It reminded me of my childhood, and I recognized that some of my fondest memories are of unsupervised play. I spent most of my childhood in the 1950s, the oldest of three kids growing up in rural New Hampshire. Our dad worked hard nurturing a business that he had started after returning from military service in World War II. Our mom was a busy homemaker in the era before preschool, play dates, ballet lessons and soccer camps.

Aside from Howdy Doody and some Saturday morning cartoons, there wasn't much of interest on our small black-and-white TV, so the command we were accustomed to from our mom was, "It's a nice day, you kids go play outside." For me, that usually meant building tree forts, playing army, or playing cowboys and Indians. Since my dad was often building something, a shed for the sheep or cottages near the ocean in Maine, there was often scrap lumber available. The understanding was that I could help myself to any scrap boards and straighten any bent nails I could find, but occasionally the lure of a beautiful, straight, 8-foot 2×4 or a fistful of brand-new galvanized spikes became too much to resist. To his credit, I don't recall my dad ever punishing me for pilfering building supplies, but I do remember his surprise at the expansiveness of one of my tree forts.

Playing army usually involved digging foxholes in tree lines, then waiting patiently, sometimes for hours, for the resident Holsteins (which represented enemy tanks) to graze their way into our ambush. Usually when we opened fire, with sticks for machine guns, the cows would bolt to the far side of the pasture in surprise, but occasionally, a frisky young bull might snort and approach our foxhole in curiosity, which added some real adrenaline to our make believe. Not surprisingly, my four-year hitch as an infantry officer in the early 1970s was nothing like what I imagined when I was ten.

Cowboys and Indians was another favorite. Roy Rogers, Gene Autry and The Lone Ranger might have been TV heroes and role models, but Tonto was much more interesting and mysterious. My cousin and I spent two weeks running around the beach in loincloths fashioned from kitchen towels after we discovered a couple of dead herring gulls that provided the feathers for (what we thought were) magnificent headdresses. Our fantasy was further enhanced when the town road crew cut several large pines and burned the brush. When the workers left at the end of the day, we coaxed the glowing embers back into a "campfire," which we secretly kept alive for almost a week.

I recognize that now it's a different world in many ways and that much of the unstructured play I took for granted as a kid would not be considered safe today. When I compare my mental image of parental involvement in organized sports like Little League baseball or youth soccer with the endless hours I spent exploring the pastures and forests around my childhood home, I feel sad for today's kids. Building sand castles at the beach or snooping around the overgrown lot down the road might not be as cool as playing video games, zoning out on your iPod, or watching MTV, but I'm afraid today's kids are missing out on something really important, which they only discover outdoors, on their own.

Thank You Ken Burns

Several years ago, I was intrigued and bewildered to learn about a young documentary filmmaker who was scheduled to present thirteen hours of antique, black-and-white photos of the Civil War on PBS. It sounded about as exciting as watching paint dry, but I watched the first episode and was hooked. Never before had history seemed so alive as listening to actual letters written from the front while viewing photos from the battlefield.

I became a loyal Ken Burns fan. Although the sport of baseball and jazz music aren't of particular interest to me, Burns' documentaries on those topics were predictably well done and informative. More recently, his epic documentary on World War II drew me in so completely, I often felt tears streaming down my cheeks as I watched the sacrifice, dedication and heroism of my parent's generation.

So, when PBS began promoting Ken Burns' offering on America's National Parks, I penciled in those evenings in September to avoid possible conflicts. I was not disappointed. I had anticipated an overview of our National Park system, perhaps with a concentration on the more popular or spectacular locations. What I didn't anticipate was the fascinating history of the park system, the influential individuals and the back-room politics.

The documentary reminded me of how often we take things for granted, especially in a country as big and geographically diverse as ours. I was impressed by the folks featured in the film who made an effort to visit all of our fifty-eight National Parks. I bought a guidebook and was surprised to discover I had already visited more than 25 percent of them. Perhaps half of my National Park visits have been related, directly or indirectly, to skiing.

In 1966, I earned a spot on the Eastern Team to the National Cross-Country Championships in Durango, Colorado. On a rest day between events, our coach, Marty Hall, took the team to see the cliff dwellings at Mesa Verde. I still vividly remember Ester, the mummified, prehistoric resident on display there.

A few years later, West Yellowstone, Montana, became a mecca for Nordic skiers determined to get on snow by Thanksgiving. A focal point of every training camp was skiing into the park from the village to Old Faithful, a distance of about 50 kilometers. It was not unusual to see bands of elk, herds of buffalo, and steaming pots of sulfurous water.

A military assignment to the Biathlon Training Center in Alaska provided the opportunity to visit Denali, Kenai Fjords, and Lake Clark, although the latter two may not count since I visited those areas before they actually became National Parks. During this time, the tryouts for the 1972 Olympic Biathlon Team were held in Jackson Hole, Wyoming, within sight of the Grand Teton.

More recently, family trips have provided wonderful memories of several other National Parks. Not long after my wife, Kay, and I were married, we escaped to Hawaii for our honeymoon. A highlight of that trip was riding bicycles down the access road from the 10,000-foot summit of Haleakala volcano.

On another family adventure, Kay, son Blair and I spent a day rafting into Canyonlands, explored the impressive rock formations in Arches National Park, and hiked into the Grand Canyon. Often when an attraction becomes highly publicized, actually seeing it in person is anticlimactic. This was not true for us at the Grand Canyon: photographs simply cannot do it justice.

Closer to home, Kay and I enjoyed a terrific getaway at Acadia, on Maine's Mount Desert Island. We packed a picnic and rode our bikes on the wonderful carriage roads, each turn revealing a more spectacular vista of the ocean and the rocky coastline. We found it well worth the effort to peddle to the summit of Cadillac Mountain to catch the sunrise.

Inspired by Ken Burns' documentary, on a recent trip to California to visit relatives, we added an overnight in Yosemite. Although November might ensure some relief from the crush of summer tourists, the weather could be unpredictable. Mother Nature smiled on us, and we spent a full day hiking in some of the most spectacular scenery I've seen anywhere. Like the Grand Canyon, Yosemite lives up to the hype, and then some.

So, thank you Ken Burns for igniting in us an enthusiasm for some national treasures we had taken for granted. And thank you to the dedicated folks of the National Park Service who have been such good stewards of the treasure, often with woefully inadequate funding.

A Dog's Example

Over the past thirty-eight years, I've had three Labrador retrievers. It would be an understatement to say that I'm a fan of the breed. All three dogs became members of the family, rather than household pets. As I think about Rode, Klister and our current Lab, Rosie, some common characteristics come to mind that make the dogs so endearing.

For starters, our Labs have all demonstrated unrestrained joy when we return from an absence. It doesn't matter if my wife, Kay, was out for a couple of hours shopping, or if I've been away for a week working, our dog can't contain her joy upon our return. Rosie wags her tail so energetically her entire body is in motion, her panting approaches hyperventilation, and her wrinkled muzzle resembles a smile. Our world would be a happier place if we all greeted each other as enthusiastically.

Another admirable trait is that Labs love to eat. Rosie has never been fussy about her food. On the contrary, if we get distracted, she'll remind us, with a nudge or a subtle moan, that it's her mealtime, and whatever we put in her bowl, she eagerly consumes. No complaints about toast that's burned, brussels sprouts that are too soggy or scrambled eggs that are too runny. Whatever's in her dish, she gratefully scarfs down.

Next to eating, Rosie loves being outdoors. Every morning, Kay and I walk her out the driveway to retrieve the paper, just over a mile, round trip. I read somewhere that dogs have a sense of smell seventy times more sensitive than ours. Whatever the ratio, the morning walk is a feast for Rosie's nose. She covers at least twice the distance that Kay and I walk, chasing down the scents of nocturnal animals, neighborhood pets, and visitors. Her body language is all excitement, fascination and enjoyment. Later in the day, if we've been focused on indoor work, Rosie will remind us it's time to get outside again. And she's always right. Even if I feel frustrated leaving a task incomplete to take her for a walk, I always feel better after being in the woods. I don't know if dogs instinctively know how to manage stress, but I suspect I'd do well to model Rosie's behavior. No matter what's going on, don't skip your afternoon walk.

Complementing her devotion to exercise, Rosie is not the least bit self-conscious about napping. If nothing requires her attention, Rosie curls up and takes a snooze. Mid-morning, early afternoon, twilight, it doesn't matter, if the opportunity arises, Rosie will catch a nap. I can remember times in the army when we were all so tired we seemed to be able to fall asleep anywhere, anytime. I swear I saw a buddy in Vietnam sleeping standing up. We'd probably all be healthier if we were able to respond to our instincts, like a dog, and take a nap when we felt tired.

Fortunately, given my background, Rosie loves winter. She's always up for an outing, but when the first real snowfall of the winter blankets the yard, she races around with total abandon. At full tilt, she'll drop her jaw into the powder, scooping a mouthful, just for the thrill of it. She'll squat and roll for the simple pleasure of feeling the cold snow all over her body. When Kay and I reach for our cross-country ski boots on a winter afternoon, Rosie begins panting. We've learned to carefully plan our outings, since Rosie would eagerly follow us until she dropped from exhaustion.

I'd be less than forthright if I didn't acknowledge a couple of drawbacks. Labrador puppies are notorious for chewing everything in sight. Sacrifice an old pair of sneakers and you may preserve the rugs, the drapes, the legs of all your furniture, your shoes and most of your clothes. Another issue, Labs shed. In fact, it's astounding that they can shed so much hair and not be totally bald. I used to think the black hairs were visible everywhere, but now I'm convinced the blond hair is more evident. Finally, you'll begin planning around your dog. Can't go to so-and-so's for the weekend, because they're allergic to dogs, and so forth.

These become minor inconveniences. Do the drawbacks outweigh the joys of having a Lab? Absolutely not. In fact, we'd probably all be a lot happier and healthier if we adopted some canine behavior.

An Outdoor Recreation Paradise

Last month, I read Bill McKibben's new book, Eaarth. It impressed me enough to devote August's column to thoughts stimulated by the book. Under normal circumstances that would have been enough, but recent newspaper headlines and NPR commentaries have kept the book on my mind.

In Russia, daytime temperatures reaching 104 degrees Fahrenheit have contributed to conditions that have spawned more than 250 wildfires, consuming more than 500,000 acres, and blanketed the much of the country in toxic smoke.

Unusually heavy rains in northwest Pakistan have created the worst flooding in that nation's history. About 1,300 people have died and as many as 13 million have been affected by the rising waters. Bridges, roads, schools, homes and entire villages have been destroyed in the path of the flood.

Closer to home (relatively speaking) the Petermann Glacier in northwest Greenland recently carved off an iceberg four times the size of Manhattan. This iceberg, as it melts over the next four years, will release the amount of water that flows down the Hudson River in four years! In other words, for those who doubt McKibben's appraisal of the world we currently inhabit, just read the newspaper.

There is a silver lining, however, in this otherwise ominous cloud. One of the changes we will probably encounter before too long is the increased cost of travel. Those of us who have enjoyed skiing in Montana, hiking in Colorado, or paddling in northern Quebec may have to find our recreational adventures closer to home. The good news, which we often take for granted, is that we live in an outdoor enthusiast's paradise.

For starters, few locations in North America have a more distinct four seasons than northern New England. Our summers are warm enough for swimming and boating, while our winters are still cold enough for skiing and skating.

In addition, we have a favorable topography for most outdoor sports: a smattering of mountains, lots of gently rolling hills and not too much flat ground. I could never understand how Jim Ryan maintained his motivation to become one of the world's best runners, when most of his training was on flat roads separating endless corn fields.

We have a wide array of recreational opportunities almost out our back doors. Here's a sample. Every Tuesday evening, Joe Defner, Thetford Academy's cross-country running coach, hosts a fun run on the school's 5-kilometer course. No entry fee, no pre-registration, just show up before 6:00 p.m. to get your name on the list. If I were in decent shape, I could jog to the school from my house.

On a recent, spectacular Sunday morning, my wife, Kay, suggested we put the canoe in the river. It's about ten minutes from our home to a boat landing where the Ompompanoosuc joins the Connecticut. Our Lab, Rosie, loves the canoe and the paddling never gets boring as she shifts from one gunnel to the other, spotting birds. Speaking of birds, bald eagles are back on the Connecticut River, and are they impressive from a canoe!

Kay and I sort of met on a hike more than a decade ago, and sometimes if the weather cooperates we return to Cube Mountain in Orford, New Hampshire, as an outdoor anniversary celebration. This year's hike was perfect: a warm, clear day, no bugs, a nice breeze and beautiful views from the top. Cube is a twenty-minute drive from home.

Last weekend, daughter Julie and her partner, Ericka, wanted to try out their new road bikes. Kay, son Blair and I joined them on a terrific loop on the New Hampshire side of the river, down toward Hanover, then north on Route 10 through Lyme, then back to the East Thetford bridge. The starting point is less than ten minutes from home.

In the winter, it's even better. We can see the Dartmouth Skiway in the New Hampshire hills to the east. Even with the bone-jarring frost heaves it's less than a twenty-minute drive. We have a pond just down the hill from the house for skating, and the surrounding woods are laced with trails for cross-country skiing.

Bill McKibben has made a believer out of me. I know we're in for some dramatic changes, probably within the next decade. But the good news is that those of us who love the outdoors and are fortunate enough to live in Vermont will probably be able to enjoy our traditional activities with only modest adjustments, for years to come.

Celebrating a Decade with Rosie

Rosie, our dog, is now ten; that's seventy in dog years. We still take her on hikes and cross-country skiing outings, which she loves, but we have to be mindful of the distance. We are very fortunate to have groomed trails nearby, where the landowner welcomes dogs. In fact, on a recent outing, he overtook us on his grooming machine, stopped to chat, and fished a small Milk-Bone out of his pocket for Rosie before he resumed his grooming. That gesture represents a deep affection for dogs, which for very legitimate reasons are not welcome at all Nordic ski centers.

If the conditions are right—packed powder, dry snow and not too many long, fast descents—Rosie can still handle ski tours up to 10 kilometers or so. The downhills are the issue, since, in spite of her advancing age, she remains determined to be first. If Kay and I pick a trail that includes several significant descents, which Rosie still attacks with abandon, for the days following the outing, we have a stiff, slow dog. I guess it says something about our priorities if we choose mellow ski trails so that we won't wear out our loyal, four-footed companion. It also says something about our dog, who values the joy of tearing down a ski trail enough to tolerate stiff, sore muscles for a few days thereafter.

Of course an obvious alternative is to simply leave her at home while Kay and I go ski the more challenging trails. Most dog owners will recognize that this is simply not an option. The highlights of Rosie's days are her outings, whether the mile round trip out the driveway for the morning paper or an afternoon cross-country ski tour. In fact, if the day begins to slip away while Kay and I become too absorbed in what we are doing, Rosie will let us know that it's time for some exercise outing. And she's always right; we always feel refreshed after a break outdoors.

Another characteristic that seems to be appearing with her maturity is a limited tolerance for juvenile behavior from other dogs. Perhaps because she was separated from her litter quite early, Rosie has always been more people-oriented. She diligently watches people, paying close attention to their activities and cues. In contrast, she has never been particularly fascinated with other dogs. On outings where other dogs are present, she will reluctantly participate in the obligatory, mutual sniff greeting, but she no longer has much interest in a subsequent game of chase. If a persistent, younger dog yips and jumps at Rosie to get her to play, one forceful bark from the old girl lets the youngster know she's not interested.

I believe I read somewhere that a dog's sense of smell is seventy times more acute than a human's! It is hard for me to imagine what it would be like to have a sense of smell seventy times more powerful. I'm not sure I would even want to try it. It does explain, however, why Rosie covers about twice the distance we do on any outing, constantly diverting from our route to chase down another exotic odor. I can only imagine that the melting and thawing snow in springtime produces an olfactory banquet for her that is beyond description.

Rosie is also remarkably committed to her schedule. Although there are plenty of times that she exhibits amazing patience, she also has a phenomenal internal clock. Kay and I typically rise sometime around 6:00 a.m., but if we oversleep, we can be assured of a nuzzle from the side of the bed indicating that it is time to get up, and more importantly, to feed the dog. Regardless of the events of the day, whether it included an exciting and stimulating hour of plunging her nose in the snow along a wooded trail, or simply lying on the living room rug, protecting the front porch from being overrun by red squirrels, Rosie will lets us know, almost to the minute, when it's 6:00 p.m., her suppertime.

It seems impossible that Rosie has been with us ten years already. It provides both a heart-warming reminder of all the enjoyment she has provided to our family over the past decade, as well as a resolution to make her remaining time with us as fruitful as possible.

Another Christmas

I'm embarrassed to admit that the last few years I've been beginning to feel like Scrooge. In spite of my best efforts to focus on the true meaning of Christmas, the overwhelming commercialism and frantic pace of the season wears me down. It seems like merchants begin shouting about their Christmas sales at Halloween. I'm all for gathering with family and friends during the holiday season, but the last few years I spend more time behind the wheel than anywhere else. And because my wife, Kay, is so good about remembering everyone at Christmas, I spend most of December helping her wrap presents.

I really feel guilty that I'm not more excited about the holiday season. I decided a little mental reminder was in order. I tried to recall past Christmases that were still vivid in my memory. When I was a kid, my maternal grandparents would arrive with the trunk of their car packed with presents. My grandfather was the son of immigrants who was forced to drop out of school to support his family but went on to become a very successful businessman. I think he went overboard with presents for his grandchildren because he had so little when he was young. We got in trouble one year when he woke me up before everyone else because he couldn't wait to see my reaction when I opened a terrific electric train set he had bought for me.

My senior year in college, my roommate asked me to be his best man at his wedding in Aspen, Colorado, during Christmas break. A blizzard struck the Rockies as I was boarding the bus in Denver for the trip to Aspen. What was normally about a three-hour ride turned into more than twelve hours. I barely made the wedding and caught a serious cold from lack of sleep. I spent Christmas sick in bed and was still recovering in early January at the tryouts for the 1968 Olympic Team. I probably wouldn't have made that team even if I'd been healthy, but I would definitely have been much closer.

On Christmas, 1970, I was in Phung Hiep, South Vietnam, helping to prepare a modest holiday dinner for my mobile advisory team and the district advisory team, together not quite a dozen Americans. As we were about to sit down, an agitated Vietnamese soldier ran in pleading for help. There had been an accident in the village and an American advisor was needed immediately. I was selected. My team medic, Sargent Boone, volunteered to go with me. In the center of the village we encountered an angry crowd of Vietnamese surrounding the scene of a fatal accident. A large, American truck, driven by a very scared, very young American G.I. had struck and killed a local Vietnamese man on a motor scooter. The scooter was crushed, a dark red pool of blood was spreading from under the man's head, and the gathering crowd appeared ready to beat the American kid to death with their bare hands. To make matters worse, when I spoke to the kid to get his side of the story, I detected the distinct aroma of marijuana.

Sargent Boone and I were able to defuse the situation, get the American kid back in his truck and out of the village, and gather information on the victim for possible compensation. But needless to say, it was not a merry Christmas.

My late wife, Mimi, died of cancer in January of 1998. To be truthful, I don't remember anything of Christmas that year.

So put into perspective, an overload of advertising and a busy schedule isn't much to complain about. And in fact, I have several wonderful, relatively recent developments to focus on. First of all, my wife, Kay, does a terrific job "keeping Christmas." There is no slacking in regard to the holiday when she's involved. For the past six years she has directed The Christmas Mystery, a community pageant in Hanover, New Hampshire, which is said to be the longest, continually running Christmas pageant in the nation. The singing never fails to bring me to tears. If I'm feeling like Scrooge, The Christmas Mystery will get me back in the spirit.

And perhaps most important, between us, Kay and I have three (soon four) grandchildren. If you feel like you are losing the true meaning of the holiday, just sit down with a three-year-old and read a couple of the Christmas classics. I guarantee that will erase any frustrations you may have and refocus you on what truly matters about Christmas.

Nothing Heals Like Cold Steel

Years ago, an article, probably in Sports Illustrated, caught my attention. It must have been an overview of common athletic injuries and a discussion of the advanced, new treatments. I clearly remember the article stating that the most devastating athletic injury, both physically and emotionally, was a knee injury. Maybe it's because knee injuries are so common. A recent study reported that nearly 50 percent of all high school athletic injuries are to knees. The high level of anxiety might also be related to the fact that until quite recently, the prognosis for a serious knee injury was not encouraging. A decade ago, a torn ACL (anterior cruciate ligament) could end a professional football or basketball player's multimillion dollar career. How quickly things are changing in medicine!

These days, total knee joint replacements are relatively commonplace, and are not just for elderly folks who want to push their grandchildren through the mall in strollers. Just over a year ago, our friend and outdoor enthusiast Will Lange invited my wife, Kay, and me to join him on an overnight hike up Tuckerman's Ravine on New Hampshire's Mount Washington. Will was filming a segment for his popular NHPTV show, Windows on the Wild. We spent a beautiful, late-summer day ascending one of the steepest trails in the White Mountains, keeping pace with a film crew, and an old Outward Bound instructor with two replacement knees!

In fact, that hike might have been a catalyst for Kay, who had been suffering increasing pain for decades from a high school knee injury. She had been a multi-sport athlete, participating in field hockey, softball and Alpine skiing in addition to cheerleading for the boys' basketball team. A fall in a slalom course resulted in a torn meniscus in her right knee, and ultimately an operation to remove the damaged cartilage. She remembers being hospitalized for ten days following the surgery, and an impressive 8-inch, vertical scar beside her kneecap.

A visit to an orthopedic surgeon (who is also a close family friend) revealed significant deterioration of Kay's knee joint where the damaged cartilage had been removed decades earlier, making her a promising candidate for the relatively new partial knee replacement, or unicompartmental knee arthroplasty. After several preliminary evaluations, Kay decided in favor of the procedure rather than face probable restricted activity and an increasingly painful knee.

Bright and early on the morning of the operation, our friend the surgeon got our attention by reminding us that if the condition of Kay's knee was worse than he expected, he would do a total knee replacement. Several hours later, I was relieved when he found me in the waiting room and reported that the partial replacement was the correct decision, the operation went smoothly and that Kay was doing well. Soon thereafter, I visited her in the recovery room, and by late afternoon the physical therapy folks were showing her how to use her crutches!

Within twenty-four hours of the operation, Kay was experiencing her second P.T. session, learning how to climb and descend stairs with the crutches. I couldn't help thinking what a change in recovery philosophy this represented from the ten days of bed rest she had endured following her original knee surgery. It was comforting to learn that some recovery advice remained unchanged. During my coaching days I advised scores of limping athletes to "I C E": apply "I"ce or cold packs to the injury, "C"ompress the site of the injury with an Ace bandage to minimize swelling and to "E"levate the injury. The physical therapist at the hospital added the letter "R" forming the word RICE, representing a reminder to "R"est. Although I totally agree with him, in practice his advice seemed comically hypocritical, since Kay rarely had more than five minutes in the hospital between nurse's visits to check her vital signs, administer medication, check the bandages, take her meal order, and so on.

Another somewhat comical (in retrospect) situation related to the several prescribed medications Kay was supposed to take following the operation. Once released from the hospital, I drove Kay home and helped her get situated before I headed to the pharmacy to fill the several prescriptions. By the time I returned, the hospital-administered pain medications were wearing off, and for the first time, Kay was aware of the trauma her knee had endured. As I scrambled to sort out the several containers of pills and the accompanying booklets of instructions and disclaimers, I was befuddled by prescription names that were totally foreign to me. It took a few anxious moments for me, and increasingly painful moments for Kay, before I discovered that the pharmacy had filled the prescriptions with generic brands.

Her recovery has progressed smoothly since then. Her goal is to cross-country ski pain-free before the winter is out. I wouldn't bet against her.

Wrestling with "Living in the Moment" During Autumn

Even though I've been an avid (some would say fanatic) skier for half a century, my favorite season is autumn. Part of my love for fall is due to the clear air, the crisp temperatures and the brilliant foliage. I'm lucky to work quite a bit outside, and autumn is ideal, thanks to cooler days and the absence of insects.

Perhaps because I enjoy the fall so much, it always seems to whiz past too quickly. The result is that I begin to dread its passing even before it arrives. Part of this outlook stems from an awareness of how many projects have to be accomplished before the winter sets in.

We are fortunate to have a few acres of forest from which I routinely thin and cull trees for firewood. We have two wood-burning stoves that augment our oil furnace, but this winter, considering the escalating cost of fuel oil, the stoves will see more consistent use. I've got plenty of wood split, stacked and covered, but if we're lucky enough to have another snow year like last winter, it wouldn't be a bad idea to relocate a couple of additional cords closer to the house. In addition, it wouldn't hurt to cut up some more kindling just to be sure we won't run short next March and early April. While we're talking wood heat, I should probably call the chimney sweep to be certain the flues aren't caked with creosote from last winter.

Of course generating heat is one thing; conserving it is another. While I've got the extension ladder out to take down the window screens, it probably makes sense to get out the caulking gun and fill any cracks or seams that would be likely to release heat next January. And of course, while I'm on the ladder, I might as well wash the windows before it gets too cold.

Then there are the gardens. My wife, Kay, spent hours during the summer tending her flowers and vegetables, but in autumn I lend a hand cutting and clearing the stalks, then tilling the soil. The compost bin is overdue for emptying and spreading so that it will accommodate this winter's vegetable scraps.

Just over the bank from the garden is the septic tank. Last summer our leach field had to be replaced. As part of the project, a new access cover and filter was installed on the septic tank, providing yet another routine, home maintenance chore. I haven't yet determined how often the filter has to be cleaned, but it certainly will be easier before the ground is frozen and the cover buried under 2 feet of snow.

The pond has been terrific for swimming this summer, but before freeze-up the dock has to come out to make room for the hockey goals.

We live at the end of a long dirt driveway featuring a couple of intimidating hills, which are especially challenging in the winter. To reassure visitors who don't have four-wheel-drive, I've located ten barrels of sand on the steepest pitches. Inevitably, a couple of the barrels get overturned by the snowplow each year, and they all need to be replenished with sand.

I can identify with the cobbler whose kids have holes in their shoes, or the carpenter whose wife is still waiting for doors on her kitchen cabinets. I have a ski trail right out the back door that I've been working on for decades. For many years it wasn't high on the priority list because the ornery old Ski-Doo Alpine I used to groom the trail rarely started anyway. Out of frustration, I finally upgraded to a more reliable Ski-Doo Skandic, just in time for several, nearly snowless winters. But last year's bountiful snow cover has me motivated to get our trail in first-class shape in the hope that we might be starting a new cycle of old-fashioned, snowy winters.

Of course autumn is the best time of year for hiking, canoeing and camping. There is also a wonderful selection of road races and fun runs, which feature scenic courses and comfortable weather conditions.

So given my long list of chores that have to get done, and the additional autumn activities we'd like to squeeze into the schedule, it's sometimes hard to "be in the moment." But I'm trying. In a few minutes I'll head out to mow the lawn, probably for one of the last times this year. I'll try to enjoy it and not worry about the empty sand barrels until next week.

A Late Winter Confession

My wife, Kay, and I are longtime listeners to Garrison Keillor's weekly radio show, A Prairie Home Companion, which airs on VPR Saturday evenings at 6:00 and again Sunday mornings at 11:00. We love Keillor's quirky humor and the impressive variety of singers and musicians (some internationally famous, others just beginning their careers) with whom he shares the stage. A few years ago, we got tickets to attend the annual broadcast from Tanglewood, just south of the Vermont border in Lenox, Massachusetts. After listening to the show for years, actually seeing in addition to hearing the production added a new level of enjoyment.

So, in a sense, we had been primed when, in the spring of 2007, it was mentioned that Garrison Keillor and the cast of A Prairie Home Companion would be sponsoring a ten-day cruise from Copenhagen, Denmark, to the fjords on the west coast of Norway. Although the idea of an ocean voyage on a huge cruise ship had never before appealed to Kay and me, this sounded like it could be different. And having visited Norway a couple of times before, I knew that seeing the fjords by ship might be the best possible approach. After only a short delay to make our decision, we were disappointed to learn that the cruise had already sold out. But we had the foresight to add our names to a waiting list, and ultimately were assigned a small stateroom with one porthole, just above the waterline.

It was a terrific vacation, one of the most memorable we've ever shared. In addition to the jaw-dropping vistas of rocky cliffs plummeting into the glassy surface of the fjords, and shore excursions to explore vibrant coastal towns, the highlight of the cruise was the daily entertainment provided by Garrison Keillor and the other performers from the radio show. When a similar cruise was offered two years ago around Italy, we didn't hesitate, and we weren't disappointed.

So when I first heard that the 2015 APHC cruise would be to the Eastern Caribbean in mid-March, I didn't even consult Kay, I simply signed us up and sent in our deposit. Well into January I felt content and even smug that I had acted quickly enough to reserve a stateroom eight decks up from the waterline that even boasted a small veranda!

Then, in February it finally started to snow, not the crippling blizzards that hit Boston, but enough to ensure terrific Nordic skiing. Sure, there were some brisk temperatures, but all Nordic skiers know that you warm up once you get going. This was the first winter in many years when we didn't have marginal snow cover, we had plenty. As an added bonus, the traditional January thaw never materialized, the snow that fell just kept accumulating.

It wasn't until February gave way to March that I began to feel twinges of guilt. For many, of course, it had been a brutally long, cold winter with frozen pipes, leaking roofs and soaring fuel bills. Ironically, for Nordic skiing enthusiasts, it was shaping up to be one of the best winters in recent memory, an unanticipated gift in the face of global warming. And I was about to abandon this blue-ribbon winter for a Caribbean cruise. I was too embarrassed to tell any of my skiing friends.

Deplaning in Fort Lauderdale, dressed in wool and corduroy, Kay and I were surrounded by travelers in T-shirts, shorts and flip-flops. We boarded the Westerdam the next day, then joined Garrison Keillor and several hundred other guests on the spacious aft deck for a sing-along as the ship steamed through the breakwater and into the Atlantic. Although Kay and I felt guilty about abandoning Vermont during the glory days of winter, we were determined to make the best of it. The ship had eleven decks and we took the stairs whenever we could between our stateroom on eight and the dining room on two. One day at sea, Holland America organized a walk supporting a variety for worthy causes. Several hundred passengers donated money and walked nine times around the promenade deck, a distance of 3 miles. On different shore excursions, Kay and I hiked around the historic forts in San Juan, snorkeled for hours in the warm water, and walked the white sand beaches.

We've already skied a couple of times since our return, and I'm back to sanding the driveway and chopping ice off the roof, but I suspect it will be quite a while before our friends forgive us.

The Prouty

The weather forecast was not promising: cloudy with showers and possible thunderstorms. The Eye on the Sky guys from St. Johnsbury explained that we were going to be hit by the remnants of tropical storm Cindy, and it was difficult to predict just how wet Saturday might be.

There may be aspects of our culture that are getting worse—traffic, pollution, and the inability of our elected representatives in Washington to compromise for the benefit of the country—but in my view, weather forecasting has become amazingly accurate. If Mark and Steve say we might get a shower, I pack a raincoat.

The following morning, my wife Kay and I were up before 5:00 to the sound of water pouring off the roof. As Kay put breakfast on the table, I checked brakes and tires, then loaded the bikes into my pickup. For the past several years we have participated in the Audrey Prouty Century Ride, organized by The Friends of the Norris Cotton Cancer Center to raise money for cancer research.

Twenty-four years ago, four oncology nurses rode their bikes 100 miles through New Hampshire's White Mountains to honor the courage of their patient, Audrey Prouty, in her fight against ovarian cancer. The nurses raised $4,000 for cancer research with their original effort.

Through the years, the Prouty has developed several facets. The signature event is still the century ride, a scenic jaunt up the Connecticut River Valley from Hanover to Woodsville, then a return to Hanover down the Vermont side of the river. For less ambitious cyclists, there are 50-mile and 25-mile options. There are also 5- and 10-kilometer walks, which are popular with families and folks who prefer to keep their feet on the ground.

By July 2004, the Prouty had grown to involve 1,250 cyclists, walkers and event volunteers, who together raised $365,000 for cancer research. There had been high expectations for the 2005 Prouty, but what would the pouring rain do to the turnout?

Although Kay and I had planned to begin our trek at 6:00 a.m., it was raining so hard I suggested a delay in the hope the storm might pass. In spite of the downpour, the parking lot filled with cars as cyclists unloaded their bikes and pinned on their numbers. By 7:00 it was evident we were going to get soaked no matter how long we waited, so we hit the road.

Having experienced the Prouty a couple of times in glorious, warm, summer sunshine, I expected to hear some grumbling from other riders we encountered along the route. I couldn't have been further off base. At the SAG stops every 10 miles or so, where riders stretched their legs, refueled with sports drink, fruit, and peanut butter sandwiches, the conversation was cheerful and enthusiastic. It was apparent that the weather hadn't dampened anyone's spirits. In fact, the steady rain seemed to strengthen the resolve of the cyclists, most of whom were riding in honor of friends and loved ones who had endured the struggle with cancer.

By Warren, New Hampshire, more than two hours into the ride, as drenched participants straggled into the SAG stop, they were greeted by an old fellow under a tarp, playing an accordion. They were also confronted by an intense, compact man who offered a handshake and his thanks. Most of the riders didn't recognize Dr. Mark Israel, a nationally prominent researcher and the director of the Norris Cotton Cancer Center. Perhaps it was because he had spent much of his career in sunny California before moving to Hanover, but Dr. Israel was clearly moved by the dedication and determination of the riders in the face of the downpour.

As midday approached, the sky began to brighten and the rain let up. Riders stripped off their sodden shells and wind pants, revealing the colorful jerseys that have become a part of cycling.

At a SAG stop on the town common in Newbury, Vermont, an energetic woman with her arm in a sling was moving through the tired riders asking questions and offering encouragement. She was Patty Carney, one of the four nurses who founded the event more than two decades earlier.

The beauty of the dairy farms along the river made the return rewarding, in spite of the growing awareness of aching muscles and general fatigue. After nearly eight hours in the saddle, the sight of the finish line is both a relief and somehow, an anticlimax. But riders are soon swept up in the festivities: music, food, and swapping stories with other participants. The electrifying buzz that flashed through the crowd was that nearly $700,000 had been generated for cancer research, far exceeding the organizer's goal!

Perhaps the lesson here is, if people of good will gather for the benefit of a worthy cause, weather is not a factor.

Sports and Life

COMMENTARY ON SPORTS AND LIFE

My First Red Sox Game

I'm more than fifty years old, and I've attended three Major League baseball games. All three were watching the Boston Red Sox play at Fenway Park. My first game was in 1958, when I was twelve. The town where I grew up was too small for Little League, so I was not much of a baseball fan, but I had certainly heard of Ted Williams and Jimmy Piersall.

A classmate's dad had acquired several Red Sox tickets to take his son and a few friends to a game. I was thrilled to have been invited. It was a big deal in those days just to go to Boston, to say nothing of seeing the Red Sox play.

My first impression of Fenway Park is still vivid. I couldn't believe that the grass on the field was real. Any baseball games I might have seen on television were in black and white, and I simply wasn't prepared for the intensely green grass and the brilliant white of the base lines.

As the stadium filled and the game began, I was overwhelmed by the feverish activity. I listened to the announcer and to the organ music. I was distracted by vendors selling programs, peanuts, and beer. My classmate's father pointed out important people sitting nearby; the team's general manager and the wives of several Boston players. I didn't realize it then, but my friend's dad had impressive connections. We were in box seats about ten rows behind the Red Sox dugout.

Midway through the game, Ted Williams strode out to the plate. I can't remember the score or the opposing team, but I remember that Ted looked serious. We all agreed, the only thing left to make it a totally perfect day would be to see Ted Williams hit a homer.

But he struck out instead. And before I could comprehend what was going on, I saw his bat launched at us like a rocket. Everything seemed to happen in slow motion. The bat hit someone in the head a couple of rows in front of us. I saw the woman collapse, as her eyeglasses spiraled lazily, high into the air. Even before the bat struck its victim, Ted Williams bounded from home plate, vaulted into the stands, and scrambled over seats mumbling, "Oh I'm sorry. I'm so sorry. God, I'm sorry."

The bat, meanwhile, had clattered across the metal pipes that divided the box seats, and had come to rest at my feet. With people screaming and shouting, and a frantic Ted Williams, bigger than life an arm's length away, it took me a while to register what was lying across my sneakers. Like every other kid at the game, I had brought my glove, hoping that a foul ball might come within reach, but I was looking down at Ted Williams' bat!

As I reached for the bat, I was mystified by the tar-like goo smeared on the handle. The instant I had it in my hands, an usher appeared, yanked at the bat, and shouted, "Gimme that!" Because things were happening so fast, and because of the sticky stuff on the handle, I held on as the usher dragged me into the isle.

Everyone's attention was still focused on Ted, the woman who had been hit, and the medics who were strapping her to a stretcher, but a couple of fans yelled, "Hey, leave the kid alone!" The usher continued to shake the bat free as he dragged me down the steps toward the field. With a quick twist of his wrists, he finally wrenched the bat loose and tossed it over the fence in front of the dugout. Then with a firm grip on my arm, he led me back to my seat.

The injured woman was evacuated, a distraught Ted Williams returned to the field, and the game resumed. In the late innings, a medic pushed the wounded spectator back to our section in a wheelchair. Her head was a turban of white bandages. I suppose they wanted us all to see that she was still alive, and that she still loved baseball.

I saw my second Red Sox game in 1979 and my third in 1984. They were both pretty boring.

The Hundred Mile Race

I love to run. I've entered footraces since high school, and though I haven't kept an accurate count, I've finished more than thirty marathons. But I've always been mystified by those hearty souls who spend their leisure time running ultramarathons, races up to 100 miles long. I remember reading about a hundred mile event held in New York's Central Park, on a 5-mile loop. I suppose in a city of seven million, it's not too hard to find a few dozen knuckleheads who get their kicks by running twenty times around the park. But it's impossible for me to imagine how it must feel, running three more 26-mile marathons without stopping, considering how miserable I am for the last 6 miles of the standard marathon distance.

So when I learned that there is a hundred miler held every year in Vermont, I was curious. It began as a cross-country horse race, over the hills and through the valleys of Woodstock, Pomfret, Reading, and Cavendish. The Vermont Adaptive Ski and Sports Association saw the potential of including foot runners in the competition, listing the event on the national ultramarathon schedule, and raising some money for Vermont Adaptive Sports in the process.

VASS is the outfit that provides equipment, instruction, and encouragement to the folks we see zipping down many of Vermont's ski slopes on one ski, or in those small, ski-equipped sleds. The organization has been so successful teaching Vermonters how to get out of their wheelchairs and onto the slopes in the winter, that by popular demand, their recreational programs expanded to include wilderness camping and canoeing in the summer.

Now in its tenth year, the Vermont 100 Mile Endurance Run is not only a big success with the participants, but a major source of funding for the Vermont Adaptive Ski and Sports. In recent years, the race has generated nearly $40,000 annually. The equestrian crowd not only opened the event to foot runners but they generously provide camping facilities for hundreds of athletes, a huge spaghetti feed before the race, and an impressive awards ceremony after the finish. Typically, the event draws more than two hundred competitors from forty states and several foreign countries.

A friend, who had been involved in the VASS for years, invited me to tag along as he fulfilled his duties on the support crew. We left home in the predawn darkness and reached his assigned position, near the 8-mile mark, as the sky grew pink at 4:00 a.m. We were on a descending dirt road, overhung with ancient sugar maples, watching a golden mist rise from nearby pastures. It was a scene directly out of a Vermont Life Calendar. We spoke in whispers, reluctant to destroy the magical stillness.

First, I saw the beams of flashlights bobbing down the road. Then, instead of labored breathing and pounding feet, I heard conversation, or more accurately, casual banter. These folks were 8 miles into a 100-mile race, on a course that included more than 14,000 vertical feet of climbing, a course that would take the leaders almost twenty hours to complete, and the runners were chatting as if they were at a church supper!

They weren't the lean, sinewy, super-endurance types I had expected. They came in all sizes, an amazing cross section of the population. When I commented that some of the runners seemed to be carrying a little extra weight, a volunteer who was a veteran of several previous ultramarathons observed, "This race has a lot more to do with determination and motivation than it does with physique. A 2:40 marathoner is seldom a threat in this event."

At the 28-mile mark, runners step on the scales and are questioned by a medic. A drop of 6% in a competitor's body weight earns a caution, a 7% drop means enforced withdrawal from the race. Next to the aid station is a table loaded with food: baked potatoes, spaghetti, soup, sandwiches, candy bars, cookies, and a wide variety of beverages. These athletes don't grab a drink on the run as we do in marathons, they sit down and really refuel!

I asked several competitors about their goals for the event, and between mouthfuls, they all gave the same answer, "Oh, just to finish."

At that race I witnessed a few years ago, 126 of the 230 starters completed the course within the 30-hour limit, led by James Garcia from Massachusetts, in a time of 16 hours, 39 minutes. The first woman across the line was Bridget Brunnick, a twenty-six-year-old Californian, who finished in 20 hours, 26 minutes. Seventy-year-old Fred Nagelschmidt, also from California, made it in under the 30-hour cutoff with more than 30 minutes to spare!

Maybe these folks aren't so crazy after all. I wouldn't mind being in condition to run a hundred mile footrace when I'm seventy.

The Olympic Torch Relay

On Friday, June 14, 1996, the Olympics came to Vermont. Well actually, the Olympic flame was carried through southern Vermont on its transcontinental route, from Los Angeles to Atlanta for the Centennial Olympic Games. In ancient Greece a sacred truce was observed between warring states for the duration of the Olympics. Heralds ran through the countryside announcing the truce and summoning participants to the Games. The custom was revived as part of the modern Olympic tradition in 1936, adding the symbolism of the torch, which was ignited by the rays of the sun on the slopes of Mount Olympus.

The 1996 Torch Relay began in Los Angeles on April 27. The ambitious route traveled through forty-two of the fifty states on its 15,000-mile, 84-day journey to Atlanta. Ten thousand torchbearers were selected to run the flame about a kilometer each, through villages, towns and cities. But the torch also traveled by bicycle, train, river boat, wheelchair and even pony express. The convoluted route brought the Olympic flame within a two-hour distance of 90 percent of the nation's population.

The torchbearers were selected in three categories. Fifty-five hundred of the runners, more than half the total, were nominated as Community Heroes. In Vermont, this group included nineteen residents who, through the years, demonstrated outstanding commitment to their hometowns. Vermonters like Carol Todd, a grandmother from Northfield, who donated countless hours helping volunteer organizations become more efficient and effective.

Robert Kalinowski, a State Trooper from Bennington and instructor at the Police Academy, dedicated much of his spare time to the Vermont Special Olympics.

Jon Gailmor, a singer and songwriter from Elmore, who, through workshops and benefit concerts, shared his music with schoolchildren throughout the state. He reached an even wider audience when he was chosen as Vermont's representative to perform at the 25th Anniversary Celebration of the Kennedy Center in Washington, D.C.

Tattie Brelsford, who grew up in Putney, carried the Olympic torch in her wheelchair. An accident many years ago cut short a promising future as a cyclist and a Nordic ski racer. But she refocused her energy, and began volunteering for nonprofit organizations working with the disabled.

Helping the Community Heroes relay the flame from Bennington to Brattleboro were seven former Olympic Team members. Understandably, most of Vermont's Olympians were skiers, like Joe Holland, a two-time, Nordic Combined competitor from Norwich, and Dennis Donahue, one of America's top biathletes at both the '72 and '76 Winter Games.

Three cross-country skiers were also selected: Terry Porter, a member of the 1976 women's team; Stan Dunklee who raced in Innsbruck and again four years later in Lake Placid; and Mike Gallagher, who represented the U.S. in three Olympic Games, '64, '68, and '72. Joining this collection of skiers was a lone Summer Olympian, Glen Whitten, who was a diver forty years ago in Melbourne.

The third group of torch bearers established a new tradition in Olympic history. Through their "Who Would You Choose?" program, the Coca-Cola company gave everyday Americans the opportunity to nominate anyone they felt deserved the honor of carrying the torch. From the thousands of entries submitted, 2,500 were drawn at random. The three Vermonters selected were Ted Doucette of Bennington, James Currier of Glover, and Tom Kaiden from Stowe.

So, for a few hours the authentic Olympic flame, kindled by the sun in Greece, traversed our state on its long journey to Atlanta. On July 19, during the Opening Ceremony, that same flame, having been handed from one American to another—men and women, young and old, rich and poor, of various ethnic origins and diverse religious beliefs, ten thousand strong, the length and breadth of this country—that same flame was finally handed to a special individual, whose identity remained a secret until he entered the Olympic Stadium with the torch held high.

Then, as millions of people around the globe watched in awe, Muhammad Ali, America's beloved boxing champion, ignited the

Olympic Cauldron and opened the Centennial Olympic Games. At that moment, the thousands of us who carried the flame on its journey, or cheered as it passed by, had a direct connection to one of the greatest sporting events the world has ever known.

Sir Roger Bannister

Some time ago, I heard an impressive lecture by Sir Roger Bannister, a British medical doctor in his mid-sixties, who also happens to be the first man in the world to run a mile in under four minutes.

Sir Roger described being a medical student at Oxford following World War II. In those days, students attended classes in the morning, but were expected to participate in sports in the afternoon. He remembered being intimidated by older, more experienced classmates who had returned to their studies after years of military service. He also admitted that he had lacked the strength and skill to succeed at rugby or soccer, so he concentrated on running.

Soon Bannister became Oxford's top miler and one of the best in Britain. But in 1948 he baffled his countrymen by passing up a chance to compete in the London Olympic Games. He had set his sights on a gold medal, and he knew he was not yet ready to win at the Olympics.

Like all successful athletes, Sir Roger had his share of disappointments. Four years after declining to compete in the London Olympics, he was confident of a gold medal at the Helsinki Games. Later, he would admit that he had been so sure of his speed, that as the Games approached, he was too casual about his training. A week before the opening of the Helsinki Games, the schedule of qualifying heats, semifinals and finals for the 1500 meters (the international equivalent of the mile) was rearranged. Events that previously had been separated by rest days were instead scheduled on consecutive days.

In the finals of the Olympic 1500, Bannister was strong through the first three laps, but racing three days in a row had taken its toll, and he was unable to hold the pace. He finished out of the medals, in disgrace. The British press was merciless. Significantly, as the sixty-six-year-old physician reflected on his failed Olympic effort, he displayed no bitterness about the last-minute alteration of the schedule. Instead, he blamed the disappointing performance on his own inadequate preparation.

Sir Roger knew following Helsinki he would be unable to train for the 1956 Olympics. He would be finishing medical school and beginning a medical rotation in 1954. But he hated the thought of ending his running career on the intense disappointment of the Helsinki Olympics.

In those days it was widely accepted that to run a mile in less than four minutes was humanly impossible. John Landy of Australia, who had several times run 4:02, was convinced that the four-minute barrier was "a brick wall."

But Bannister had frequently run three, fifty-nine-second quarters back-to-back, and he was quite certain that a sub-four-minute mile was possible. He also believed that under the right conditions, he could be the first to do it.

Although admitting it might sound odd by today's standards, he revealed that patriotism provided strong motivation for his effort to shatter the four-minute barrier. "Britain was in shambles after the war," he said, "there was a pervasive attitude that we couldn't do anything well anymore."

He made an attempt at the sub-four-minute mile in 1953 and failed. "I messed up my pacing," he said candidly. Then, on May 6, 1954, Bannister enlisted the help of two running buddies to make a second attempt. It was a significant gamble. It was a windy, rainy day. If Bannister ran in the foul weather and failed again, it would take several weeks for him to recover sufficiently for a third attempt. During that time, other talented runners seeking the same goal might succeed. Yet the same thing could happen if he postponed his attempt and waited for better weather.

By five in the afternoon, the rain had stopped and Bannister's running buddies had become impatient. They convinced him to go for it. On the first lap, Sir Roger urged his friend to go faster, but the training partner wisely stuck to the prearranged pace. On the third lap, Bannister's second friend took the lead, also holding steady to the record- breaking pace. Then, in Sir Roger's words, "I took over on the last lap, and that was that!"

There was no posturing for television cameras, no end zone dramatics, no victory lap draped in a national flag. Roger Bannister achieved one of the most notable milestones in the history of sport, then quietly hung up his racing shoes, and dedicated himself to a distinguished forty-year career in medicine. That's an example of keeping sports in the proper perspective.

Atlanta's Centennial Olympic Games

The Olympic flame was extinguished, the flag was entrusted to the Mayor of Sidney, Australia, and we survived another, emotional roller coaster of televised sport. Although my firsthand experience with the Olympics is limited to the Winter Games, I watched the Atlanta extravaganza with great interest. It's easy to bash the television coverage of the Olympics, but let's be fair; even VIPs in Atlanta with free passes couldn't have seen, in person, all the events we did at home courtesy of NBC. Of course, the broadcast wizards prepackaged most of what we saw, and determined for us what was important and what was not.

Obviously, women's gymnastics was very important, yachting was not; track and field was important, soccer was not. This is a problem for me because I don't always agree with their evaluations. Women's gymnastics is a troubling sport in my view. I am astounded by what those girls can accomplish, and I use the word girls intentionally: most of those gymnasts are not yet women. But at the same time, I'm certain the physical and emotional demands of that sport are not healthy for young teenagers. The litany of serious fractures and sprains endured by members of the U.S. Team is reminiscent of professional football.

And women's gymnastics highlights another disturbing trend: the celebrity status of coaches. In my opinion, the role of the coach is to guide, instruct, and support the athlete in preparation for competition. Then, ideally, the coach fades into the background as the athlete performs. It does not seem healthy to me that after every routine, each young American gymnast runs to her coach for the obligatory hug, which of course is broadcast to millions of TV viewers, coast to coast.

None of our tiny gymnasts appeared to derive from their competition the unrestrained joy that was so evident in softball's Dot Richardson. Now there's a worthy Olympic Champion: a woman who clearly loves her sport, who worked very hard with her teammates to prepare for the Games, and who, two days after winning a gold medal, was back at her job as a medical resident in a Los Angeles hospital.

The same exuberance was evident on the women's soccer team and the women's basketball team, both of which not only won the gold, but appeared to truly enjoy the process. In contrast, the members of the men's basketball "Dream Team" were totally in character: very talented, but grossly overpaid professionals, working at their occupation. I would prefer to send a collection of college all-stars to the Olympics, even if it meant risking the basketball gold medal.

And how about poor Carl Lewis? Only nine gold medals in four Olympics! Undeniably, he's America's most talented track and field athlete, yet his twelve-year Olympic odyssey began beneath a cloud of selfishness, and it ended the same way. I'll bet Carl is secretly delighted he was not added to the sprint relay, since the Canadians were probably unbeatable, regardless of who ran for the U.S.

I think I'm as patriotic as most Americans, and I love to see our kids do well, but I have a real problem with our athletes taking their victory lap wrapped in the Stars and Stripes. I know it's unrealistic to hope we could eventually ignore nationalities and simply applaud outstanding athletic achievement, but wrapping our winners in the flag and chanting "USA...USA...USA," does not contribute to the harmonious global community the Olympics strives to create.

If Baron Pierre de Coubertin, the French nobleman who a century ago founded the modern Olympic Games, had been a spectator in Atlanta, he might have been frustrated by the inadequate transportation system and disgusted by the commercialism, and he certainly would have grieved for those who suffered in the explosion at Centennial Park.

But I believe de Coubertin would have admired Dan O'Brien's determination in the decathlon; he would have marveled at Fu Mingxia's perfection in diving and would have celebrated Josia Thugwane's victory in the marathon (the first gold medal for a black man from South Africa).

The Olympic Games may not have evolved as de Coubertin had envisioned; but for seventeen days the world was united by the accomplishments of the athletes in Atlanta, and many of us were inspired and enriched by what we saw.

Of Snowstorms, Airplanes, and the North Woods

"Life is either a daring adventure or nothing at all."
—Helen Keller

December 24, 1996, brought typically miserable winter weather to the Upper Connecticut River Valley: freezing rain and dense fog. A Learjet flown by Patrick Hayes and Johan Schwartz of Aircraft Charter Group, Inc., from Bridgeport, Connecticut, requested clearance to land at Lebanon Airport. As they made their instrument approach through the storm, the pilots aborted the landing and climbed out of the pattern for a second try. Moments later, about 7 miles northeast of Lebanon, the Learjet disappeared from radar.

What ensued was the most extensive air and ground search in New Hampshire's history, involving dozens of organizations and hundreds of volunteers who were inspired by the unflagging efforts of the families and friends of the two young pilots. More than a dozen army helicopters were committed to the effort. Scuba divers were even recruited to scour the depths of the Hanover Reservoir and Post Pond in Lyme.

Federal officials called off the search after six days, while state agencies like the Department of Fish and Game continued the effort for another week. By then, all reasonable hope of the pilots' survival was gone, and additional snow accumulation made it highly unlikely that the sleek jet would be discovered until after the spring thaw. Even so, dozens of Upper Valley residents continued to donate their time and resources to locate the missing airplane.

It would be almost three years, November 11, 1999, before the scattered wreckage of the Learjet was found by a forester on a remote shoulder of Smarts Mountain. It had been completely camouflaged by branches and treetops dislodged by the devastating ice storm of January 1998. Even when the exact location of the airplane had been pinpointed on aerial survey maps taken after the crash, no trace of the wreckage was visible in the photographs.

One of the reasons so many Upper Valley residents refused to abandon the search for the two young pilots from Connecticut, was the still vivid memory of an equally tragic airplane accident in 1959. Ralph Miller, M.D., was Head of Pathology at Dartmouth Medical School, Director of Laboratories at Mary Hitchcock Memorial Hospital, and Senior Consultant in Pathology for the Veterans Administration Hospital in White River Junction, Vermont. At sixty years old, Dr. Miller was at the peak of his career. When Dartmouth President John Sloane Dickey decided in 1956 to rebuild the college's medical school, Ralph Miller was the logical choice to lead pathology, one of the six basic science departments.

When he wasn't teaching at the medical school or performing autopsies, Dr. Miller was an avid outdoorsman. He maintained a connection with the Dartmouth Outing Club, which he had joined during his undergraduate years at the college. His love of Alpine skiing inspired his son, Ralph Jr., to establish the world speed record on skis in 1955 and earn a spot on the 1956 U.S. Olympic Ski Team. Both father and son were known for their love of the rugged outdoors, and for going fast.

But perhaps Dr. Miller's greatest joy was flying. He was an experienced pilot with more than twenty years in several varieties of private aircraft. He frequently flew his own plane to medical conferences throughout the country and had even flown two research expeditions for Dartmouth in the Arctic. He was a charter member of the Lebanon chapter of the Civil Air Patrol. It was not uncommon for Dr. Miller to combine his passion for flying with his medical work, and he was a frequent visitor to the small airstrips of New Hampshire's remote, northern towns.

On the morning of February 21, 1959, Dr. Miller had agreed to fly his colleague Dr. Robert Quinn to see a patient in Berlin, New Hampshire, north of the White Mountains. Dr. Quinn, thirty-two years old, was a highly respected cardiologist, one of the promising young doctors recruited in 1956 as part of President Dickey's plan to reinvigorate the medical school. After earning his medical degree from Yale, Dr. Quinn served two years in the Army Medical Corps and did research at Harvard before joining the faculty at Dartmouth's medical school and attending patients at both Mary Hitchcock Memorial Hospital and the Veterans Administration Hospital in White River Junction.

The weather was not good when Dr. Miller's cream and red Piper Comanche departed Lebanon airport, but the weather in northern New England is seldom ideal for flying, and Dr. Quinn was urgently needed in Berlin, New Hampshire. Dr. Miller had filed a six-hour round-trip flight plan that would bring them back over Gorham and Littleton, then down the Connecticut River to Lebanon. While Dr. Quinn was treating his cardiac patient in Berlin, Dr. Miller had planned a short flight to the airstrip in Whitefield, where he would perform an autopsy in nearby Lancaster, before returning to Berlin for Dr. Quinn and the trip home.

All went according to schedule until Dr. Miller returned to Berlin from Whitefield in the mid-afternoon for Dr. Quinn. The weather was deteriorating, and before 3:00 p.m., Dr. Miller canceled his original flight plan. The two doctors then went into nearby Milan for a quick lunch, presumably hoping the weather would improve. Sometime around 3:30 the cream and red Comanche was seen taking off from the Berlin airport, in spite of serious snow squalls in the vicinity.

Although he had been flying for twenty years, Dr. Miller had only eight hours of instrument flight training, so he flew low enough to follow the highway. The plane was identified over Route 2 in Jefferson at 3:35 p.m. At roughly the same time, an army pilot in the clouds over Concord overheard Dr. Miller twice radio the Whitefield Airport. According to the army pilot, there was no response from Whitefield.

At 9:00 p.m., Dr. Modestino Criscitiello, a medical school colleague of the missing doctors, and a close friend of the Quinns, informed the Civil Aeronautics Authority that the two physicians had not returned as expected. Despite sub-zero temperatures and continued snow squalls, a search was launched before dawn Sunday morning. It quickly became one of the most extensive searches in the state's history, covering hundreds of square miles from Vermont in the west, Maine to the east, and as far south as Keene, New Hampshire. Although hampered by several days of bad flying weather, the air search involved the Civil Air

Patrol, the national guard, the army and the air force, as well as dozens of private planes.

On February 25th, four days after the doctors' disappearance, seventy aircraft were involved in the search over northern New Hampshire. Two hundred sixty-eight reported sightings had been investigated, but none produced the missing Comanche. Before the air force withdrew their assets in early March, they had contributed nearly 450 sorties amounting to almost 700 hours of flying time and 5,000 gallons of fuel.

Meanwhile, a massive ground search was underway, covering some of the wildest terrain in the Northeast. Soldiers from the national guard, state policemen, and conservation officers from the Department of Fish and Game joined members of the Dartmouth Outing Club who were inspired by the tireless efforts of Dr. Phil Nice, a pathology colleague of Dr. Miller's from the medical school, and Ralph Miller Jr., the pilot's son who, at the time of the accident, was a second-year medical student at Dartmouth. In spite of heroic efforts by hundreds of volunteers on the ground, who endured extended exposure to severe winter conditions, after five days, hope eroded that the doctors would be recovered alive.

In retrospect, Dr. Nice mentioned three issues that hampered the rescue effort. Although there was a massive mobilization of resources during the week following the doctors' disappearance, it lacked cohesion and a systematic organization. So many well-intentioned but misguided possible sightings were reported that it seriously diluted the search effort far beyond the realistic location of the downed aircraft. And finally, had the military been able to grant an urgent request for a high-flying night search during a break in the weather on the evening of February 22nd, a signal fire made by the two doctors might have been spotted.

More than eight weeks after the accident, a private plane chartered by colleagues from Dartmouth Medical School and Mary Hitchcock Memorial Hospital, piloted by Richard Stone and carrying New Hampshire Conservation Officer Richard Melendy, was searching the Pemigewasset Wilderness, east of the impressive Franconia Ridge. The "Pemi," as it is known to hikers and camping enthusiasts, is the large, uninhabited heart of the White Mountain National Forest. Logging operations in the 1800s left a network of overgrown skid roads and even an abandoned railroad bed, which had once served to extract millions of board feet of timber.

Today, the southern boundary of the Pemigewasset is the popular Kancamagus Highway, which bisects the White Mountain National Forest between Lincoln and Conway. But in 1959, the Kancamagus was still on the drawing boards, and the heart of the Pemi was about as far from a paved road as one could get in New Hampshire.

About 4:00 p.m. on the fifth of May, Officer Melendy spotted the wreckage of a small plane across the Thoreau Falls Trail, nearly the geographical center of the Pemigewasset Wilderness. Stone reported the sighting to John Rand, Executive Director of the Dartmouth Outing Club, and by 4:00 the next morning a search party, including Dr. Miller's colleague Dr. Phil Nice and Ralph Miller Jr., had been mobilized. It was slow going due to patches of deep spring snow and streams that were bank full with runoff. A mile from the crash site a searcher discovered an unusual knife in the snow. Ralph Miller Jr. identified the instrument as a surgical scalpel identical to those used by his father. It was the first indication to the search party that the doctors had survived the crash.

Further on, the wreckage was sighted. The plane was upside down, partially supported by birch saplings, its crumpled left wing overhanging the trail. Dr. Miller's body was found under the wing. He was wearing a winter overcoat and boots. About 200 feet from the aircraft, Dr. Quinn's body was discovered. He wore only street clothes and was missing his shoes, which were never found. Dr. Miller's jaw had been badly broken in the crash, but Dr. Quinn appeared to be uninjured. Near the bodies, hanging from birch saplings were two sets of crude snowshoes, fabricated from branches and surgical tape. Under the left wing of the airplane, near Dr. Miller's body, was a neat pile of firewood that had been cut with a surgical saw. Nearby were the remnants of the signal fire that had never been seen from the air.

But the most poignant discovery was a plastic bottle found in the cockpit of the plane, a line carefully inscribed two inches up from the base and marked "CUT HERE." Inside the searchers found what amounted to a journal of the two doctors' struggle to stay alive in the four days following the crash. On Monday, February 23, Dr. Miller wrote:

When carb ice set us down here Saturday about 4:30 we made camp. Fair night. -5° F. Good wood cut with hacksaw.

Sunday noon we went south on snowshoes (home-made) but the road petered out and we returned with enough energy to secure wood for the night. Again, fairly comfortable.

It is +5 this morning but reached -10 last night.

It is cloudy and I see little prospect of any planes reaching us today.

We will go north with the chance this abandoned railroad leads somewhere. My charts do not give enough details to be sure where we are. Should we not return, regrets to all. We will keep trying to our limit.

The ice formed so fast on the carb heat control it would not come on. This because I was throttled down so the engine heat was not up to standard 200°.

It was the first time I have had any icing with N5324P.

Later that same morning he wrote:

Monday 10 AM-snowing-decided against any snoeshoing (sic). All energy used for wood cutting-I have little hope-good bye Betty-it has all been wonderful- No regrets except for Bob. Have fun.

That same day Dr. Quinn wrote:

Up until today we were hopeful of being found, but no signs of rescue ship.

Tried to walk out yesterday. No luck. I have become particularly weak. Fighting cold is hard.

The next day, Dr. Miller wrote:

Tuesday noon
Still trying -though tools broken.
Snow
No hope left.

On Wednesday, Dr. Miller wrote in crayon on the seat fabric:

My last and most important message!! Survival instinct fights pain.
R.E.M. Goodbye all. This is saving a lot of experiments I hope.

For Dr. Ralph Miller Jr., today a physician in Lexington, Kentucky, the
forty-one years since his father's death have not dulled some of the tragic
ironies of the accident. The night before the ill-fated flight, father and son
had a spirited conversation about the weather. Dr. Miller Sr. felt the severe
storms of the winter were over, while his son argued confidently that
more storms and significant snowfalls were on the way. They bet a bottle
of wine on their predictions.

The next day, as Doctor's Miller and Quinn were flying to Berlin,
young Ralph Miller was skiing at the Dartmouth Skiway with Dr. Phil
Nice, and both noticed the cold windy weather, punctuated by harsh
snow squalls that dumped an accumulation of new coverage.

In retrospect, Ralph Miller Jr. sees his father's accident as an
unfortunate series of relatively minor misjudgments, taken individually,
none of them serious, but in succession, tragically fatal. Even the night
before the flight, the weather was threatening, but Ralph Miller Sr. was a
man who enjoyed calculated risks, and challenging weather was simply
part of flying in northern New England. Ralph Jr. remembers that the
airplane left Lebanon with less than full fuel tanks: again, not a serious
oversight in itself. When the plane left Berlin for the return flight, Dr.
Miller might have climbed up through the snow squalls, but he felt more
comfortable staying below the clouds so that he could maintain visual

contact with terrain features that he recognized. As the ceiling lowered, however, returning to Berlin became impossible since the narrow valley between Gorham and Jefferson would have been too tight for a turn.

Low on fuel and blinded by the swirling snow, Dr. Miller dropped the Cherokee's landing gear and applied full flaps to reduce airspeed as much as possible. It will never be known for certain whether lack of fuel or carburetor icing brought the airplane down, but Miller's poise and experience clearly avoided a catastrophic impact with the ground. The fact that both doctors survived the crash is a tribute to his ability to handle an airplane under extreme conditions.

Sadly, once on the ground the ironic misjudgments continued. Dr. Miller, a veteran of two flying expeditions in the Arctic owned a comprehensive winter survival kit that he often carried in his plane. Apparently, the kit had been removed from the airplane for a previous flight to the South, and never replaced. The Cherokee's radio was not damaged by the crash, but the wrecked plane was surrounded by 4,000-foot ridges that effectively blocked any radio transmissions. Had the weather cooperated, Dr. Miller almost certainly would have been able to contact a search plane overhead the morning after the accident, but ironically, the winter storms he had bet his son were over, kept the search planes out of the skies until Wednesday, the day the doctors finally succumbed to the cold.

A final tragic misjudgment, for which the doctors cannot be blamed, involves their aborted effort to walk out from the crash site. After their ingenious attempt to fabricate snowshoes from the materials they had on hand, they followed the abandoned logging railroad bed more than a mile from the airplane. Given the severe cold and the deep snow, it is unlikely they could have managed the 12-mile hike to the town of Lincoln, but less than a mile from the point where Dr. Miller's scalpel was found, a Forest Service cabin overlooks the trail. Although they had no way of knowing it, the two doctors were eight tenths of a mile from the food and shelter that would have allowed them to survive well beyond Wednesday, when the air search began.

Ralph Miller Jr. acknowledges that his father enjoyed taking calculated risks. Dr. Miller enjoyed reading the accounts of the Arctic and Antarctic explorations of Perry, Shackleton and Byrd. His chosen field of medicine brought him in contact with death almost daily, so for him, death was not a terrifying philosophical concept, but instead an inevitable part of life. His journal entries during the final four days suggest an objective, scientific detachment, rather than any sense of fear or desperation. His only regret was for his young colleague.

Although the loss of Ralph Miller and Robert Quinn was a devastating blow to their families, a shock to the Dartmouth medical community, and an enduring mystery to the people of the Upper Connecticut River Valley, the last four decades have brought changes that would have pleased the two men. Dr. Quinn was honored by naming the Rare Book Room at the Dartmouth Medical School Library in his memory. A medical school lecture series was established in Dr. Miller's honor. The Dartmouth Outing Club remembered the men by building the Miller/Quinn airstrip in the College Grant to provide safe haven for other small planes caught in similar circumstances over New Hampshire's north woods.

In addition, both men would no doubt be proud of their sons, who carried on the medical legacy. Dr. Ralph Miller Jr. practices medicine in Lexington, Kentucky, while Dr. Jeffrey Quinn is a physician at Cornell.

What would also intrigue Dr. Miller, however, would be the advancements in search and rescue techniques since 1959. Lieutenant David Hewitt, the New Hampshire Conservation Officer who played a central role in the effort to find the missing Learjet in 1996, outlined some of the technological improvements of the past four decades.

Following the disappearance of the Learjet from Lebanon's radar, the New Hampshire Department of Fish and Game, which has responsibility for organizing searches in the state, had immediate access to the F.A.A.'s radar records and taped transmissions of the aircraft's radio communications. The search for the missing Learjet was underway within an hour, using snowmobiles and all-terrain vehicles.

Today there are far more people in the woods than there were in 1959: hiking, snowshoeing, cross-country skiing and snowmobiling. Though not densely populated, much of the northern part of the state is now crisscrossed by trails that didn't exist four decades ago.

As the 1990s drew to a close, searchers had access to high-tech instruments that enhanced the range of their eyes and ears. Computer-generated topographical maps and global positioning instruments allowed search teams to precisely identify what ground had been covered and where to look next. Cellular telephones and small, portable radios allowed search parties to stay in contact with each other, and with the command center. Military satellites were even recruited into the 1996 search, and intelligence analysts suggested five different sites that might have concealed the wreckage of the Learjet.

Several teams of search dogs, capable of picking up the scent of a human from half a mile away, were pressed into service. Of the fourteen helicopters provided by the military, some were equipped with forward-looking infrared radar, capable of locating sources of heat on the ground, even at night.

Perhaps two advancements would have held special significance for Dr. Miller. A technological marvel that would have made all the difference in 1959 is the emergency locator transponder. This device is automatically activated in an emergency and emits a powerful radio signal that allows authorities to pinpoint the location of a downed aircraft within minutes. ELTs are currently required equipment on all piston-driven aircraft, though still optional on turbine-powered aircraft. Had the ill-fated Learjet been equipped with an ELT, Civil Air Patrol officials theorize the crash site would have been located within an hour.

The second significant advancement has been organizational. Forty-one years after losing his mentor in the crash, Dr. Philip Nice still voices frustration about the disorganization and fragmentation of the critical, preliminary search efforts. There were several state and federal agencies, as well as many volunteer organizations involved, but no clear operational leader, and as a result much duplication of effort. Today letters of agreement exist between the various emergency response agencies, clearly defining the Incident Command System, which assigns areas of responsibility, points of contact and cooperation between agencies, and even provides a common language to be used during an emergency. An observer at the command center of the search for the Learjet would have seen a much more organized and systematic interagency approach than what Dr. Nice experienced in 1959.

And yet, all of these technological and organizational advancements did not find the missing Learjet. A forester, engaged in a routine timber stand evaluation almost three years after the accident, found the Learjet. As Lieutenant Hewitt of the New Hampshire Fish and Game pointed out in a press conference, 2,800 square miles (the search area for the missing Learjet) of predominantly forested wilderness is a huge expanse to methodically cover on foot and by air.

Though much has changed since Doctors Miller and Quinn wagered with the weather forty-one years ago, much remains the same. Mother Nature and the mountainous northern forests are every bit as unforgiving today as they were four decades ago.

An Exercise Program that Works

Not long ago, C. Everett Koop, the former surgeon general of the United States, courageously announced what many of us have suspected but have been afraid to admit; we have become a nation of couch potatoes. In a widely broadcast press conference, Dr. Koop asserted that an alarmingly high percentage of Americans are overweight due to poor nutrition and lack of exercise.

The more things change, the more they stay the same. As a high school student in the early 1960s, I remember the enthusiasm and optimism inspired by John F. Kennedy. Physical fitness was a high priority for our young president more than thirty years ago. Even though we have known for decades that exercise is a key to good health, why has it been so difficult making it a part of our daily lives? Although fitness centers have sprung up all over America, most of them are forced to employ an aggressive sales staff, since it is common to have a 50 percent turnover in health club memberships every year.

In the frigid hours before dawn, on a recent January morning, I was searching for the secret to maintaining an exercise program. I had heard about two women in a nearby town who have walked together for years, almost every morning, summer and winter, rain or shine. In January that means bundling up in sweatshirts, mittens, neck gaiters and reflective vests. It also means starting and finishing in the dark. They have become so comfortable in their routine that they rarely permit guests on their walks, although a one-time exception was made in my case.

Four years ago, Prudence and Nancy, friends who live a half mile apart on a dirt road, agreed to walk together as part of a New Year's resolution to lose weight. Both are busy wives and mothers, so the only time available to walk the 4-mile loop through their rural neighborhood is before breakfast. Both admit that even after four years, it is often difficult to get up and out into the cold on dark winter mornings while their families still sleep. But as we begin walking, they talk cheerfully.

Each house we stride past prompts a story. A barn reminds them of the spring they interrupted their walk to return escaping lambs to their ewes. The snow crunches underfoot as we pass an expensive spec house that remains unsold. As we approach one darkened home, the cheerful banter stops abruptly and they explain in whispers that the residents once announced in the post office that they had been awakened by Nan and Pru's predawn renditions of Patsy Cline's all-time hits.

There has also been plenty of excitement through the years. One morning they encountered a defiant skunk. Pru says it attacked; Nan rolls her eyes at her friend but does admit the small animal blocked the road and refused to let them pass. They are accustomed to dogs, and once before sunrise, they almost overtook what they thought was a Lab or a Newfoundland before they realized it was a black bear! During a blizzard, Nan probably saved Pru's life, by pulling her out of the path of an oncoming snowplow. And one springtime, Pru was nearly swept away when she stubbornly waded through a stream that had overflowed its culvert.

So what has kept these two women walking their 4-mile loop, day after day through the years? They both admit that the original objective of losing weight is no longer their primary concern, although they agree the exercise is good for their bones and their hearts. Over the years what has emerged as the most important reason for getting up at 5:30 every morning, is the chance to talk. They both confess, not entirely joking, that their morning walks have probably saved thousands of dollars in professional counseling fees. Nan has an emotionally demanding job as a visiting nurse. Pru served on her local school board during a contentious and highly publicized budget dispute. Within the past couple of years, Nan's two daughters have headed off to college. Because Pru's four kids are all enthusiastic athletes, she always seems to be bringing someone to the Emergency Room. And both families have lost beloved pets in recent years.

For Prudence and Nancy, the opportunity to share their joys and sorrows on a daily basis with a sympathetic listener has been so therapeutic that they continue to brave the ice and the slush, the black flies and the mosquitoes.

Perhaps the real trouble with sticking to an exercise program is going it alone. Find a friend you can talk with while you're working out. Like Nan and Pru, you'll be more likely to stick to your training schedule, and no doubt, you'll get far more out of the arrangement than physical fitness.

The Long Swim

For years I've heard about the benefits of swimming: how it's refreshing recreation, effective exercise, and an excellent form of therapy following an injury or illness. The swimmers we see in the Summer Olympics every four years certainly are impressive athletes. But competitive swimming seems to me to be painfully monotonous. For most swimmers, it's endlessly back and forth, back and forth, in a 25-meter pool. I'm sure many people consider running and cross-country skiing equally as boring, but at least in those sports the scenery and weather provide variety. The swimmer normally trains in a controlled environment: air temperature about 81°, water temperature about 78°, and lane markers 5 feet apart.

Running, hiking and cross-country skiing are social sports. I often train with a group of friends who chatter and joke throughout the entire workout. Swimmers can't enjoy that kind of diversion while they're practicing their sport. So, for years, I have both admired and been baffled by the dedication of swimmers to a sport that seems so painfully dull.

As a result, I was intrigued when Dr. Harry Briggs, a marine combat veteran and former college professor, planned to swim the 10 mile length of New Hampshire's Lake Sunapee. The event was dedicated to raising funds for the Lydia Briggs Endowment Fund for Athletics at Tilton School, a fund that Dr. Briggs established in memory of his wife. He planned to enter the water at 6:00 a.m. in Georges Mills, and arrive at the Newbury Public Beach at 6:00 p.m. I may not be a big fan of swimming, but twelve hours of continuous exercise in any form is impressive, so I planned to be at the Newbury Beach when Dr. Briggs finished his swim.

Although I parked in Newbury an hour before the estimated conclusion of the swim, I was late. A small group of enthusiastic fans surrounded a tanned, solid man who was drying off with a towel and chatting casually. The only clue that he had spent the previous eleven hours plowing through the brisk chop of Lake Sunapee was a faint bluish tinge to his lips and the pale, wrinkled skin of his hands and feet.

Swimming the length of Lake Sunapee had not been some hair-brained scheme for Harry Briggs. He has an impressive history of forty-three long-distance swims. In 1957, Dr. Briggs was the first person to swim across Lake Erie, an achievement that took thirty-five hours and fifty-five minutes from Sandusky, Ohio, to Point Pelee, Ontario. That event was especially rewarding since Briggs had failed in two previous attempts to cross Lake Erie.

Two years earlier, Dr. Briggs was the first person to swim from the French island of Corsica to Italy's Sardinia, a distance of 15 miles. The former marine also crossed Lake Winnipesaukee from Alton Bay to Wolfeboro, and then back to Weirs Beach, a distance of 36 miles. More recently, "the paddlin' professor," as he was called by the New York Times, swam 10 miles on Big and Little Squam Lakes and the 12-mile length of Lake Winnisquam.

When asked about the hardest part of his distance swims, Dr. Briggs responds without hesitation, "It's tough to stay warm when you're in the water that long. I eat every hour, glucose or some type of sport drink. You burn a lot of fuel just trying to keep your body temperature up.

"Sometimes the weather's a problem," he continued. "Midway through this swim the wind kicked up the waves and it was hard to stay on course. I usually sight on a mountaintop every few strokes, but the waves made that difficult today.

"But the toughest part of distance swimming is definitely mental," he concluded. "When the wind picks up, or my back gets stiff, I ask myself, can I keep this up another seven hours? You really have to overcome the negative thoughts, and that's never easy."

I know Harry Briggs is right, although I can only imagine the intensity of the negative energy when your back stiffens and you still have seven hours to go to reach the finish line. But Harry Briggs seems to have mastered even that difficult challenge, especially when you consider he completed this 10-mile Lake Sunapee swim at seventy-six years of age!

"When you get to be my age," he says, "you have to have goals. There is so much over which you have no control, like retirement or the death of a spouse. But if you set a goal and reach it, you feel great. After all, there's no shame in failure, only in not trying."

How right you are Dr. Briggs and thank you for showing us how it's done!

Memories of a Christmas Past

Like everyone else, I get overwhelmed by the holidays. I never start early enough to find meaningful gifts for my family, putting up all the decorations can become a chore rather than a joy, and every year I seem to burn out on holiday concerts, church services, and social gatherings. But the memory of a Christmas nearly thirty years ago helps me to keep today's holiday overload in perspective.

I was a mobile advisory team leader in the heart of South Vietnam's Mekong Delta. Our mission was to "win the hearts and minds of the people," but as the big American combat units pulled out, leaving our Vietnamese allies to be mauled by the North Vietnamese, we weren't winning many hearts or minds. In the autumn of 1970, Phung Hiep District was dicey enough that our five-man advisory team was attached to a larger, district advisory team to improve our security.

In spite of the stifling heat, daily artillery barrages, and the constant threat of Viet Cong mortar attacks, by mid-December, I was actually looking forward to Christmas. One of our guys knew a mess sergeant at a big American base and was able to trade something for a turkey. Another advisor scrounged a case of Lancers rosé. But the real bonus was an olive drab, number 10 can of dehydrated shrimp. Not only would we have turkey and wine for our Christmas feast, we'd actually start things off with

honest-to-goodness shrimp cocktail!

On the morning of the Big Day, after reading letters from home and opening a couple of packages, everyone pitched in to prepare the meal. All was ready by noon, but as we were sitting down to eat, a Vietnamese soldier burst in with news of an accident in the center of Phung Hiep. Our team medic, Sergeant Boone, and I grabbed our M-16's, recruited an interpreter, and raced through the muddy back alleys of the village.

The accident scene was encircled by a mob about to explode. Angry Vietnamese villagers threatened a terrified American soldier, who couldn't have been older than eighteen. Long, angry skid marks on the pavement led to a massive U.S. Army truck, which idled in the middle of the road. At the other end of the burned rubber stripes was a mangled motorbike and its Vietnamese driver, his head in a pool of congealing blood.

"Sergeant Boone," I pleaded, "is there anything you can do for this guy?"

Boone didn't even need to check for a pulse. "'Fraid not sir, he's very dead."

The crowd had been distracted by our arrival, but they soon began to close in on the American kid. He was scared stiff, and probably stoned on pot, but when we tried to get his version of what had happened, he acted arrogant and unconcerned that a man had just died under the wheels of his truck. I made a show of taking notes, studied the soldier's identification, and recorded the unit markings on the vehicle.

With the interpreter's help, we interviewed Vietnamese witnesses for their version of the accident. They all agreed the truck was going too fast and struck the man as he was trying to get his motorbike out of the way.

It was obvious there would be more blood on the road if we didn't do something quickly. I told the kid to get in his truck and return to his base. Then I asked the interpreter to assure the bystanders that the Military Police would conduct a thorough investigation of the accident. The huge truck drove away, leaving the body of the Vietnamese man, Boone, the interpreter, and me, surrounded by angry villagers.

For several tense moments, it was impossible to tell if their frustration would boil over, but eventually they allowed us to leave. Walking through the squalid back streets of Phung Hiep, I was overcome by the sickening feeling that, although my intentions were correct, I had just betrayed the villagers I was supposed to be advising.

By the time Boone and I returned to the team house, Christmas dinner was over. They had saved some turkey, but neither of us had much of an appetite.

I can't remember the name of the Vietnamese man who died that Christmas Day in Phung Hiep, and I never learned what happened to the kid who was driving the truck. But since then, at Christmas, I consider myself very lucky that the only stress I now endure is an overload of social obligations, a few frantic holiday shoppers, and the occasional rock musician butchering a Christmas carol on the radio.

Don't forget to count your blessings. Most of us have far too many we take for granted.

A Return to Baseball

I got off on the wrong foot with baseball. Although our town was too small for Little League, an enthusiastic, junior high phys. ed. teacher tried to pull together a team, so for one spring, I lugged a baseball glove everywhere I went.

My devotion to the game was challenged one afternoon when we were lined up to practice fielding grounders. The ball seemed to leave the coach's bat like a bullet, then ricochet off the uneven ground at crazy angles. The coach had carefully instructed us to block the ball's path with our bodies and "watch" the ball into our gloves. We were just beginning to gain some confidence when Alan Welsh stepped in front of a real zinger that took a bad hop, missed his glove, and caught him squarely in the crotch. He collapsed instantly in the dirt, his mouth gaping frantically like a beached trout, but no sound came out. The coach tried to be reassuring, "That-a-boy Welshy, you didn't let that one get past you." I wondered if you had to die stopping a grounder to earn praise from a baseball coach.

Soon thereafter, I miraculously connected with a pitch in a scrimmage. It was such a surprise, I let the bat sail as I bolted for first. After rounding the bag and heading for second, I noticed everyone else was sprinting for home. I had thrown my bat with such abandon that it struck the next batter, Gussy Rogers, squarely in the forehead, and he was stretched out on the grass, unconscious. Since Gussy's dad was our town's policeman, I was convinced my only base hit would result in a life sentence for murder.

The final episode of my short baseball career came in our first game. It was a road trip to a neighboring town. Playing on a different field, against kids we didn't know, with spectators in the bleachers, was almost more excitement than I could handle. Amazingly, I got another hit and even remembered to drop my bat before knocking someone else senseless. I sprinted to first, knowing the throw would be close. I dove as the first baseman leapt for a high toss from his shortstop. As I clutched the bag, the first baseman landed on my hands, and the umpire howled, "Yerrr Out!"

I looked up in confusion. The first baseman was still standing on my hands, proving I had reached the bag before he did. The ump just scowled and pointed toward our dugout. That was the last time I played baseball.

Since then, if I hear some horror story about abusive Little League parents or self-absorbed Major League players spitting on umpires, it simply fuels my distaste for the game. But a friend in Reading, Vermont, has coached elementary school kids every spring for years, and my curiosity finally got the best of me.

The town of Reading may have only 700 residents, but the Claude Bartley Memorial Field is impressive with a sturdy fence surrounding the diamond, cinder block dugouts, and a tall backstop behind home plate. Many of these improvements were made by employees from Ben & Jerry's, who volunteered their time during a recent Community in Action project.

The home team, in T-shirts the color of John Deere tractors, was hosting their worthy rivals from Bridgewater, who wore bright, turquoise blue. Each coach pitched to his own kids, overhand to the experienced players, underhand to those still getting the hang of it. And they kept pitching until every batter got a hit!

My fears about overzealous parents were completely unfounded. The moms in the bleachers were fully engaged in conversations with each other while keeping watchful eyes on a rambunctious assortment of younger kids.

Meanwhile, the activity on the field was a mixture of mind-numbing boredom and frantic activity. One outfielder amused herself by playing the harmonica, while her teammate sat in the clover and studied insects. Then a batter would connect, and the fielders would watch in awe as the ball sailed or dribbled past. Base runners would sprint, overtake each other, turn back, change their minds and race on to the next bag, while the fielders scrambled after the ball, then heaved it in the general direction of the infield.

When one team pulled ahead by five runs, it was time for the other team to bat. The game lasted two hours, as they always do, regardless of the number of innings played. Bridgewater squeaked out a victory, 17 to 16. But Reading is famous for their post-game "2-4-6-8-who-do-we-appreciate" cheer, as well as their impressive, vertical hat toss, so all the players went home winners. This is baseball at its best. I may even become a fan.

Dudley Weider's Denali Vacation

"Dudley, you're a doctor aren't you?" The question came from Chris Morris, leader of a twelve-person expedition on 20,320-foot Mount McKinley, the highest peak in North America.

Totally exhausted from post-holing for eight hours through deep spring snow under the weight of a sixty-pound backpack, Dartmouth Hitchcock Medical Center's globe-trotting adventurer and respected otolaryngologist (ear, nose and throat doc) had just staggered into the 14,200-foot camp after five days of ferrying food and supplies from the Kahiltna Glacier, more than 7,000 feet below.

"Yes, I'm a doctor," Dudley Weider managed to gasp between deep gulps of the thin air. "What's the problem?"

"Would you follow me?" the guide asked urgently. The National Park Service maintains a medical tent at 14,200 feet to support the 1,300 climbers a year who face frostbite, exhaustion and death to conquer America's highest summit. Doctors and medics from throughout Alaska and the western United States volunteer their time for three-week rotations during the mountaineering season, but the Anchorage physician who was scheduled to be on duty had slipped a disk in his back and was unable to make the climb. Scott Darsney from Dutch Harbor, Alaska, an experienced climber and qualified medic was stretched thin in the first-aid tent, and he wanted the reassurance of a medical doctor.

Although Dudley Weider is no stranger to ultra-endurance expeditions in hostile environments, his first days on Mount McKinley had not been pleasant. He had trained diligently in the months prior to his arrival in Alaska by mowing his lawn under the weight of a sixty-pound backpack, by attending technical mountaineering courses in North Conway, New Hampshire, and by wearing his heavy, plastic-shelled climbing boots at every opportunity. But there was no way Dr. Weider could have prepared for the jet lag, the altitude, and the mind-numbing fatigue of repeated treks hauling supplies from the Kahiltna Glacier, where bush planes on skis deposit the climbers, to high on the shoulder of Denali, as the Native Alaskans call their majestic peak.

The twelve-person expedition, of which, at age fifty-nine Dr. Weider was the eldest member, had been grounded in the village of Talkeetna for four days by bad weather. When the skies finally cleared and the ski planes delivered the expedition to the Kahiltna, there was an eagerness to get climbing. Taking advantage of Alaska's famous midnight sun, the group left the glacier airstrip at 12:00 a.m., each mountaineer staggering under a sixty-pound pack and pulling another forty pounds of supplies in a plastic sled.

They arrived at the 7,800-foot elevation, a distance of four and a half miles and nearly 1,000 feet higher than the glacier landing strip, at 8:00 the following morning. After establishing a camp and having a bite to eat, they collapsed in their tents to sleep through the day. On the lower slopes, the deep snow is often soft during warm summer days, so climbers frequently move up the mountain during the twilight of Alaskan nights, when the frozen crust is more apt to support their weight.

The second evening on the mountain, the group took half their gear from 7,800 feet on up to 9,800, and cached it before returning to the lower camp to rest. The following day they broke camp at 7,800 feet and ferried the remaining supplies to 9,800. Once a camp was established at 9,800 feet, the expedition began hauling supplies to 11,000, and then leapfrogged on up to 13,500.

Although the first days on the mountain had been torture, and Dr. Weider cursed himself for inadequate training, by the fourth day he was starting to feel better, while paradoxically, a couple of his teammates were beginning to suffer from the high altitude. When the expedition reached the 14,200-foot camp at 11:00 p.m., Dudley Weider was physically exhausted by the climb, but he had overcome earlier misgivings about his ability to reach the summit.

Nearly asleep on his feet, Dr. Weider followed his expedition leader to the National Park Service medical tent, where he found a sixty-year-old man with a history of angina who was suffering from acute chest pains. The climber's electrocardiogram was clearly abnormal and two sublingual doses of nitroglycerin seemed to have had little effect. In spite of the patient's desire to continue his climb, Dr. Weider recommended a helicopter evacuation, and eventually convinced the patient to accept a chopper ride off the mountain. It was 1:30 a.m. when the exhausted doctor finally stumbled back to his tent for the night.

Dudley Weider has had a lifelong fascination with remote locations and severe winter weather. As a child in Cleveland, he remembers being so captivated by Admiral Bird's film describing Little America, the research station on Antarctica, that he phoned home from the theater for permission to stay and see the film a second time. While at Bay Village High School, Weider played football in the fall, but his primary sporting interest was speed skating, at which he eventually earned a national ranking as a junior.

When Weider began to consider colleges, Dartmouth quickly became his top choice. Not only was Hanover a rural location blessed with relatively severe winters, but Baker Library housed the Stefansson Collection, the world's most comprehensive assortment of books, articles, and artifacts from the Arctic, with the exception of a similar collection in Moscow. Viljhalmur Stefansson was an Icelandic-born, Canadian-American anthropologist and adventurer, who early in the twentieth century made several expeditions to the Arctic. He was one of very few explorers to learn the Upik language, which he did by speaking with Inuit children in Barrow. Dudley Weider was so fascinated by Stefansson that Dartmouth was a logical choice.

He graduated from the college in 1960 and went on to Tufts Medical School. In 1965, Dr. Weider achieved a lifelong dream when he was assigned to the Public Health Service Clinic in Kotzebue, Alaska, 25 miles north of the Arctic Circle. After two years in the frozen North, Dr. Weider returned to tropical Cleveland, but the lure of Alaska was strong, and in 1971 he returned to Anchorage for three more years. His fascination with Mount McKinley intensified, thanks in part to Minus 148°, Art Davidson's famous account of his winter ascent of Denali, and also thanks to Weider's almost daily view of the majestic, snow-capped cone rising from the tundra.

"Dr. Weider, sorry to wake you, but they need you again in the medical tent." It was 6:30 a.m., and the situation was serious. A twenty-six-year-old Mexican climber was in a coma, suffering from severe pulmonary edema. Apparently, he had climbed for three days, directly from 7,000 feet on the Kahiltna Glacier to 14,200 feet, without taking the recommended rest days for acclimatization. At sea level a healthy individual has a blood oxygen saturation level of nearly 100 percent. Halfway to the summit of Denali, 88 percent O2 saturation is typical, but the Mexican climber registered only 37 percent, and his lungs were so full of fluid that his breathing was barely audible. By administering 100 percent oxygen, Dr. Weider was able to get the patient's saturation up to 52 percent, which was enough to keep the climber alive until a helicopter evacuated him to the hospital in Anchorage.

An hour later a Japanese mountaineer was brought into the medical tent, also suffering from pulmonary edema. When tested, his O2 saturation registered 58 percent, and a helicopter evacuation was recommended for him as well. By 10:00 a.m., the medical tent was quiet, so Dr. Weider rejoined his group for the descent to 13,500 feet, where they retrieved the remainder of their gear and began the 700-foot climb back to 14,200.

At 6:30 the following morning, Dr. Weider was again awakened with an urgent request for his medical expertise. Thousands of feet above, just below the summit of Denali, a terrifying drama was unfolding. Six British military mountaineers, less than a thousand feet below the peak, were climbing in two teams of three, when one group fell, injuring two of the soldiers and sweeping away most of their equipment. Sgt. Martin Spooner suffered severely sprained ankles when attempting to arrest the fall, and his teammate, Lance Corp. Steve Brown appeared to have sustained head injuries. Brown began acting irrationally, removing his clothing in the howling, sub-zero gale just below the summit. With no tents, sleeping bags, or food, and with Spooner immobile, the entire expedition was doomed unless help arrived quickly.

Phil Whitfield, who had been only slightly injured in the fall, and Johnny Johnson were selected to descend for help. The fastest route to the medical aid station was down the infamous Orient Express, a 55-degree, 4000-foot face of windblown snow the consistency of concrete. The route appears deceptively benign, but one misstep can result in a bone-smashing tumble down thousands of feet of bulletproof hard pack. Over the years, fifteen climbers have lost their lives on the Orient Express, many from Japan and Korea, thus giving the deadly slope its name.

Johnson and Whitfield successfully descended, arriving at the medical tent with the news not only of the British accident near the summit but also of two injured American climbers at the base of the Orient Express. A rescue mission was immediately launched from the medical aid station to assist the downed Americans. With the arrival of the two Brits, Dr. Weider was again pressed into action: this time sewing up one soldier's scalp lacerations with a first-aid kit and Leatherman pocket tool that the doctor had brought from home.

Ten hours later, the rescue team returned with Jeff Munroe and Billy Findley, both residents of Anchorage. Their 3,000-foot fall had left Findley with fractured ribs, as well as knee and ankle injuries, while Munroe was unconscious and in critical condition. Fortunately, by that time two other climbers with medical experience had arrived at 14,200 feet. Like Dr. Weider, Dr. Ed Donovan was a nose/ear/throat doc, and also a Dartmouth graduate who practices in Nashua, New Hampshire, while David Moon worked in an emergency room in the Denver area.

Due to the severity of Munroe's condition, the medical aid station was communicating by radio with the emergency room in Anchorage, and at their suggestion, Dr. Weider installed a nasal tracheal tube that facilitated the administration of oxygen and medications. Munroe's symptoms suggested to Dr. Weider a subdural hematoma, but CAT scans would later reveal a more serious diffuse axon shearing.

Helicopters were poised for two missions, to evacuate the injured climbers from 14,200 feet, and to snatch the stranded British soldiers from a narrow ledge at 19,000 feet. But throughout the afternoon and evening, the winds howled and the clouds swirled. At midnight, there was a momentary break in the clouds, the pilots scrambled, rescue personal at 14,200 feet talked the chopper in by radio, and the injured Americans were whisked off the mountain.

Fifteen minutes after Dr. Weider collapsed in his tent, he heard the alarming news, "Grab your gear boys, there's been another fall on the Orient Express!" Roger Robinson, a National Park Ranger had been watching a pair of climbers descend the treacherous snowfield through a telescope, when the trailing climber fell, dislodged the lead climber and they both tumbled 1,500 feet to the spot where the Americans had been discovered the day before.

The British expedition leader, Capt. Justin Featherstone, weathered in just below the summit, had watched the condition of his men deteriorate and had elected to guide the still disoriented Lance Corp. Brown down the mountain to medical help. Corp. Carl Bougard, who had not been injured in the original fall, volunteered to remain at 19,000 feet with his immobile teammate, Martin Spooner. With Featherstone leading down the deadly Orient Express, Brown stumbled, dislodging them both and puncturing his Captain's leg with his sharp crampons.

When their terrifying fall finally ended, Featherstone had sustained a broken leg in addition to the puncture wounds, but the disoriented Brown unclipped from the tangled safety rope and wandered across the snowfield. Almost immediately he fell into a crevasse, but soon clawed his way back to the surface only to disappear into a deeper crevasse several meters away. Brown was so disoriented he didn't realize that he had lost his mittens, and by the time the rescue team reached the two British climbers, Brown's hands were severely frostbitten.

The rescue team returned with the injured climbers by 9:00 a.m., and Dr. Weider went to work again, first installing an I.V. and then stabilizing Featherstone's broken tibia and fibula. At the lower altitude, Lance Corp.

Brown appeared to be acting more rationally, but his hands were so severely frostbitten he would eventually lose most of his fingers.

That left two British climbers stranded on a narrow ledge of packed snow at 19,000 feet. Spooner and Bougard had little in the way of survival gear, no food, and no radio. Spooner was immobile due to his severely sprained ankles, and Bougard had long since lost feeling in his feet due to a wind-chill factor that reached 100 below. The stormy weather would not permit a helicopter rescue attempt.

Meanwhile, with a welcome lull in activity at the medical tent, Dr. Weider's climbing partners elect to push on to 16,000 feet. It was an exhausting and frustrating day. Several members of the party had decided to turn back. The next oldest member of the team had headed down after four days on the mountain. Another climber in the group, whose mother had recently passed away, turned back under pressure from his family. Jim Jurens, Dr. Weider's tent mate and the DHMC operating room nurse who had originally proposed the expedition, was having difficulty sleeping and couldn't lie flat without experiencing significant shortness of breath, so he reluctantly also started down. And a thirty-four-year-old Texan in the group simply ran out of steam and called it quits.

That left Dr. Weider trying to keep pace with two thirty-four-year-olds and a forty-four-year-old marathoner, who was the most physically fit member of the group. For the first time on the expedition, Weider asked his teammates to slow down, but he felt badly, knowing he might be jeopardizing their chance to reach the summit. Having pushed himself to exhaustion many times before, Weider knew his physical limits better than most endurance athletes.

In 1987, Dr. Weider and his buddy of many wilderness adventures, Willem Lange of Etna, New Hampshire, skied the 210-mile Ididaski race on the same trail used in the world-famous Alaskan sled dog event. More recently, Weider was part of a Norwegian expedition that skied 240 miles across the Greenland ice cap. His tent mate for part of that trip was Steve

Faucet, the adventurer famous for several attempts to circumnavigate the globe in a hot air balloon.

Dr. Weider was one of several Dartmouth grads who skied the Haute Route, a two-week trek in the Alps that begins in Chamonix, France, and culminates in Zermatt, Switzerland. Put Blodgett, who organized that trip, says of Weider, "Amazing man! He does not at first glance seem especially strong, but in fact, he's very tough. He also has the unique ability to appear attentive when he's actually sound asleep!"

And in January 1998, Dr. Weider ran a full, 26-mile marathon, the first ever to be held on the continent of Antarctica. So more than most people, Dudley Weider knew his limits, and he wasn't certain he had the conditioning necessary to reach the summit, and to descend safely. Rather than force his teammates to slow down, and perhaps risk their chance for success, Dudley offered to remain at 14,200 feet and practice medicine while the others pushed to the summit.

The drama continued near the peak. Finally, the weather broke and a helicopter located the stranded British soldiers. The pilots were astounded to see Spooner and Bougard alive and waving after several days of exposure to 80-mile-an-hour winds and temperatures that dipped to minus 30° F. The rescue pilots dropped a survival package containing food, sleeping bags, a radio, and two "screamer suits," body harnesses that allow climbers to be suspended from lines below a helicopter. Later, with the chopper refueled and the winds calm enough for the delicate maneuver, rescue pilot Jim Hood hovered over the injured climbers, who had donned the screamer suits, while they "clipped in" to the lines hanging from the aircraft.

Three minutes later Hood landed at 14,200 feet, where the British mountaineers were rushed into the medical tent and their condition was evaluated. Spooner was in good spirits in spite of his badly sprained ankles, but Bougard's feet were so badly frostbitten that eventually all of his toes would be amputated. Once the helicopter returned from a refueling run to the Kahiltna Glacier, the injured climbers were loaded aboard and flown to Talkeetna, where a Life Flight jet waited to transport them to the hospital in Anchorage.

After Dr. Weider made his decision to stay at 14,200 feet, the three remaining members of his expedition pushed on to 17,500 feet, where they were weathered in for four days. On the fifth day they summited, but clouds obscured the view. After a few moments on the top of North America, they descended quickly to 14,200 feet and Dr. Weider joined them for an agonizing race down to 8'000 feet. After a successful expedition, most mountain guides are determined to get their clients off the mountain as quickly as possible, before the weather turns sour, which eventually, it always does.

More than a year after his adventure on Denali, Dr. Dudley Weider remains in contact with many of the people he met there. Billy Finley wrote from Anchorage with an update on the slow, but promising recovery of his climbing partner, Jeff Munroe.

"I want to thank you for your help on the mountain. You were very professional and without your help Jeff would have died."

Mountaineering Park Ranger Roger Robinson wrote to inform Dr. Weider that he had been awarded the Denali Pro pin. "Thanks to your support, the complicated British and American rescue operations went smoothly and successfully. In recognition of your efforts, we present you with the 1998 Denali Pro pin. This climber recognition program is designed to recognize and reward mountaineers who reflect the highest standards in the sport for safety, self-sufficiency, assisting other mountaineers, and 'no impact' expeditions."

Later, Dr. Weider learned that he had received Honorable Mention as "Denali Pro" of the 1998 climbing season. In nominating Weider for the recognition, Park Ranger Robinson said, "I was amazed at his strength and determination. He was covered in sweat, carrying a heavy pack and pulling a sled on his own climb." Robinson continued, "Within minutes of arriving at the 14,200-foot camp, he was assisting a climber suffering from serious chest pains."

Many adventurers who have survived the bone-numbing cold and crippling exhaustion of high-altitude mountaineering, when asked if they would ever return, answer simply, "Nope, once is enough." But Dr. Dudley Weider grins as he admits he has remained in touch with many of the people he met on the slopes of Denali.

"Captain Featherstone, the British expedition leader is determined to climb the mountain again, and he's asked Michael Dong, the medic from San Diego, and me to join him. Those guys wouldn't push the pace so hard. I'd do a lot more hiking with a heavy pack to get ready. Yeah, I'd love another crack at reaching the top!"

I almost missed the small photo and the brief obituary in an issue of Newsweek. It read, "Emil Zatopek won the 5,000 meters, the 10,000 meters and the marathon at the Helsinki Olympics in 1952, a record that stands as one of the most enduring in track-and-field history. The ungainly Czech runner was 78."

What an irony! A few months earlier, prior to the Games in Sydney, Newsweek devoted its cover and a comprehensive lead story to the growing scandal of doping at the Olympics, yet the passing of one of the twentieth century's greatest champions rated only two sentences and a tiny photo.

At age nineteen, working as an apprentice in a shoe factory in the depressed coal-mining region of northern Czechoslovakia, Emil Zatopek reluctantly entered a cross-country race, finishing second. That caught the attention of a coach, and Zatopek was encouraged to join the local track club. When the Nazis invaded in 1939, the opportunity to travel for competitions disappeared for several years. But after the war, Zatopek made up for lost time. In 1946 he finished fifth in the 5,000 meters at the European Championships. Two years later, at the Olympic Games in London, he shocked the running world by winning gold in the 10,000 and silver in the 5,000, a back-to-back performance previously thought impossible.

Zatopek was not a pretty runner. His success resulted from a voracious appetite for training, and his ability to push himself to complete exhaustion during competitions. He enjoyed training in heavy army boots, through deep snow, because it made his track shoes feel so light when he raced. On the track, it was not uncommon for Zatopek to run fifty 200-meter intervals in one workout. "Why should I practice running slow," he said. "I already know how to run slow. I must learn how to run fast."

In the 1952 Helsinki Olympics, Zatopek defended his gold medal in the 10,000 meters, and won the 5,000 as well. Then, after encouraging his wife to victory in the javelin, he announced his intention to enter the marathon, a distance he had never before raced. Famous for his gregariousness, during the race Zatopek asked the Olympic favorite Jim Peters from England, "Jim, the pace is too fast, no?" Peters responded facetiously, "No, it's too slow." But Zatopek took the Brit at his word, picked up the pace, and finished his first marathon far in the lead, cheered on by 80,000 spectators.

The adoration of his countrymen was demonstrated after the Soviets crushed the Czech uprising in 1968. Attempting to disgrace the Olympic champion, the Russians relegated Zatopek to driving a garbage truck in Prague. But the Czech citizens emptied their own trash cans into the truck, refusing to let their national hero handle their rubbish.

Emil Zatopek's athletic accomplishments include eighteen world records and five Olympic medals, four of them gold. But Zatopek's true greatness was his sportsmanship. He gladly shared training discoveries with rival competitors, he never gloated over his victories, and he was gracious in defeat.

In the 1960s, a competitor emerged who had the talent to challenge Zatopek's legacy. Ron Clarke of Australia also set eighteen world records, but in six Olympic races, although heavily favored, he was able to earn only one bronze medal. Heading home after a visit with Zatopek in Czechoslovakia, Clarke opened a small package that the legendary champion had given him. Inside was an Olympic gold medal and a note. "Dear Ron, I have won four gold medals. It is only right that you should have one of them. Your friend, Emil."

The world needs more champions like Emil Zatopek.

Mother Nature's Gift to Runners

The wind howled and sheets of rain swept the landscape. As forecast, the remnants of Hurricane Lili drenched New England, but after such a dry summer, no reasonable person could complain about the weather. In Thetford, Vermont, however, there were plenty of furrowed brows.

Saturday, October 5th, was the twelfth annual Woods Trail Run, a gathering of high school athletes that has grown to attract almost 2,000 competitors, from as far as Pennsylvania.

Dan Grossman, the organizational guru who originated the event, has a list of more than 400 volunteers, all eager to donate their time and energy as a member of "Dan's Team." You can count on Byron Hathorn and Dave McGinn to judge the close calls at the finish line, while Linda Ide controls the P.A. system and broadcasts "Chariots of Fire," "The William Tell Overture," or even Scottish bag piping tunes as hundreds of runners stampede from the starting line.

Fortunately, Lili left only a few branches on the trail, and a brilliant autumn sun broke through as the races began. Roots, rocks and occasional slippery footing are part of cross-country running, but angry yellow jackets are not, so when several finishers reported to the first-aid tent for treatment of stings, a volunteer was dispatched to deal with the insect hazard.

Eavesdropping on the comments of high school runners from urban communities to the south provided a great reminder of how lucky we are to live and run in the natural beauty of Vermont.

The following day, Sunday, October 6th, was classic Vermont autumn, crisp and clear. The foliage was close enough to peak to validate the popular Leaf Peepers Half Marathon and 5-K in Waterbury. The race is well organized and attracts a good field of runners. There is something for everyone: a challenging 13-mile event for the dedicated competitor, and a manageable 3-mile course for those who aren't interested in the longer distance.

At the starting line, eager runners listened to a recording of the "Star Spangled Banner," a tradition initiated the previous year following the terrorist attacks. I glanced at a competitor whom I had just met in the parking lot, a young guy wearing an Annapolis T-shirt. He was a retired naval aviator who had seen combat in the Persian Gulf and Bosnia. I doubt listening to the national anthem was simply a formality to him, nor was Vermont's remarkable autumn beauty something he took for granted.

The course, a combination of paved and dirt roads, rolled gently beside the Winooski River, in the shadow of Camel's Hump. We ran past diehard anglers casting into pools that reflected the fiery maples and sumacs. I smelled a wood-burning stove from one of the farmhouses, and I heard the excited honking of geese overhead as they followed the spine of the Green Mountains south for the winter.

No matter what your level of conditioning, a half marathon is a demanding race. But the fatigue evident at the finish line of the Leaf Peepers was tempered by the joy of experiencing to the fullest one of Mother Nature's spectacular autumn gifts.

Different Spotlight on Figure Skating

I'll admit right up front that I've had issues with figure skating for a long time. I also confess that part of my bad attitude is probably the result of envy. You see, Nordic skiing isn't much of a spectator sport, except, perhaps in Scandinavia. A long time ago, I participated in a North American Championship cross-country ski race. The only fans were a few dedicated parents. No crowd of journalists clamored for quotes when Bill Koch won America's first Olympic medal in Nordic skiing at the 1976 Winter Olympics in Innsbruck. So I get frustrated seeing ranks of photographers and dozens of TV cameras breathlessly follow a figure skater's every move, even in practice sessions!

Often at the Winter Olympics, the Nordic skiing events are relegated to some remote location, an hour or more away from the host city, the spectators and the media. Figure skating, of course, is the primary attraction at the main Olympic Village. The only exception in recent history was in 1994 at Lillehammer. The Norwegians had constructed two magnificent ice arenas in Lillehammer, but to spread the Olympic facilities among several communities, they had built the famous Viking ship speedskating oval in Hammer, 50 kilometers to the south. When international figure skating officials arrogantly insisted that the skating events couldn't be separated, the Norwegians shocked them by relocating the figure skating events to Hammer as well. It turned out to be a brilliant move, since it kept the Tonya/Nancy soap opera 50 kilometers away from the rest of the Games.

And how much do we hear every four years about how hard the figure skaters train? Okay, so they have to get up early to get ice time. So what? Most dedicated athletes get up early. The skaters practice their spins and jumps in a climate-controlled arena, and after every short routine they skate over to their coach, or choreographer, or costume designer, or sports psychologist for a hug. If I remember correctly, those private coaches can cost the skater's family a hundred thousand dollars a year, for several years in a row. Of course, there is a payoff. If the skater medals in the Olympics, there is usually a contract worth a million dollars a year with Disney on Ice.

In contrast, when a Nordic skier goes out for a three-hour distance workout, the athlete is skiing for those three hours, usually non-stop, regardless of the weather, which is often below zero. And if an American skier astounds the Nordic world by earning a trip to the podium, there are no lucrative endorsements, no pro tours, no celebrity series. At best, the skier will be invited to speak at a local high school or Rotary Club, then it's back to the regular job. If the skier is a member of the National Guard, as many of America's biathletes are, their unit could be called to serve in Bosnia or Afghanistan, and the Olympian will be activated right along with the rest of the unit.

I truly admire the talent, the athleticism, and especially the composure displayed by many figure skaters. I'm especially impressed by the strength and teamwork of the pairs skaters. But, since my first Winter Olympics at Sapporo in 1972, I've thought the judging in figure skating was fickle at best, and occasionally downright unfair.

I think Janet Lynn was robbed of the gold in Sapporo. In Calgary, sixteen years later, tiny Midori Ito from Japan stole the show, but according to the judges, wasn't worthy of a medal. Surya Bonaly of France was arguably the most athletic woman figure skater at Lillehammer, and the only one capable of an astounding back flip. She finished fourth.

Thanks to recent revelations that a Russian mobster influenced international skating judges in Salt Lake to assure Olympic victory for the Russian pairs and the French ice dancers, my suspicions have been confirmed. But there's nothing to worry about. Apparently, in figure skating, if there is impropriety by the judges, duplicate gold medals are awarded, and everyone goes home happy. Go figure.

Small Town Hoops, Basketball as It Was Meant to Be

My brother-in-law referees high school basketball games. He drives throughout Vermont most of the winter, usually after dark. He endures screaming fans, sweating athletes, and occasionally, abusive remarks about his judgment or his eyesight. He does it for the love of the game. Recently, he officiated a game near our home, so we went.

Having been forewarned that the rivalry between neighboring high schools would draw a crowd, we arrived early. The school has a small gymnasium, typical of many Vermont towns, so seating was limited. Even half-an-hour before the tip-off, we were lucky to find seats.

Promptly at 7:00 p.m., a member of the school's Athletic Booster Club reached for the microphone and began introducing the teams. There was polite applause for the visiting athletes, but wild yelling and stomping of boots for the home team. Then four local barber shop singers performed the national anthem as everyone stood facing the Stars and Stripes. It might be my imagination, but I've noticed a deeper respect for the flag since September 2001.

As the crowd reclaimed their seats, a deafening buzzer sounded and the two teams circled into huddles to get psyched up. There was pushing and shouting, high fives and tousling of heads. Anyone who worries that young men in our society are emotionally damaged by a lack of physical touching, hasn't seen a high school basketball game lately.

With the start of the game, I was immediately impressed by the speed and intensity of the players, as well as their consistent ability to hit long, three-point shots. Having seen several college games and one NBA battle recently, I had expected rural high school hoops to be clumsy and perhaps even boring. Boy, was I wrong.

And that wasn't all. I was afraid the high school coaches would be frustrated former athletes, living out their competitive fantasies through their players. But the only time a coach raised his voice in anger was when one of his own players performed a little victory dance following a dramatic dunk. It was great to see rival coaches shaking hands and congratulating opposing team's players after the final buzzer.

I was also concerned that the three officials would dominate the game. But I was proud of my brother-in-law. He and his two colleagues kept the game moving by letting the kids play.

My final concern was the crowd. I had been warned about poor sportsmanship by overzealous fans at high school athletic events. Happily, I was wrong again. There was lots of cheering and clapping for successful efforts, but no booing or shouts of "AIR BALL" when a shot went astray.

I can't say I've become a full-fledged basketball fan quite yet, but small town, high school hoops is certainly the purest form of the game. And for the admission price of three bucks, how can you go wrong!

A Different View of Teenagers

Lately, I've felt hopelessly out of touch with the younger generation. I can't relate to the blue spiked hair or the baggy pants that threaten to drop to the floor with every step. I can't stand rap music and I think video games are a total waste of time.

So, it came as a pleasant surprise when three recent interactions shattered my stereotype of teenagers. Last summer, I designed a cross-country trail for Hazen Union High School in Hardwick, Vermont. Laying out a new trail is the easy part; cutting the route through a dense forest is hard physical labor that seems to take forever. But in Hardwick, all the back-breaking work was done by thirteen boys and one girl in Hazen Union's Forestry and Natural Resource Program.

After training his students to work safely in the woods, instructor Marc Luneau issued the chainsaws and set his young lumberjacks loose. The students finished a 5-kilometer loop that was so popular with local skiers that an extension trail is already taking shape this summer. Some of these kids may wear baggy pants under their Kevlar chaps, but it doesn't slow them down in the woods.

Not far from Hardwick, at Lamoille Union High School in Hyde Park, Vermont, another trail is taking shape. Once the project got underway last summer, the contact person became a student who had created an independent study project focused on the trail. He tagged along as I designed the route, often helping me find boundary lines or significant terrain features. By using email, he contacted almost one hundred volunteers and organized them into work crews that cleared the first 2.5-kilometer loop by autumn. He even took his turn in the excavator, burying sumps and installing culverts. To cap it all off, he created a compact disc that documented the creation of the trail. This young Vermonter might have honed his computer skills playing Nintendo, but he couldn't have had much time for games during the past year.

Then, on the morning of May 7th, two strapping eighth-grade boys arrived in our yard, ready to get dirty as part of Operation Day's Work.

Students first select a developing country to study, then they contact community members willing to hire students for a day. All the proceeds are contributed to a worthy project in the selected country. Over the past four years, $140,000 has been raised for education programs in Haiti, San Salvador, Nepal and Ethiopia.

I may never appreciate the noise that throbbed from the boom box as the two Thetford students sweated in our front yard, but I certainly admire their hard work in support of educational projects in Bangladesh.

A Wonderful Winter

So, this neighbor of mine has an audience of about fifty people, and he's going on and on about what a horrible, dark winter it's been, bitterly cold for endless weeks, snow drifts over his head, and finally, how grateful he is that the endless month of February is mercifully behind us. By the time he finally sat down, I was about steamed up enough to reach over and pop him. That wouldn't have gone over too well, since he was speaking during the "joys and concerns" segment of our Sunday church service.

I've been equally frustrated with these slick TV meteorologists who try to convince us that every winter snowstorm is an impending national disaster. They don't just forecast the weather anymore, they suggest how much earlier we should leave for work in stormy weather, they explain how to drive on snowy roads, and they recommend what to wear to avoid frostbite.

I think this whole concept about "wind chill" is a marketing gimmick developed by the Weather Channel, which allows them to incorporate even more drama to the weather report. Be honest now, which makes you sit up and take notice: a temperature reading of 6° below zero, or a wind-chill factor of 42° below?

I've had it with all that negativity. From my perspective, this has been a wonderful winter. Much of New England got 2 feet of beautiful powder on Christmas Day, followed by a comparable blanket a week or so later. While the northern mountains received their customary allotment; these storms were special because they buried central New England, a region that has been starved for natural snow for more than a decade. Nordic skiers, snowshoers and snowmobilers took to the trails in record numbers.

Mother Nature even gave us a break on the traditional January Thaw. We did have a couple of days where the mercury rose above freezing, but it never threatened the snowpack, and we continued to enjoy excellent coverage well into March. I acknowledge what a heavy burden snow can be for some folks. I've spent a few anxious hours on our roof, shoveling snow and chopping away at ice dams. Although our two woodstoves are just backup for the oil furnace, I've split, stacked and hauled enough firewood this winter to develop a sincere respect for those rural families who depend on wood to heat their homes.

It strikes me like the death of a neighborhood friend when I see a once-proud barn collapsed under the weight of a blizzard. And I know it can be tough for wildlife during the dead of winter, although I've been assured by one of Vermont's wildlife biologists that the white-tail deer can manage just fine for up to eight weeks in severe cold and deep snow. But for me, the thrill of waking up to a thick blanket of powder covering the landscape far outweighs the challenges that come with one of those howling Nor'easters. I'm still deeply concerned about global warming, and I have a nagging fear that this might have been Mother Nature's swan song in terms of old-fashioned Vermont winters.

But in the meantime, I'm grateful for one of the most bountiful ski seasons in recent memory. Now if I could just convince those TV meteorologists to adjust their attitudes along these lines: "Tomorrow we will be enjoying some INVIGORATING temperatures thanks to a Canadian high-pressure system, and by the weekend we are expecting a WONDERFUL blizzard which could PROVIDE 18 inches of SPECTACULAR powder across central New England ... "

Taking a Stand on Guns

Recently, our family saw the film Bowling for Columbine. Michael Moore, the activist filmmaker who took on General Motors a few years ago, has turned his attention toward America's deadly fascination with firearms. I wasn't happy with some of the methods Moore used in his film, but I have to admit, he prompted me to reconsider my opinion of guns.

Like many boys growing up in the New England countryside, I learned to shoot as a kid. I had my own hunting rifle and shotgun before I had a driver's license. As a teenager, I hunted deer and partridge, spending many enjoyable autumn afternoons in the woods.

A four-year hitch in the army intensified my shooting experience. As a member of the U.S. Biathlon Team stationed at Fort Richardson, Alaska, it was not unusual for me to fire two hundred rounds a day in training, probably ten times the number of bullets a typical deer hunter shoots during an entire season.

When we weren't training or competing in biathlon races, we were capitalizing on Alaska's well-deserved reputation as a hunter's paradise. As the leaves began to turn in mid-August, we'd hunt moose or caribou, either of which could provide enough delicious, healthy meat for a year. Then we'd head out for several days chasing Dall sheep or mountain goats—often without much luck—across windswept ridges and rocky peaks. This was hunting for the pure joy of hunting.

Rounding out my firearms experience was a tour in Vietnam, where I carried an M-16 in the Mekong Delta. Ironically, I did less shooting during half a year in combat than I had in a typical day of biathlon training.

Returning to Vermont after the military, my attitude toward firearms began to change. In my opinion, rifles and shotguns are intended for hunting, and hunters have made important contributions toward the sustainability of our wildlife populations by funding important biological studies and conserving vital wildlife habitat.

On the other hand, pistols, even those intended for personal protection, and assault weapons are designed to kill people. When the Bill of Rights was ratified more than two hundred years ago, granting citizens, among other things, the right to "keep and bear arms," our fledgling nation had just broken free from one of the world's strongest colonial powers, and the unchartered wilderness to the west was a wild and dangerous place.

The threats confronting our country today are very different. A computer hacker determined to cripple our communications, a saboteur striking a weak link in our power grid, or a suicide bomber prepared to detonate himself in a crowded subway will not be deterred by an M-16 in every American closet, or a Smith & Wesson .38 under the driver's seat of every car. In today's world, firearms are no longer part of the solution. They are part of the problem.

Hiking at Dartmouth

Hiking is a favorite outdoor recreation for many Dartmouth undergrads and thousands of loyal Dartmouth alums. Dartmouth boasts the oldest collegiate outing club in the nation. For almost a century the Dartmouth Outing Club has maintained trails, built cabins, and encouraged undergraduates to explore the forests and mountain tops of the region.

Over the past few decades, most Dartmouth students began their college experience by participating in Freshman Trips, five-day wilderness adventures, almost entirely orchestrated by student members of the Dartmouth Outing Club. Incoming first-year students can choose between hiking, canoeing or bicycle trips, ranging from physically challenging to relatively humane. Groups of six to eight students, under the guidance of an experienced trip leader, are issued food and a map, then transported to their departure point.

Days later, the often bedraggled and usually hungry groups are rounded up and delivered to the Moosilauke Ravine Lodge, a magnificent log building constructed by Dartmouth students prior to World War II, at the of the base of the southernmost 4,000-foot summit in New Hampshire's White Mountains. At the Ravine Lodge, the outing club thoroughly indoctrinates the new students in Dartmouth tradition: songs and square dancing before a roaring fireplace, ghost stories after midnight, and breakfast the following morning of green eggs and ham, made famous by Dartmouth alum, Dr. Suess. It is no surprise that hiking remains a favorite recreation during many students' undergraduate years and for the rest of their lives.

Hiking also thrives at Dartmouth thanks to the school's location. The Appalachian Trail, that famous 2,150-mile path from Springer Mountain, Georgia, to the summit of Mount Katahdin in Maine, runs right through Hanover. In addition, Dartmouth students can, quite literally, step out of their dorms and within minutes be hiking one of many local trails to nearby hilltops with sweeping vistas of the Connecticut River Valley.

There are few colleges or universities in the nation that enjoy such a convenient location for the outdoor enthusiast.

Of course, college students are notoriously energetic and adventurous, which has resulted in some legendary hikes. The Dartmouth Ski Team traditionally culminates fall training with a time trial up Mount Moosilauke. From the Ravine Lodge, the Gorge Brook Trail climbs almost 2,400 vertical feet in about 3 miles, a route that the college's top Nordic skiers have accomplished in a few minutes over half an hour. Back in the early 1980s, after a summer of working on the lodge crew and training on Mount Moosilauke, former ski team captain Kirk Siegal established a record by racing from the lodge to the summit and back down in under an hour!

Another Nordic skier who spent a summer at Moosilauke was Andy Wells, from Bozeman, Montana. Not blessed with Kirk Siegal's speed, Andy set an impressive record of a different sort. The Dartmouth Outing Club maintains ten trails on and around Mount Moosilauke, totaling almost 30 miles. Starting and finishing at the Ravine Lodge, Andy covered all the trails on the mountain in under twenty-four hours. In addition to the obvious test of physical endurance, "The Moose," as Andy's accomplishment was called, required careful planning and a sophisticated strategy.

Through the years, many Dartmouth Outing Club alums have gone on to significant achievements in hiking and climbing. Former ski team members have climbed Alaska's Mount McKinley and hiked the Appalachian Trail, end to end. Former Dartmouth skier Ned Gillette made a career out of trekking and skiing some of the most desolate places on earth.

But perhaps the golden age of Dartmouth hiking occurred during the 1920s, inspired by the wiry and tenacious Sherman Adams, who years later would serve as President Eisenhower's Chief of Staff. Adams and his classmate, William Fowler, were responsible for an informal competition to determine which Dartmouth man could walk the farthest in a day. After failing in an attempt during the spring of 1919 to reach Springfield, Massachusetts, 75 miles from Hanover, Adams decided to train for a record-breaking attempt. In May, 1920, he and Fowler set out from the Skyline Cabin, 3 miles north of Littleton, New Hampshire. Hiking on trails and back roads, they reached Hanover, a distance of 83 miles, in 23 hours, 47 minutes! Hiking at Dartmouth certainly does have a long and impressive history.

A New Year's Resolution

I am making a New Year's resolution inspired by two popular slogans: "You don't know what you've got until you lose it," and "Don't kill the goose that laid the golden egg." For the past couple of decades, our little town of Thetford has benefited from the boundless energy and intense civic commitment of Dan Grossman. Through the years, Dan and his wife Dana have served our community in a variety of positions, including members of the school board, members of Thetford Academy's board of trustees and moderator of town meetings. But many consider Dan's greatest contribution the 5-kilometer trail that winds through the woods behind Thetford Academy, and the dozens of major cross-country running events that he has organized on that trail over the past thirteen years.

In 1990, Dan learned that the New England High School Cross-Country Running Championship annually rotates between the participating New England states, with Vermont scheduled to host in 1992. Within a few weeks, Dan had won the bid to conduct the '92 meet at Thetford Academy, had generated community support for the creation of a new trail suitable for the Championship event, and had started recruiting community members willing to volunteer on race day.

Thanks to Dan's persistence and vision, the new 5-kilometer course was completed in '91 and an invitational meet was scheduled to provide high school runners the opportunity to test the course before the '92 New Englands. This also gave Dan's volunteers a dress rehearsal before the big event. That first Woods Trail Run drew 275 athletes. The following year, a few weeks prior to the New England Championship, the Woods Trail Run swelled to 700 competitors. In spite of some anxiety among the volunteers (those working the finish line for example, often faced more than 100 exhausted runners each minute), that '92 New England Championship was a resounding success.

The annual Woods Trail Run has now grown to accommodate more than 2,000 high school runners, who travel to Thetford from as far away as New Jersey, Maryland and Pennsylvania. Participants frequently comment on the enthusiasm of the crowd, the scenic beauty of the site and the challenge of the course. Coaches rave about the race organization and Dan's amazing attention to detail. But the future of these wonderful events is uncertain. Following the Vermont State meet a few weeks ago, Dan announced he will no longer be directing running events at Thetford Academy. Considering the time, energy and personal finances he has invested during the past decade, he has ample justification for stepping down. But the actual reasons behind his retirement should be a lesson for all of us who benefit from the generosity and hard work of others.

Although Dan willingly invested about 1,000 hours of his own time every autumn, many of the volunteers he counted on to set up, conduct, and clean up after the events had become cavalier about last-minute conflicts, forcing Dan to scramble to fill the vacancies. A second headache, ironically, was Thetford Academy, the school that has gained so much positive recognition from Dan's efforts. Rather than celebrating the success of the running events, feedback following the races often focused on mud tracked into the gymnasium by spectators or divots left by runners on the soccer field.

Perhaps the straw that broke the camel's back was supplied by the Vermont Principal's Association, which oversees state championship athletic competitions. Along with amenities like inspiring music broadcast during the races, hot soup and sandwiches for his army of volunteers, and results available on the internet even before the competitors arrived home, Dan also established a tradition of extremely popular commemorative T-shirts. These shirts became a successful source of funding, most of which Dan poured back into trail maintenance and equipment needed to support the events, such as a powerful public address system. At last November's state meet it was announced that T-shirts at future championships would be sold by the Principal's Association.

Historically, the Principal's Association provided awards for the top ten finishers in several categories at the State Meet. When Dan was supplied with awards for only the top five competitors, he phoned the Association's office and was told the decision had been made to reduce the number of prizes: With hundreds of high school runners from across the state expecting prizes to tenth place, Dan provided the missing awards, but mentioned the decision by the Principal's Association to restrict the number of awards in the future. Within days, an article appeared in the Burlington Free Press claiming a misunderstanding, that the principals had never intended to change the number of awards presented.

So, one of my New Year's resolutions is to be lavish with my praise of those I see donating their time and effort to benefit our communities. I hope the big cross-country races at Thetford Academy continue, but they won't be the same without Dan Grossman. On the positive side, he certainly set the standard for how these events should be conducted.

Does Pete Rose Deserve to Be in Cooperstown?

I'm not much of a baseball fan, but the recent controversy surrounding Pete Rose's new book My Prison Without Bars emphasizes a complex ethical issue in sport. As a Major League player, Rose earned the admiration of fans and teammates through his fierce determination and legendary competitive zeal. Although gifted with neither size nor speed, he remains baseball's all-time hits leader.

Sadly, Rose's accomplishments on the field have been overshadowed by his compulsive gambling. Many celebrity athletes have difficulty adjusting to fame and fortune, too often resulting in broken marriages, addictions to alcohol or drugs, and financial ruin. Pete Rose's unforgivable transgression was the implication that he bet on Cincinnati Reds games while serving as the team's manager in 1987, an accusation that he vehemently denied for thirteen years, but finally acknowledged in his book.

Why the confession now, after thirteen years of denial? Because time is running out for Rose to be reinstated, and thus eligible for baseball's Hall of Fame, a recognition he desperately seeks. Pete Rose's predicament highlights an intriguing question. Have we become so enamored with athletic talent that we willingly ignore serious character flaws in our sport heroes?

Rose was undeniably one of the greatest players in baseball, but he also broke one of the game's most sacred rules, then he lied about it for more than a decade. Should we forgive his human failings now that he has finally confessed, and celebrate his athletic accomplishments by enshrining him in the Hall of Fame? I don't think so.

Since our earliest memories of childhood games, we are told by our parents and coaches that participation in sport builds character, teaches teamwork and instills discipline. Sports provide a microcosm of life, the opportunity to learn and grow by experiencing "the thrill of victory and the agony of defeat" in a safe environment.

But our devotion to sport is based upon the assumption of fair play. We are outraged when we discover that the starting pitcher of the Little League World Series is actually a couple of years older than the other kids on the field, or that Johann Muehlegg, the skier who dominated the Olympic cross-country events in the 2002 Salt Lake Games, owed his success to performance-enhancing drugs.

Perhaps Rose's situation is slightly different, since there is no evidence that he actually influenced the outcome of any ball games on which he had placed bets, but the central issue is still integrity and character. In my view, our sports heroes should be recognized for more than a specific athletic talent.

Those truly worthy of the Hall of Fame inspire us with their dedication, their concern for their teammates and perhaps above all, their sense of fair play. They are worthy because of not only how they play the game, but how they live their lives.

Sorry, Pete, you don't make the cut.

A Trip to the Sea, on the Clock

This story actually begins three years before the start of the American Revolution. In the spring of 1772, John Ledyard, a freshman at Dartmouth College in Hanover, New Hampshire, had endured all he could of classrooms and lecture halls. On the bank of the Connecticut River, he felled a giant pine, from which he made a canoe, then escaped downstream to Hartford, Connecticut. Thus began his impressive career of global exploration. He was an associate of John Paul Jones and he also served as an officer under Captain Cook. He sailed the world's oceans and explored remote lands. He foresaw the wealth of America's Pacific Coast and anticipated the future significance of trade with the Far East. All this before his untimely death at age thirty-seven, while in Cairo, preparing to cross Africa.

Although students at Dartmouth continued to explore the rivers and mountains surrounding their campus, it was more than a century later that Fred Harris generated the enthusiasm for a winter carnival, and founded the organization to host it. In December, 1909 the Dartmouth Outing Club was established, the first of its kind in the nation. The spring of 1920 marked the birth of the Ledyard Canoe Club, and almost immediately thirteen men in five canoes reenacted John Ledyard's down-river adventure, this time paddling past Hartford, all the way to Long Island Sound, 210 miles from Hanover. The Trip to the Sea became an annual rite of passage for devoted Outing Club members during the spring of their senior year. But even in its infancy, the Trip wasn't a leisurely float down the river. Since excused absences from classes and church were limited, participants paddled through the night to complete the trip in four days.

A 1959 article in Life magazine recounting that year's Dartmouth trip caught the attention of some rival paddlers at Amherst College, who issued a challenge. In response, the Ledyard Canoe Club organized a race in the spring of 1960, which drew twenty-two boats from several colleges and universities along the river. With the winter runoff especially high and the competitive juices flowing, Dartmouth sophomores Peter Knight and Jonathan Fairbank paddled non-stop to reach Old Saybrook in 33 hours and 50 minutes, a record that has endured for nearly half a century.

Two factors have helped to preserve that record. Since many of the twenty-two boats in that 1960 challenge swamped or became entangled in snags along the route, Dartmouth's administration prohibited future competitions. In addition, recent revisions have made the portages around some of the falls and power stations longer and more difficult than they were forty-four years ago.

But that did not deter four Dartmouth Nordic skiers, who on the cold, overcast morning of April 3, 2004, slid a couple of sleek racing canoes into the muddy Connecticut from the Ledyard dock in Hanover. Eben Sargent of Barton, Vermont, Andy Hunter from Readfield, Maine, Brad Martin from Oakland, Maine, and Tucker Murphy who lives in Bermuda, were in peak physical condition, following an arduous winter of Nordic racing. Brad and Eben were experienced paddlers, having completed impressive expeditions in Northern Canada, while Tucker had rowed crew, and therefore was accustomed to tippy boats. A day prior to their departure, the skiers had hidden peanut butter and jelly sandwiches, cheese and water at each of the six portages along their route.

Their launch was smooth and devoid of fanfare. Moments later, they jogged the canoes around the first portage at the Wilder Dam. Thick brush, chunks of ice and a menacing brown chop in the outflow below the dam made launching tense, but soon the two delicate racing canoes and their paddlers were swept out of sight down the river. Word of their fate came the following day. They had reached the Vernon Dam at dusk, 80 miles from Hanover in record-breaking time, after eleven hours of smooth paddling. In the gathering darkness, one boat swamped in the turbulence below the dam, then the second boat flipped attempting to aid the first. Wearing life jackets, the paddlers were never in danger, but recovering their boats and gear from the torrent consumed enough time to put the record out of reach.

Although three of the four athletes were graduating the following spring, they hinted that a future attempt at the record was probable. Among other things, they learned that a powerful spring runoff is more essential to a record breaking expedition than a super light racing canoe.

In an age when too many young people are finding their excitement playing video games, and too many outdoor recreation programs are paranoid about risk management, I salute these four Dartmouth students and their effort to keep John Ledyard's spirit alive.

I Want to Believe in Lance

On July 19th, with less than a week remaining in the 2004 edition of the Tour de France, Lance Armstrong was on track to win for an unprecedented sixth time. To most sports fans, the Tour represents the ultimate test of athletic endurance. Of course, ironman triathlon events require incredible stamina, and Alaska's Iditarod sled dog race pits mushers and their teams against some of the toughest terrain and weather on the planet. But few annual competitions can compare with the physical demands of the three-week bicycle race around France each July.

Perhaps that is why for decades the Tour has been plagued by rumors of performance enhancing drugs. Recently, the French authorities decided the doping had become intolerable, so they began cracking down. Prominent teams and famous cyclists were caught red-handed and forced to withdraw. Through it all, Lance Armstrong, the cocky Texan, and his team of international riders, sponsored by the U.S. Postal Service, continued to dominate the Tour. This must be especially grating for the French, considering their national pride and the recent political rift between our countries regarding the war in Iraq.

Quite simply, the French press and their knowledgeable cycling fans have difficulty believing that Lance Armstrong can so dominate their event without the aid of performance-enhancing drugs. His invincibility is even more phenomenal considering that less than a decade ago, he was fighting for his life against cancer. Struggling back from the ravages of the disease and the chemotherapy treatments, Armstrong seemed more determined and motivated than ever before. Armstrong admits in his book, It's Not About the Bike, that even though he is regarded as one of the toughest trainers on the Tour, nothing he has ever done was as grueling as recovering his strength following chemotherapy.

So, I desperately want to believe Lance is clean. America could use an honest to goodness, old fashioned hero right now. Although Greg LeMond opened the door by winning three Tours back in the '80s,

Americans have never dominated cycling, and there is tremendous satisfaction in beating someone at their game.

But I must admit to some nagging doubts. For starters, the Tour has been plagued by rumors of doping for so long, it's illogical to believe that one rider could be so dominant without the use of drugs, and an American at that.

Then there is the recently published book, L.A. Confidential: Lance Armstrong's Secrets, by cycling journalist David Walsh and freelance writer Pierre Ballester, in which Emma O'Reilly, Armstrong's former masseuse, suggests he used EPO prior to the '99 Tour.

And it certainly doesn't help Armstrong's credibility that his longtime training advisor, Italian physician Michele Ferrari, is under investigation for advising pro cyclist Filippo Simeoni and other athletes in the use of blood booster, EPO, according to a recent article in USA Today.

Although it was subtle and easily overlooked, Armstrong's response to a press conference question following one of his previous Tour victories was unsettling. When asked directly whether he or any of his Postal Service team used performance drugs, Armstrong answered, "We have done nothing illegal." That response speaks volumes, since unethical athletes, coaches and team doctors are constantly developing innovative, new methods of boosting performance that are not yet specifically banned.

I sincerely hope that Lance Armstrong is racing drug-free. If reputable evidence surfaces that in earlier Tours, Armstrong used EPO or something similar, I'd like to believe it was related to his cancer treatment rather than performance enhancement. Even if Armstrong is beating the Europeans at their own game, both on his bike and at the pharmacy, six consecutive Tour de France victories is an incredible accomplishment. It's just that the victories would be even more sweet if he is winning drug-free.

Two Perspectives on Foot Races

On Sunday, May 30th, my wife, Kay, and I were in Burlington for the Vermont City Marathon. Kay anchored a women's relay team, while I enjoyed the first 23 miles of the marathon, then staggered through the final 3. A week later, we were in Quechee, Vermont, to support friends who were competing in the Covered Bridges Half Marathon. Attending two of Vermont's premier running events, the first as participants, the second as spectators, gave us an interesting insight into how different these races appear from the "back in the pack" or on the sidelines.

Even as a seasoned competitor, with more than fifty marathons under my belt, I usually feel intimidated lining up for the start. I glance around at hundreds of eager runners filling the street: fit, well-trained athletes who exude confidence. I subtly scan the crowd for the typical weather-beaten faces and gray hair of my age group. This is depressing, since all the prime candidates are lean, muscular and determined.

Then the gun goes off and the sea of runners surges forward. The first couple of miles are consumed by searching for "running room." In the crush of competitors, it's not easy to see obstacles ahead, like storm drains or parked cars.

Since the Vermont City Marathon begins early on Sunday morning, many Burlington residents view the action from the comfort of their front porches, in some cases still sporting their bathrobes and cradling their first cup of coffee. The spectators on Church Street and in Battery Park are more vocal, enthusiastically cheering all the runners but saving extra volume for individuals whom they recognize.

Participants in the race also experience a broad spectrum of smells. At the starting line the air is thick with muscle liniments like Bengay and Atomic Balm, as well as sunscreens and tanning lotions. In downtown Burlington the restaurants have begun preparations for a busy lunch, while later, in the residential neighborhoods, hamburgers and hot dogs sizzle on barbecue grills. And depending upon the wind, runners will be treated to either a fresh breeze off the lake or a whiff of the wastewater treatment facility.

Frequently, in long races, participants will settle into a pace next to a runner they've never met. Often the shared effort generates mutual support and lasting friendships. An encouraging word or a positive observation from a fellow runner can restore motivation and dispel discouragement.

On the other hand, some coincidental running partners can become irritating. One of my training buddies recounts a race in which a competitor he refers to as "Talkative Guy" tagged along and babbled incessantly, nearly driving my buddy crazy.

Years ago, in one of my first Boston Marathons, I found myself running stride for stride with a young guy wearing a T-shirt that read:

I'M RICH

I'M AVAILABLE

(617) 234-6789

At first, I smiled at the fellow's ingenuity, but after several miles of the crowd screaming in my ear, "Hey look, he's rich and available," I forced myself to pick up the pace, just to get away from the guy.

Of course, as a spectator on the sidelines, it's an entirely different picture. Watching the final stretch of the recent Covered Bridges Half Marathon, Kay and I were struck by what an eclectic sport running has become. Participants of all ages and all shapes trotted past, drawn to the finish line.

It's a mistake to assume that all distance runners are the lean, sinewy gazelles we occasionally see on television leading the Boston Marathon or in the Olympics. Kay and I watched runners of all sizes and physiques. Some had an obvious aptitude for running, but others looked more like football players or boxers. And a surprising number, especially considering they were in a 13-mile race, didn't look athletic at all.

There was also an amazing variety of styles, from the flamboyant, bouncy gait of an athletic young woman, to the economical, efficient shuffle of an elderly man. And from the sidelines, very few participants appeared to be really suffering, which was reassuring considering the way I felt during the final miles a week earlier.

Finally, we were impressed by the dedication and energy displayed by many of the spectators, cheering all the runners, not just for a few minutes, but for hours.

Like most running enthusiasts, I'm more of a participant than a spectator, but the opportunity to watch the recent Covered Bridges Half Marathon gave me a new and encouraging perspective on the sport.

In Praise of Summer Camp

Several years ago, I sat nervously in a plush office overlooking Portland Harbor in Maine. I was there with two friends, seeking funding from a charitable foundation to reestablish Nordic skiing in northern Aroostook County. In an effort to put us at ease, the president of the foundation mentioned that the previous day Maine's best-known author, Stephen King, was seated at the same conference table, also seeking funding. King believes that the opportunity to attend summer camp during his troubled childhood in Lewiston, changed the course of his life.

The author's request to the foundation was to match his own financial commitment in forming a scholarship fund that would make it possible for disadvantaged children in Maine to experience summer camp. The previous year almost 4,000 kids received $1,000 each to attend the summer camp of their choice. It is impossible to quantify the social and emotional benefits this program bestows upon its participants, but everyone agrees, it's an overwhelming success.

In recent years, a handful of visionary Dartmouth College students established an innovative mentoring program for children living in a nearby, low-income housing development. The college students provide the disadvantaged children with educational and recreational opportunities that otherwise might not be available, in addition to serving as role models.

The unqualified success of the original partnership quickly led to similar programs at St. Michael's, UVM, Norwich University and Castleton State. The award-winning organization is now recognized statewide as The DREAM Program, Direction through Recreation, Education, Adventure, and Mentoring.

Although the program thrived during the academic year, it soon became apparent that the summertime, when the children were out of school and most of the college students were off campus, posed additional challenges. The solution was a summer camp, and after a year of searching, the DREAM program purchased 50 wooded acres on beautiful Metcalf Pond, in Fletcher, Vermont.

With the youthful optimism that has been the cornerstone of the entire DREAM program, groups of disadvantaged children and their mentors camped at Metcalf Pond and explored the surrounding woods that first summer, even before any permanent buildings were constructed. The vision, energy and dedication of a small group of college students is having a profound impact on the lives of some of Vermont's neediest children.

At a time when our popular culture seems to be dominated by unfettered consumerism, hedonism, and the avoidance of physical exertion, one Vermont summer camp holds firm to traditions more than a century old. Camp Keewaydin and its sister camp, Songadeewin, both on Lake Dunmore, teach youngsters the skills needed to enjoy extended wilderness hiking, canoeing and camping trips.

Affiliated camps on Lake Temagami in the heart of central Ontario's vast labyrinth of lakes and rivers, serve as a base for impressive, extended canoe expeditions. Young campers learn to work together while negotiating a whitewater rapid, to pull their own weight during strenuous portages, and to endure clouds of mosquitoes without complaint. The culmination for many experienced campers is a seven-week excursion, often by original routes, to Hudson Bay. It is not an exaggeration to say that for the past century, Keewaydin's paddler's have departed on their adventure as boys, and returned from the Bay as men. And not too long ago, six young women from Songadeewin, accompanied by an experienced staff member and a guide, inaugurated what might well be a century of women paddling to Hudson Bay.

These camps instill the traditional values of living simply with minimal environmental impact, providing rustic challenges in beautiful, natural settings, and nurturing within their campers a character that will last a lifetime. America's summer camps are national treasures, and the dedicated people who direct, staff and support them are our unsung heroes.

The Sad State of Sports, 2005

I try to be the kind of person who sees "the glass as half full." As a former coach, I know the value of a positive attitude, and I try to find the opportunity for growth or improvement from even the most discouraging situation. But it seems to me that the world of sports has provided us with some pretty troubling images lately.

I grew up playing pickup pond hockey. I vividly remember Sunday afternoon games on a local frog pond, which began after lunch and ended only when it became too dark to see the puck. In those marathon contests, skaters of all ages and abilities were welcome, and nobody bothered keeping score.

More recently, as a member of several Olympic biathlon teams, I enjoyed the privilege of seeing firsthand some of the best ice hockey ever played, including the unforgettable, "Miracle on Ice" at the 1980 Lake Placid Winter Games.

But the pleasure I derived from watching ice hockey waned as the level of violence seemed to escalate. As more NHL players skated for their nations in the Olympics, the crisp passing and impressive teamwork gave way to physical intimidation on the ice, and brutish behavior off the ice.

Now the NHL players and owners are deadlocked in a contract dispute that threatens the entire season. I can't pretend to understand the intricacies of all the issues, but I'll bet that greed plays a major role on both sides. Considering what they have done to the game in recent years, the NHL owners and players might be distressed to learn that many of their former fans are getting along just fine without an NHL season.

Things aren't much better in the NBA. After months of titillating speculation regarding the fate of the Los Angeles Lakers' star Kobe Bryant, who faced charges of rape in Colorado, a brawl broke out at a recent game between the Detroit Pistons and the Indiana Pacers that horrified even veteran basketball fans. What began as a shoving contest between Ben Wallace of the Pistons and Indiana's Ron Artest quickly expanded to the stands when a Detroit fan doused Artest with a cup full of beer, and Artest stormed into the bleachers, swinging. Other players joined the melee while fans poured onto the court. For ten minutes the brawl continued, resulting in nine people requiring medical attention, five of whom were taken to the hospital.

So much for all the character virtues we attribute to participation in sports: discipline, self-control, teamwork, fair play, etc. Perhaps the most revealing insight from the recent NBA debacle is that Artest, who presumably had the most egregious loss of self-control, will be suspended for the remainder of the NBA season, forfeiting $5 million of his $6.2 million annual salary! I can't help thinking that there is something desperately wrong with the priorities of our culture when high school teachers struggle to support their families, while we pay a short-fused basketball player over $6 million a year.

But it's unfair to lay all the blame on overpaid professional athletes. The NBA brawl probably would have remained a pushing contest between players on the court were it not for mean-spirited, confrontational spectators. Somehow, sports fans in America have come to believe it's their right to heckle and verbally abuse players and officials.

Earlier this fall, Texas Rangers relief pitcher Frank Francisco was charged with felony assault after throwing a chair at a heckler during a game in Oakland. It later came out that the abusive Oakland fan and his wife (who was hit by the chair), specifically picked their season ticket seats near the visiting team's bullpen, a location ideal for heckling, which he described as, "an American tradition." The line seems to have blurred between freedom of speech and sportsmanship.

But all of the self-centered greed and juvenile behavior associated with professional sports pales next to the horrifying confrontation of deer hunters in Wisconsin. Allegedly, Chai Vang, a Hmong immigrant from St. Paul, Minnesota, was observed occupying a tree stand on private property. According to local hunters, when Vang was asked to leave, he opened fire, killing six, including a father and son. After his arrest, Vang claimed the white hunters fired first, after taunting him with racial slurs.

Whatever the actual scenario, six people are dead and the sport of deer hunting will operate under an ominous cloud for years to come.

In the interest of seeing the glass half full, I shouldn't forget the Red Sox's phenomenal pennant and World Series performances, the Patriots' record-breaking, twenty-one-game winning streak, or Bodie Miller's early season World Cup victories. But for a while this fall, it's been tough to overlook the sad state to which some sports have fallen.

New Year's Resolutions—Goal Setting

I've never taken New Year's resolutions too seriously. Often, it seems to me, folks make resolutions that are unrealistic or impossible to evaluate and, almost inevitably, a few days or weeks into the new year, the old habits reemerge.

Actually, athletes and coaches are very experienced at making and keeping resolutions, only they think of it as setting goals. Everyone, from Little Leaguers to Olympic champions, has set goals and strived to achieve them. But successful goal setting is more complicated that it might first appear. To begin with, a worthy goal must be a reach. If the objective is easily accomplished, it is probably not a worthy goal. On the other hand, there must be a reasonable chance of achieving the objective. A target that is too lofty might actually create a sense of discouragement rather than inspiration toward reaching the target.

One solution to this dilemma is to establish multiple goals: perhaps short-term, intermediate, and career or lifetime goals. A worthy short-term goal might be to get some quality exercise at least five days each week. This would support an intermediate goal of finishing in the top 25 percent of your age group in a local road race, while your lifetime goal might be simply to maintain your body weight, cholesterol and blood pressure at healthy levels.

One helpful tip for establishing goals is to avoid the temptation of linking your objective to someone else's performance. For those of us who routinely compete in sporting events, it doesn't take long to recognize the "hotshot" in your age group, who typically takes home the hardware. It's very tempting to succumb to the temptation of thinking, "If I could just beat 'ol What's His Name, I know I'd be doing well." A better approach would be to figure out how fast a pace it would take, on a typical day, to finish ahead of the hotshot, and build your goal around achieving that pace.

One of the things experienced athletes learn to recognize is that life frequently interferes with training plans. Sickness, family obligations and the unpredictable nature of the weather often throw a monkey wrench into the best made plans. It is important to remember that you established your goals as guideposts for your journey toward health or athletic success, and if necessary, you can adjust them.

Sixteen years ago, after a decade of coaching the men's Nordic skiers at Dartmouth, I wrote a book that illuminated the five areas that I felt a promising athlete must address to reach full potential. Since then, I have been gratified by the feedback the book generated, not only from skiers but from coaches of other sports and even from non-athletes.

The first requirement of Nordic skiers is physical fitness. To excel at cross-country skiing or biathlon, you must be in shape. Physical conditioning is a science in its own right, but in simple terms a successful athlete must have a balance of explosive, muscular power and aerobic endurance.

Nearly as important as conditioning is skiing technique, the ability to use that power effectively to move over the snow toward the finish line. This category was complicated back in the 1980s by the addition of the skating technique to the sport of cross country.

Since Nordic skiing has long been recognized internationally as the most demanding of endurance sports (as evidenced by the consistently top oxygen uptake testing scores by skiers), it follows that the fuel used to generate all that energy output might be important. Through the years nutrition has gained more and more significance in the development of top athletes and the achievement of championship performances.

Equipment and waxing are important components to success in skiing. During recent decades, technological advances in ski construction, base structuring, and waxing breakthroughs have created significant performance improvements.

Finally, there is the area of sports psychology or mental preparation. In my estimation, this is the area about which the least is known, yet it holds the secrets to the most outstanding improvements. Regardless of the sport, if we think back to truly remarkable performances like Joan Benoit's 1984 Olympic Marathon victory, Bill Koch's 1976 silver medal, or the 1980 U.S. Hockey Team's "Miracle on Ice," the deciding factor is rarely better conditioning, technique, equipment or food, but instead some inner fire, a mental desire that overpowered self-doubt, and allowed the athletes to perform their best.

Now, back to those New Year's resolutions: no more desserts, less TV and more exercise…

Terry Aldrich Retires from Ski Coaching

It seems that I've been engaged in friendly competition with Terry Aldrich my whole life. It all began in high school, when I was forced into Nordic ski racing when a teammate was injured, and I filled his slot to salvage the team score. By senior year, I was doing well enough in cross-country skiing to risk a trip to Old Forge, New York, and the Junior National tryouts. There seemed to be thousands of enthusiastic spectators at that race, and they were all screaming for their hometown favorite, Terry Aldrich, who cleaned my clock!

During our college years, we raced against each other every weekend for four winters. I occasionally finished ahead of him in cross-country only because Saint Lawrence needed him in all four events. I got exhausted just watching Aldrich changing clothes and ski boots all weekend.

After college a fortunate few of us collegiate skiers went off to Alaska and the Biathlon Training Center, just outside of Anchorage. There, the competition between Aldrich and me intensified. We compared ski times and shooting scores. We kept a careful tally of kilometers on snow from the start of skiing in October. Every workout became a race, and weekly time trials were like the Olympics.

In our precious off-duty hours, we played fiercely in an Anchorage soccer league. And of course, at every opportunity we took advantage of Alaska's world-famous fishing and hunting. It was not just about who bagged a moose, but how many shots it took to drop the animal, how many trips it took to hike out the meat, and how many pounds of steaks, roasts, burger and sausage was put in the freezer. In those days, the Elmendorf Air Force Base Officer's Club had a monthly, all-you-can-eat Alaskan Buffet, complete with king crab, smoked salmon, and caribou steaks. We used to fast for a couple of days prior to the buffet just to be able to compete well against our teammates.

The one time I remember getting the upper hand on Aldrich was actually an accident. During a long, hot, summer road race in Fairbanks,

I asked my wife, Mimi, to stand a couple of miles prior to the finish with a drink. Today, we have scientifically engineered competition drinks with precisely the correct balance of electrolyte replacement, glucose, and fluid. But years ago, I concocted a thick combination of Tang, tea, and honey.

I was running pretty well, in spite of the unseasonable Fairbanks heat, but Terry was steadily gaining on me. As I approached Mimi, who waited with the critical feed, I struggled with an ethical decision. If 1 shared the mixture with Aldrich, he almost certainly would overtake me, and probably beat me to the finish line. If I grabbed all the juice and threw away what I didn't drink, Terry might fade in the final miles.

Friendship won out. "Give the rest to Terry," I shouted as I grabbed the thick mixture that Mimi held out for me. She quickly poured a second cup of my secret formula and held it out as Terry approached. Worn down by the heat and thinking it was water, Terry shouted, "In my face, throw it in my face." With no time for explanations, Mimi shrugged, and tossed the mixture into Aldrich's face as he ran past.

Moments later, as I waited in the recovery area, I couldn't understand why Terry hadn't blasted past me in the final mile. Then he staggered through the finish line, his hair plastered to his forehead, squinting through eyelids glued together with honey.

Of course, he got me back. Many years later, we were still competing, he as Middlebury College ski coach, I as the Dartmouth ski coach. Loading the vans at the Mt. Van Hoevenberg Nordic Center in Lake Placid after an exhausting weekend, we simply exchanged glances. Fortunately, I got the skis tied down and my athletes loaded in time to be first out of the parking lot.

By using all the short cuts I knew, we were still in the lead at Port Henry, but on the straight stretch before the Crown Point bridge, I saw headlights gaining on us fast. The Middlebury van roared past just before the toll booth. When I rolled down my window, the attendant announced,

''Your assistant coach said you'd be paying for both vans.'' My Dartmouth skiers never let me live that one down.

Now that Terry is retiring after three decades of college coaching, he's apt to have more time for friendly competition. I'm not sure I'm looking forward to that.

Too Many Guns

Like everyone else, I was horrified by the shooting rampage that took place on the campus of Virginia Tech University on April 16, 2007. How could Cho Seung-Hui have become so alienated and so full of hate that his only recourse was to kill thirty-two fellow students and instructors before turning the gun on himself? It inevitably brought back images of the twelve students and one teacher at Columbine High School who were gunned down by their classmates, Eric Harris and Dylan Klebold, in 1999.

These tragedies strike a slightly different chord with me because for many years, firearms were a central part of my life. As an infantry officer in Vietnam for nearly a year, I was rarely more than arm's length from my M-16. The army also gave me the opportunity to compete in the sport of winter biathlon, which combines cross-country skiing and rifle marksmanship. As a result, almost every day for the best part of a decade, I could be found caressing the trigger of a custom-made, .233 caliber, Model 700 Remington rifle. We shot so much (200 rounds a day was not uncommon), we kept log books of our workouts, including a running total of shots through the barrel. This was important since it was actually possible to wear out a barrel, which drastically reduced the rifle's accuracy. The barrel of my biathlon rifle had to be replaced sometime after 20,000 rounds.

I also had the army to thank for introducing me to Alaska. The Biathlon Training Center was located at Fort Richardson, just outside of Anchorage. For those of us who relished the outdoors, and especially winter, an assignment to Alaska was nearly paradise. We typically got on snow in October and were still skiing dry powder in April. And that was what we did for work! In our spare time we had unfettered access to world's best hunting and fishing. It was easy to keep the freezer stocked with salmon and rainbow trout, and every autumn, I eagerly anticipated hunting season.

Moose hunting was very rewarding, but hard work. If you were skillful and lucky enough to be able to drop an animal within a mile or so from your truck, you had a relatively easy hike. Several of mine were much longer. One year we put 589 pounds of moose meat in the freezer. You can calculate how many 100-pound loads through the muskeg and alders it took to get that animal to the truck. I can still feel the straps of the pack frame digging into my shoulders.

In contrast, Dall sheep hunting was almost pure joy. These magnificent animals inhabit the rocky crags high above the tree line in Alaska's formidable mountains. With their incredible agility in terrifying terrain combined with phenomenal eyesight, which allows them to spot an intruder more than a mile away, Dall rams are among the most prized hunting trophies in the world. Only the rams with the biggest horns (at least five-eighths of a curl) are legal to shoot, the same animals that have passed their reproductive prime and are facing imminent starvation, having worn down their teeth. For more than a decade, I anticipated sheep hunting all year long.

This background information is to establish the fact that I am experienced with firearms and that for many years rifles played an important role in my life. But I have become increasingly troubled by what seems to be a dramatic increase in gun-related violence. I recognize this is a complex issue and that there are no easy solutions, but some aspects of the problem seem to require little more than common sense.

I admire the dedication and skill of competitive shooters. The men, and very often women, who excel at target shooting are fanatic about safety, and frequently donate their time and energy to programs that instill the principles of safe marksmanship in young athletes.

I also have a high regard for hunters, especially those who cherish the experience of the hunt over the fleeting glory of simply bagging a trophy animal. It is the license fees of sport hunters that underwrite the Departments of Fish and Game in many states across the country. And organizations like Ducks Unlimited have raised millions of dollars through the years to buy and preserve critical waterfowl habitat that otherwise might have been lost forever to industrial or residential development.

But marksmen and hunters have little use for assault rifles or semiautomatic pistols like the 9mm Glock 19 that Cho Seung-Hui used at Virginia Tech. These weapons were originally designed, and refined through the years, for one purpose: to kill people. Although Amendment II in our Bill of Rights ensures our freedom "to keep and bear arms," I don't think our Founding Fathers envisioned an M-16 in everyone's closet and a 9mm Glock under every car seat.

According to Newsweek magazine, Americans own 270 million firearms, far more per capita than anywhere else on earth. As the world's leader in firearms exports, the U.S. earns more than double that of Italy, the runner up in global gun sales. Perhaps the tragedies at Virginia Tech, Columbine, Red Lake, Minnesota, and Springfield, Oregon, are an illustration of the old adage, "you reap what you sow."

Tough Decisions

A family friend's recent wedding in Anchorage provided a welcome opportunity to return to Alaska. In many ways, Vermont and Alaska are quite similar. Both states are noted for their scenic beauty, which has stimulated a significant tourist industry. Vermont and Alaska share well-deserved recognition as year-round outdoor recreational playgrounds. Hunting and fishing are extremely popular in both states. Although separated by most of the continent, Alaska and Vermont endure relatively harsh climates, and take pride in a reputation for fiercely independent residents.

One notable difference, however, is that Vermont seems older, more grounded in tradition, while Alaska feels younger, wilder, and perhaps, in a way, more reckless. Two centuries ago, as our country expanded westward, little thought was given to protecting the abundant natural resources those first European settlers encountered. The fertile plains were plowed and planted with crops, pristine streams were dammed to generate power for mills, and vast herds of buffalo were decimated, almost to extinction.

More recently, the pressure of increasing population and improved accessibility from nearby urban areas has forced Vermont to adopt strong measures to protect its environment and scenic beauty. For more than a generation, the Green Mountain State has forbidden roadside billboards, which, in contrast to its neighbors, has become an important factor in the impression of natural, scenic beauty admired by Vermont's millions of visitors.

Alaska, in contrast, is more freewheeling. I lived in Anchorage during the controversial Native Claims Settlement Act that preceded the construction of the 800-mile, Trans-Alaska Pipeline in the mid 1970s. The oil fields at Prudhoe Bay, the haul road created for the construction project, and the pipeline itself could be viewed either as marvels of engineering or as disastrous violations of one of the earth's most pristine and fragile ecosystems, depending upon one's perspective. The fears and dire predictions of many environmentalists were realized only a decade after the completion of the pipeline, when the Exxon Valdez ran aground in Prince William Sound, spilling 11 million gallons of crude oil.

It must be noted, however, that the residents of Alaska have reaped significant benefits thanks to North Slope oil. From the auction of the original drilling leases, and a subsequent tax on every barrel of oil to flow through the pipeline, the state established the Alaska Permanent Fund, which pays every resident about $1,000 a year! In Anchorage, oil revenues funded one of the most extensive urban recreational trail systems in North America. During the long Alaskan winters, residents of the state's largest city can enjoy hundreds of kilometers of groomed cross-country skiing, which link many neighborhoods. Several of those loops are lighted for night skiing, an important feature considering Anchorage's short winter days.

Soon after the oil began flowing, someone noticed that Alaska suffered a higher rate of drownings than the national average. This is not surprising since the water is so cold that few Alaskans swim for fun, yet fishing is a major industry as well as a popular sport. Oil money was used to build swimming pools at many of the state's schools, even in remote villages in the bush, where swimming then became part of the physical education requirements. The incidence of drowning in the forty-ninth state is now in line with the rest of the nation.

Finally, the oil companies and the wide array of service industries that support the oil industry in Alaska provide excellent jobs for a significant number of the state's residents. The oil companies also make an effort to be generous members of the community (motivated, in part perhaps, by the desire for positive publicity), including the funding of new soccer fields, a world-class biathlon shooting range, and the reconfiguration of vital ski trails.

As so often seems to be the case recently, there are no easy, straight-forward solutions to the challenges we face. Most everyone would agree we must do more to protect our environment and to reverse, if possible, the effects of global warming. But if that means banning sports that have a negative environmental impact, like snowmobiling, all-terrain vehicles, Alpine skiing and NASCAR, it is unlikely those measures will meet with widespread approval. Even outdoor activities generally regarded as environmentally friendly, like hiking, canoeing and cross-country skiing are not immune to criticism when the consumption of fossil fuel getting to the site of the activity is considered.

As the evidence grows demonstrating the negative impact we are having on our environment, we will be faced with increasingly difficult decisions to reverse the trends. Even in the area of sports and recreation, I suspect we'll face some tough decisions.

Tough Times for Sports

For the past few weeks, the bad news from the world of sports seemed to just keep coming. The Tour de France, which has been plagued by incidents and allegations of illegal doping for years, finally imploded. Almost daily, athletes were failing drug tests, or in the case of the tour leader, Michael Rasmussen from Denmark, failing to even show up to be tested. Those attempting to put a positive spin on the carnage suggest that the increased vigilance of the Tour officials and their commitment to rid the event of illegal doping is finally having an effect.

Things aren't much better in the NFL, where Michael Vick, the star quarterback of the Atlanta Falcons, was recently indicted for his involvement in a dog-fighting operation. If Vick is implicated in the dog breeding, training and competitive events that allegedly took place at a house he owns in Virginia, he may be trading his red and black Falcons uniform for an orange jumpsuit.

The bad news in the National Basketball Association centers on former referee Tim Donaghy, who is accused by the FBI of betting on games in which he was an official, giving inside tips to gamblers, and under pressure from organized crime, influencing the outcome of games. Donaghy's dishonesty and personal weakness in a position that should be beyond reproach is bad enough, but the movers and shakers of the NBA are terrified that Donaghy is not the sole bad apple in their organization and may implicate others before the investigation is complete.

To round out the current sad state of American sports, we have Barry Bonds' assault on Hank Aaron's career home run record of 755. Here's the dilemma: Barry Bonds, the San Francisco slugger (who has probably surpassed Hank Aaron in career home runs by the time you read this), has never admitted to, nor been convicted of using illegal steroids, although the circumstantial evidence appears overwhelming. A best-selling exposé by two respected investigative reporters for the San Francisco Chronicle develops a convincing case that Bonds, through his personal trainer, Greg Anderson, had close ties to BALCO, a sports medicine laboratory investigated and closed down by the FBI for distributing steroids and other illegal performance enhancing drugs.

Not long ago, a family gathering drew me to the north end of Otsego Lake in the heart of New York's Leatherstocking Region, made famous by James Fennimore Cooper. Just a few miles south is Cooperstown, a beautiful village of 2,500 and home of the Baseball Hall of Fame. A week earlier Cooperstown had welcomed 75,000 visitors as baseball heroes Tony Gwynn and Cal Ripken Jr. were inducted into the Hall of Fame. I thought a short road trip to the birthplace of baseball might be interesting.

I arrived at Doubleday Field in time to see older players in Orioles uniforms heading for the parking lot. They were guys who had met at a fantasy baseball camp years earlier and had enjoyed the experience so much they gather every year to play a few games. I asked their thoughts about Barry Bonds and his run on Hank Aaron's record. Billy Hatfield of Richmond, Virginia, responded, "You know, we play this game because we love it. Most of all, we love the comradery."

Dominic Staiti from Baltimore added, "You're the first one to mention Bonds all week."

Their teammate, David Vidi, chimed in, "It is what it is," referring to Bonds' record attempt.

Across the parking lot, Larry Petraglia and Pat Narciso operate the Batting Cage, where Little League hotshots and Major League wannabes swing at machine-launched fastballs. Regarding Barry Bonds, "Most locals seem generally negative," admitted Larry, while Pat's opinion was that Bonds is arrogant and the record should be followed by an asterisk.

In the Baseball Nostalgia Shop, Bruce Andrews, a high school football, basketball and track coach had a different view. "Bonds is a great ball player. Back in the days of Mantle and Maris the season was 160 games, now it's effectively year-round. Today's players are expected to achieve an unrealistic level of performance. Besides if A Rod and Ken Griffey, Jr. keep up the pace, Bonds' record won't last long."

On Cooperstown's Main Street I spotted a sign for the Vets Club. Down a narrow staircase, half a dozen men watched a ball game, nursed beers and exchanged jokes. When I asked their opinion of Bonds, Jim Laden, a twenty-year U.S. Air Force veteran responded, "Who's Barry Bonds?"

Homer Lindstadt, who served in Korea from '68 to '71, said defiantly, "He's a champ! He hasn't been convicted of anything. It's the system that's screwed up, not Barry Bonds."

Mark Rowley, a former U.S. Marine who served in Beirut in '82 and '83 was "just sick and tired of hearing about it. Hank Aaron didn't use drugs to hit his home runs."

Rich Bailey, another member of the club, shifted the focus. "I met Cal Ripken last week when he was in town. What a first-class guy! He signed autographs and shook hands all weekend. Had his whole family here. 75,000 people came to see him inducted! There wasn't a vacant motel room within two and a half hours of here! There have never been more people here for an induction ceremony. What a tribute to Ripken and Gwynn!"

Thanks for the reminder, Rich. If you can't say something good about someone, don't say anything at all.

A Changing Perspective on America

Even though it's been a terrific autumn in the sports world, I've been distracted by seemingly endless negative headlines on the world scene. That's not to say I wasn't thrilled by the Red Sox's convincing victory in the World Series. I've also been following the fortunes of the New England Patriots, both their quest for that elusive, undefeated season, and the scandal that resulted from a Patriots' coach illegally videotaping an opponent's defensive signals. Finally, there was track star Marion Jones' emotional confession, after years of denials, that she did, in fact, use steroids to achieve her phenomenal Olympic success, three years ago in Sydney. Although her confession transforms her from an Olympic champion to a cheat and a liar, at least Marion Jones finally came clean, admitted her guilt and returned her Olympic medals. Sadly, there are dozens of other prominent sports celebrities who also achieved their fame unethically but continue to deny any wrongdoing.

In spite of these fascinating sports stories, I can't ignore a growing sense of dread regarding the direction our country seems to be heading. In June of 1971, I remember boarding a "freedom bird" at Tan Son Nhut airfield in Saigon, for my flight back to "the world," after nearly a year in Vietnam. At the time, I struggled to think of any positive results that might offset the misery and destruction I had observed during my tour. All I could come up with was the assurance that at least our government must have learned to be very cautious about committing American troops to far flung conflicts, many of which have been simmering for centuries.

I can remember feeling a knot in my stomach in 1983 when President Reagan ordered U.S. troops to invade the Caribbean island of Grenada, and again three years later when he ordered U.S. aircraft to bomb targets in Libya. In 1989, when the first President Bush ordered the 82nd Airborne Division to invade Panama, one of my Vietnam buddies (who had made the military a career) was in the first flight of paratroopers. Then, in

February 1991, I remember watching the television coverage of the U.S.-led coalition invading Kuwait to dislodge Saddam Hussein's forces.

All of those military exploits filled me with a sense of dread, but at least the missions had been clearly stated, adequate forces had been deployed, and once their objectives had been accomplished, our troops came home. In contrast, our involvement in the conflicts in Afghanistan and Iraq began with the cockiness and bravado of a schoolyard bully: "Shock and Awe," "Bring it on," "Mission Accomplished." The more our politicians try convince me that the war in Iraq is not another Vietnam, the more convinced I am that it is. Our troops are halfway around the world, in a country whose culture and language they don't understand, fighting an enemy they can't see. And perhaps to an even greater degree than during Vietnam, our involvement in Iraq has turned our former allies against us.

It has been said that warfare brings out the best and the worst in humanity. Although there have been dozens of stories recounting the courage and self-sacrifice of our troops in Afghanistan and Iraq, there are also the horrifying revelations of Abu Ghraib prison and the Haditha massacre. As an infantry officer in Vietnam, I was aware of isolated incidents of brutality committed by Americans, but it was certainly understood that torturing prisoners was forbidden by the Geneva Convention, and that waterboarding and similar techniques constitute torture. If our newly appointed attorney general, Michael Mukasey, can't say whether or not waterboarding is torture, maybe the CIA could give him an opportunity to experience the procedure firsthand. I'll bet that would clarify his view pretty quickly.

For most of my life I've felt proud and privileged to be an American. Watching Ken Burns' recent PBS special on World War II gave me a renewed sense of gratitude for my dad's generation and what they accomplished in Europe and the Pacific. I also have great respect for today's active military, many of whom have already served two or three combat tours.

But I am increasingly frustrated by our country's leaders in Washington. The decisions of the current administration undermine the foundations on which our country was established. As the world grows smaller through advancements in communication and transportation, we seem less willing to collaborate with other nations, and instead we arrogantly pursue "our national interest."

I guess I'll be able to enjoy sports again when I'm confident the country's back on the right track.

Olympic Politics

There must be an Olympics coming up. The headlines are filled with threats of boycotts, demonstrations and protests. All the clamor hit closer to home when demonstrators in Paris and London disrupted the Olympic torch relay. Max Cobb of Westford, Vermont, was one of a handful of Americans selected by the U.S. Olympic Committee to run the torch during its brief visit to San Francisco, en route to China, host of the Olympic Games in Beijing. Max earned this impressive honor by demonstrating his enthusiasm for the Olympic movement through his skillful guidance of the U.S Biathlon Team during the past two decades.

Max and his family traveled from Vermont to San Francisco for the event. Shortly before the torch run was scheduled to begin, the route was relocated and shortened. The thousands of spectators and dozens of protestors who had lined the original route through San Francisco waited in bewilderment while the torchbearers, running in tandem, quickly completed the revised course before the protesters could reorganize and disrupt the ceremony. Of course, most of the spectators, some of whom had traveled a considerable distance to watch the torch pass by, were also tricked by the revised route.

My first thought was, how sad that something as noble and idealistic as the running of the Olympic flame has become a target of political demonstrations. That thought was almost immediately replaced by the awareness that nothing seems simple, straightforward, right or wrong any more. Although I have experienced firsthand the magic and unifying power of the Olympic Games, I also sympathize with those who oppose China's repression of the Tibetan people. The Chinese government has a notorious record on human rights, but it is also eager to showcase to the world, through the Beijing Summer Games, recent economic and social advances. I can understand why now, with the world's attention on the Games, is the time to try to convince the Chinese leaders to revise their policies on human rights.

Of course, the Olympic Games have been a forum for political activists since the beginning. Who can forget the horror of watching the hostage crisis unfold on television from the '72 Munich Games? In the early morning of September 5th, Palestinian terrorists broke into the Olympic Village, shot two members of the Israeli Olympic Team and held nine others hostage. During a failed attempt to free the hostages, the nine Israeli athletes, five Palestinians and one German police officer were killed. Perhaps because of the Olympic idealism, the brutality of those events seemed especially obscene.

Four years later in Innsbruck, Austria, as hundreds of athletes and Olympic officials lined up for the Opening Ceremony under the incessant whirr of helicopters, a rumor tore through the throng. It was said that a small, private plane breached the restricted airspace above the Opening Ceremony and after refusing to alter course, was shot down.

In 1980, President Jimmy Carter pressured the U.S. Olympic Committee to boycott the Moscow Games in protest of the Soviet Union's invasion of Afghanistan. I have always admired President Carter's character and integrity, but I believe he received bad advice on the 1980 Olympic boycott. Those in his administration will always claim that the boycott led to the Soviet defeat in Afghanistan, but I'm more inclined to believe the recent film Charlie Wilson's War that billions of dollars in military aid, especially stinger missiles, made the difference.

At least partly in retribution, the Soviet Union led a boycott of the 1984 Summer Games in Los Angeles. Peter Ueberroth, the head of the Los Angeles Organizing Committee, miraculously convinced a couple of the Communist nations to ignore the Russians and participate. In so doing, Ueberroth preserved a television broadcast contract that left Los Angeles and the USOC a legacy worth many millions of dollars.

Thanks to satellite television and the internet, more people around the world will be watching the Games from Beijing than any previous Olympics. It follows that those with a political agenda will use the Games as a platform from which to broadcast their message to the world. I just hope the inspiring performances of the athletes and the international goodwill fostered by the Games aren't lost in the clamor.

A Sporting Look at the Election

By now we're all suffering from information overload regarding the presidential candidates and their running mates. Thanks to countless magazine articles, endless radio interviews and a constant flow of television sound bites, we know what the candidates would do to end the war in Iraq, establish a health care system that works, slow the pace of global warming, and resolve the nation's financial crisis. So, as is often the case in these pivotal decisions of international significance, the truly decisive factors are related to sports.

Given his personality, his experience as a prisoner during the Vietnam War, and his well-publicized feisty temper, it is no surprise that John McCain was a boxer during his time at Annapolis. It also stands to reason that since his wife, Cindy, inherited one of the most successful Budweiser distributorships in the nation, the McCains are avid NASCAR fans.

According to an August issue of Newsweek, after returning home bruised by a schoolyard bully, the pre-teen Barack Obama was handed a pair of boxing gloves and given a lesson by his Indonesian stepfather. The core message, as related in Dreams from My Father, Obama's 1995 book, was that there were two types of men, weak and strong. It was up to the childhood Obama to decide which he would be.

In spite of that early introduction to boxing, a love of body surfing that evolved from living close to the beach in Hawaii, and an interest in professional sports that is mandatory for residents of Chicago, Barack Obama's most significant sports connection seems to be basketball. He was a standout player for his Punahou high school team in Honolulu, and still shoots hoops with friends to release tension and relax. It is reported that his address to the 2004 Democratic convention, the speech that many say was the starting point for his current presidential bid, was written while a televised basketball game was blaring in the background. One additional connection to the sport is that Michelle Obama's brother is a Division I basketball coach in Oregon.

Basketball also figures strongly in Sarah Palin's background. As a feisty guard on tiny Wasilla High School's team, Palin earned the nickname "Sarah Barracuda" as she led her team to a state championship. The daughter of a high school cross-country running coach, Alaska's governor still runs, and is said to prefer hills. Much has been made of Palin's hunting and fishing exploits, but it should be remembered that the line between sport and subsistence is easily blurred in Alaska. Many Alaskans fill their freezers with salmon and moose every year, in the same way gardeners in "the lower forty-eight" stock their pantries with tomatoes, and their root cellars with potatoes and carrots from their gardens.

It is often said that "everything's bigger in Alaska," and that seems to describe Todd Palin's accomplishments on his snow machine. Four times he has won the Iron Dog Race, an annual event from Wasilla to Nome to Fairbanks, covering nearly 2,000 miles in mid-winter Alaskan conditions. To put that in perspective, it's roughly equivalent to wrestling your Ski-Doo from Boston to Atlanta, Georgia, then on to Oklahoma City in sub-zero temperatures and howling snowstorms. While his accomplishments certainly helped his wife's campaigns for Alaskan voters, it remains to be seen if voters in the rest of the country might view Todd's exploits as masochistic.

The final member of the foursome, Senator Joe Biden of Delaware, has a strong affinity for football. As a youth growing up in Pennsylvania, Biden struggled with a speech impediment that made the classroom intimidating. He found refuge in sports and admitted decades later during a visit to the Football Hall of Fame in Canton, Ohio, that he had dreamt of being inducted there.

Biden still gets emotional when he remembers the thoughtfulness of Pittsburg Steelers owner, Art Rooney, who sent his star running back, Rocky Bleier, to visit Biden's sons when they were hospitalized following the car accident that killed their mother and sister. Biden admits that although most people who live in Delaware root for either the Philadelphia Eagles or the Baltimore Ravens, he will always be a Steelers fan.

Regardless of how the vote comes out on November 4th, it looks like we'll be getting a couple of sports enthusiasts in the executive branch. Perhaps that's not too surprising. It stands to reason that a nation of sports fanatics would select one of their own to lead them.

The Turning Point

The trouble with a turning point is, you don't always know when you've reached one. I spend quite a bit of time in the woods designing trails, frequently following the shoulder of a hill, an old logging road or a gently tumbling brook. Occasionally, the routes I walk make changes in direction so subtle that I end up far from my intended destination. There must have been many, imperceptible turning points, but added together they leave me a long way from my truck.

I see the same dilemma in our contemporary world. Few of us will ever forget the gut-wrenching feeling as we watched endless replays on television of jetliners smashing into the World Trade Center. There was little doubt that our lives would be significantly changed. That turning point was starkly evident.

But how about the ongoing war in Iraq? At the outset, the liberation of the Iraqi people from a certifiable tyrant like Saddam Hussein didn't seem like such a bad idea. And though many of us might have had misgivings about the effects of Rumsfeld's "shock and awe," on Iraq's civilian population, the invasion and capture of Bagdad went smoothly enough. But then, soon after the statue of Saddam came down, violence erupted in the streets, the priceless heritage of the country was looted from its museums and libraries, mosques were destroyed, and violence reined. Was this another turning point?

Then we learned of hundreds of detainees being held without due process at Guantanamo Bay, Cuba, the physical and mental abuse of Iraqi prisoners by American guards at Abu Ghraib in Bagdad, and the President of the United States claiming that the Geneva Convention's prohibition of torture didn't apply to our war on terror. Maybe this, too, was a turning point.

Next, investigations revealed that the justification for the invasion, the destruction of Saddam Hussein's stockpile of weapons of mass destruction, was a hoax. There were no weapons of mass destruction.

Furthermore, no credible link could be found between Saddam and the 9/11 terrorists. That had to be a turning point.

And I think we reached another one almost five years ago, on May 3, 2003, when President Bush landed on the deck of the aircraft carrier, Abraham Lincoln, under a banner that read, "Mission Accomplished." And again, recently, when we reached a new benchmark in the conflict, 4,000 American dead.

It's hard to know if there was one turning point or many, but I do know our country is badly off course. I only hope it's not too late to find our way back.

Thoughts on the Beijing Olympic Summer Games

It is two days before the Opening Ceremony of the Beijing Summer Olympic Games, although you are reading this at least a week after the Olympic flame has been extinguished and the Olympic flag has been handed over to the officials from Vancouver. But as the Games are about to begin, I have some decidedly mixed feelings about the impending extravaganza.

By way of a disclaimer, I should acknowledge right up front that I'm a lifelong fan of the Olympics. I was an athlete on two Winter Olympic teams and participated in five other Olympics as a coach, team leader or organizing committee volunteer. I am not an objective observer of the Olympic Games.

My first area of concern relates to the television coverage, which is both a miraculous achievement and a mind-numbing curse. Having attended seven Winter Olympics I can confirm that there is no way an individual could possibly see in person even a fraction of the events covered on television. When Bob Costas casually remarks from his studio command center, "While the hockey teams break between periods, let's go to the Women's Slalom for the start of the second run," he's providing a viewing opportunity that would be physically impossible at the site. Standing in the freezing wind, halfway up the Men's Downhill course can certainly give a spectator an appreciation of the terrifying speed that the athletes generate as they plummet down the mountain, but if you want to see more than a series of blurs rocketing past, watch the event on TV.

Nordic skiing is terrific on television as well. At the Olympics and other major competitions, the television production crew typically has dozens of camera locations at strategic positions around the course, and they are constantly shifting their coverage to capture the excitement of the event as it unfolds. A spectator on the course or in the start/finish stadium actually sees very limited fragments of the race.

Even figure skating and ice hockey, both sports enjoyed by spectators in comfortable, climate controlled areas, are enhanced by the televised feature of instant replay.

Unfortunately, we pay a very stiff price for these technological wonders. For starters there are the seemingly endless network introductions, incessant studio commentaries and constant commercial interruptions. I believe it was during the 1988 Calgary Games that the director of the Lake Placid Olympic Training Center taped every minute of the more than 100 hours of Olympic coverage. After she had edited her tape down to the actual coverage of Olympic competitions, she had less that 50 percent of the advertised "coverage" of the Games.

To be fair, I understand that NBC will make more of the competitions available on their cable affiliates, but since we don't have cable, I'm bracing myself for more exciting network coverage of our perky female gymnasts having lunch with their teddy bears and gargantuan wrestlers and weight-lifters shopping for souvenirs in downtown Beijing.

A second area of mixed feelings is the media coverage. I participated in a sport so obscure we had to explain it to any reporter who stumbled into our area (usually by mistake, trying to find the figure skaters). In those days, any publicity was good publicity, with the potential to help generate modest corporate sponsorship and perhaps draw young Olympic hopefuls into the biathlon development program. I think it's terrific that Dara Torres, a forty-one-year-old mother competing in her fifth Olympic Games, is getting tremendous press coverage, and that other deserving athletes who have trained for years in obscurity are gaining the attention of the media. But how would you like to be Michael Phelps? If this twenty-three-year-old wins seven golds and a sliver, thanks to all the pre-Games hype, he'll be regarded by some as a failure for not winning eight golds!

Finally, I have severe misgivings about the expectations for victory being so high that athletes and coaches succumb to taking advantage of unethical performance enhancement. Most prevalent, of course, is doping, and unfortunately, I'm confident doping will impact the results in Beijing. Sadly, unethical coaches, team doctors and athletes seem to be one step ahead of the Olympic officials, as we have seen in previous Games where cheaters were awarded medals only to have them revoked months or even years later.

On a positive note, Beijing will be the most expansive Olympic Games yet, viewed by more people on earth than ever before. Perhaps the commercialism, petty nationalism and doping will be overshadowed by good sportsmanship, athletic excellence and international good will. Let the Games begin.

Reestablishing the Coming-of-Age Ritual

Not long ago I had the opportunity to attend a small graduation ceremony at an outdoor education center in North Carolina. It was a rewarding trip for a number of reasons. My prior experience in the South had been limited to nine weeks of infantry training at Fort Benning, Georgia, back in 1968. Not the ideal setting in which to appreciate the beauty of the natural surroundings. On my recent trip, I was amazed by the hills and forests of western North Carolina. An afternoon hike not far from the education center in Ashville was one of the most scenic and enjoyable I've had anywhere, which includes New Hampshire, Colorado, Alaska and Vermont. I was reminded that much of the movie The Last of the Mohicans had been filmed in North Carolina, but only now do I really believe it.

The graduation ceremony was inspired by Native American stories and drumming. The graduates and their family members sat in a circle and listened to the leader relate the legend of Singing Stone, the Native American youth who impatiently seeks permission from the tribal elders to set out on his vision quest. His lonely and dangerous journey takes the youth to the four corners of the world, along the way guided by animal spirits. After countless miles and many months of walking, he is welcomed warmly back to his village, discovering that what he sought on his quest was actually within him all along.

Many of the most universally admired stories of all time are of quests. The Odyssey by Homer and Don Quixote by Cervantes are classic examples. More recently, all the Harry Potter novels, as well as the seemingly endless series of James Bond movies are all quests. On the surface the story might be a conflict between good and evil, man against nature or the hero overcoming his own shortcomings. But in the classic quests, the hero is to some degree transformed by the experience, perhaps gaining wisdom, tolerance or compassion. In short, the best quests are about growing up, coming-of-age.

Many indigenous cultures have a coming-of-age ritual that might involve hunting, surviving alone in the wilderness or even combat with an enemy. Although contemporary American culture does not seem to have a universally accepted coming-of-age ritual, some current activities have filled the void. For many young Americans, heading off to college has become a coming-of-age ritual, primarily because college administrators are typically more permissive regarding student alcohol consumption than are the student's parents. Since another common theme in the classic quest stories is hardship and sacrifice, college doesn't constitute an authentic coming-of-age ritual.

Violent team sports share many traits with the classic quests. There is often hardship and sacrifice as well as an element of danger in college football or ice hockey. Certainly, athletes are welcomed home as heroes by their community after winning a championship, and athletes are frequently transformed by the intense emotion of agonizing defeats and glorious victories.

Tragically, the most authentic coming-of-age ritual we currently offer our youth is service in the military. There are many aspects of the military that are highly commendable, but sending thousands of eighteen-year-old recruits into the meat grinder of combat in Iraq or Afghanistan is not one of them. Thousands of these young soldiers and marines have lost their lives, while others have been horribly wounded. Even those who escaped physical trauma may return home mentally scarred by the horrors they observed or were forced to participate in. There is no doubt that for the survivors, combat is a legitimate coming-of-age ritual, but the price of this ritual is too high.

I believe we should have a national service corps comprised of young people who devote a year to public service, perhaps following high school, before heading off to college or starting a career. Students might have a choice of different organizations, like the Red Cross, the Peace Corps, VISTA, the military, Habitat for Humanity, Hospice, etc. Students would be granted a modest cost of living stipend, but the work would be demanding, insuring a modest amount of sacrifice and discomfort, in other words creating a legitimate quest. Imagine the worthwhile public service projects that could be accomplished by this youthful army of volunteers. Think of the maturity and focus these veterans of the Peace Corps, the Red Cross and the military would apply to their college careers.

I believe the best gift we could provide the "entitled generation" would be to establish a year of national service, which would soon become our national coming-of-age ritual.

Veteran's Day

Good Morning! Thank you for pausing in your busy schedules to remember Veteran's Day, which is actually on Thursday this year. For the sake of clarification, a veteran is any citizen who has served in the military during war or in peacetime. Memorial Day, at the end of May, is set aside to honor those who died while serving in the military, while Veteran's Day recognizes the contributions of all veterans.

Our first president, George Washington, said, "If we desire peace, it must be known that we are, at all times, ready for war." Sadly, every generation of Americans, since the founding of our country more than 230 years ago, has had to send troops into combat. The total number of veterans in our nation's history is around 42 million.

Sixteen million Americans served in World War II, and it is widely acknowledged that it was their effort that made the difference in the defeat of Hitler's Germany and Hirihito's Japan. About 2 million of those World War II vets are still with us, but they are slipping away at a rate of nearly 1,000 per day. If you know a World War II vet, give him a call and thank him for his service. We would all be living in a very different world were it not for his efforts.

Our nation's involvement in more recent conflicts is more complicated. The fighting in Korea and Vietnam was intended to stop the spread of Communism. The first Gulf War was to assist an ally whose tiny country had been overrun by a ruthless dictator, while the current conflicts in Afghanistan and Iraq were launched as an attempt to disable the terrorist organization responsible for the attacks on our country on 9/11.

Our elected officials determine our nation's foreign policy, leaving the military to carry it out. In spite of extremely difficult conditions in both Iraq and Afghanistan, our troops have, in general, done an admirable job. They deserve our praise and continued support, especially considering many have served multiple combat tours with precious little time at home. The families of our troops deserve recognition as well, since they have endured years of painful separations and the constant fear of knowing that their loved one was in danger.

The population of America is around 310 million, roughly 23 million of whom are military veterans. Another way of looking at it is, less than 10 percent of our population is willing to put their lives on the line to defend the freedoms that we all take for granted. We owe them our gratitude. Thank you.

The Long Haul

If, as a young athlete, you have a lot of motivation but limited talent, you eventually end up in the endurance sports. I don't mean that there aren't talented people running marathons or Nordic skiing, but many find their way to the distance events because they weren't much good at hitting a baseball or threading their way through slalom poles. Athletes endowed with great talent are typically drawn to sports with thousands of adoring fans and professional salaries rivaling the GDP of a mid-sized country.

I have run about sixty marathons, hiked most of the mountains in the northeast and skied across Finland in seven days, so it's evident how I was in Little League. But there is a straight-forward honesty to distance sports; the harder you train, the better your results. Success has little to do with physical size, hand-eye coordination, reaction time or fast-twitch muscle ratio.

Endurance athletes win on mental characteristics like persistence and consistency over the long haul. Perhaps it's human nature, but many distance enthusiasts develop the urge to go even further. After skiing a few 50 kilometer events, (that's just over 31 miles), the Canadian Ski Marathon begins to sound intriguing (100 miles in two days). Then the annual Border to Border, Ski Across Finland, 444 kilometers from Russia to Sweden, just south of the Arctic Circle, seems like a cool thing to try.

Eventually, a pattern emerges in these endurance events. The first third of the race is characterized by high energy, positive expectation and enthusiasm. Experienced athletes often hang back at the start, knowing that the early leaders often falter later on. By the middle third of the event, the participant becomes introverted, concentrating intensely on pace, hydration and mile markers.

The final third usually holds the real test, either that precipitous drop in blood sugar known as "hitting the wall," or a more subtle "fade," where the athlete is simply unable to hold the pace. Either way, it's a real struggle to reach the finish.

Occasionally, however, for no discernible reason, the fatigue evaporates and the final miles become a euphoric celebration of life. Those rare instances keep endurance athletes coming back for more.

A Terrific Event

Judging by current 2010 headlines, we appear to be overwhelmed by natural disasters, political conflicts and economic uncertainty. Catastrophic floods, tornados, tsunamis and earthquakes have temporarily been forced off the front page by the ongoing nightmare of millions of barrels of crude oil, natural gas and dispersant chemicals fouling the abundant fishery and wildlife habitat of the Gulf of Mexico.

In addition to the ongoing violence in Iraq and Afghanistan, a belligerent North Korea apparently torpedoed and sunk a South Korean naval vessel while, on the other side of the world, Israel and the Palestinians continue to provoke each other toward full-scale armed conflict.

On top of the natural disasters and the politics, we have what appears to be a very tenuous global economic recovery that could unravel at any moment, triggered by the insolvency of the Greek economy, the shaky finances of Portugal and Spain or some soon-to-be-revealed Wall Street investment scam.

Things aren't much better in the world of sports. Over the past several months, revelations about the private life of Tiger Woods, arguably the most successful athlete ever, have transformed his image from a poised, seasoned champion to that of a pathetic, sex-crazed, adulterer. Perhaps almost as disappointing, disgraced cyclist Floyd Landis, who for years challenged the positive doping test that stripped him of his Tour de France victory, recently conceded that he did, after all, use illegal performance enhancement during his international cycling career, and even more disturbing, Landis asserts that his teammate at the time, Lance Armstrong, did as well.

In spite of this apparent flood of bad news, every spring I can look forward to a celebration of health, fitness and community pride. For twenty of the past twenty-two years, I have traveled to Burlington to participate in the Vermont City Marathon. I have seen the event grow from a few hundred dedicated distance runners to the most recent edition, where eight thousand entrants participated either in the full 26.2-mile marathon or as a member of more than seven hundred relay teams. In my view, the concept is brilliant. While for many the challenge of the full marathon is what motivates their training and fuels their dedication, for others, joining friends, colleagues from work or family members on a relay team is what makes the day so special.

The organizers of the VCM have also been extremely skillful in configuring the course. Historically, endurance competitions have provided woefully little to lure spectators. Typically, a handful of loyal parents and friends cheer at the start of a distance event, find some way to amuse themselves for an hour or more, then encourage their exhausted athletes toward the finish line. In contrast, the architects of the Vermont City Marathon designed a course that loops repeatedly through the start area at scenic, Battery Park, so that spectators can watch the race develop at just over 3 miles, about 8.5 miles and at 15 miles. The loops that radiate from Battery Park, and ultimately, to the finish line at Waterfront Park, take the runners through downtown Burlington, several residential neighborhoods and along the scenic lakeshore bike path, featuring impressive vistas across Lake Champlain to the Adirondacks.

In addition to the creative course layout, which deserves much of the credit for the event's growth to eight thousand runners, and perhaps an equal number of family and friends who fill Burlington's hotels and restaurants for Memorial Day weekend, there are a couple of other successes that deserve mention. With a staff of less than a dozen, Run Vermont, the outfit that organizes the Vermont City Marathon as well as several other fitness and running programs, depends upon 1,700 volunteers each year to host the marathon. In exchange for a T-shirt and the pride of being a part of a successful event, these volunteers take care of everything from distributing race numbers at registration, to awarding medals to the marathon finishers as they stagger through the finish line. After more than twenty years, no doubt many of these volunteers have developed a justifiable sense of accomplishment for the role they play in the hosting of Vermont's largest participatory event.

Finally, the marathon brings the entire community together. Garden hoses stretch across lawns to provide a cooling spray for the runners. Kids offer sliced oranges, bananas and cups of water. An amazing variety of musicians, from bagpipers to blues bands and the impressive Taiko drummers, encourage the runners throughout the course.

If the news of the world is getting you down, convince some friends to enter a relay team in next year's Vermont City Marathon. You won't be disappointed.

Rest and Hydration

With the arrival of summer, many outdoor enthusiasts are gearing up for physically challenging events like charity bike rides, overnight hiking expeditions and distance-running races. Many of us consider ourselves physically active, trying to make a point of getting some type of exercise every day, but training for a specific event suggests an intensified level of commitment. For starters, training for an event suggests the creation of a training plan, actually anticipating particular workouts for specific days, weeks or even months in advance. The training plan may be in the form of a calendar with projected workouts penciled in up through the day of the big event. In the case of elite athletes, these plans can become quite technical and complicated, incorporating principles like "hard day followed by easy day" or alternating endurance training with interval and tempo training. Also woven into the training plan is a careful balance of cross-training activities that emphasize different muscle groups, for example, an afternoon spent paddling a canoe, predominantly upper torso exertion, might be followed the next day by a bike ride, primarily leg work. Another characteristic of training is the athlete's commitment to recording actual workouts, usually including time and mileage, in a training log or journal.

In the complexity of creating a successful training plan, a couple of very simple principles are often overlooked: the need for adequate rest and hydration. The basic assumption of all athletic training is simple, judiciously overstress a muscle group or entire system, then allow the system the opportunity to rest and recover and it will rebuild itself stronger than before. There are a couple of important corollaries, however. First that the stress administered is carefully monitored: too severe and injury will result, too moderate and no significant gain will be achieved. The other assumption is that the muscles are given adequate opportunity to recover. This is often a problem with many athletes because of the prevalent attitude, "the harder I train, the better I'll get." A more accurate approach might be "the smarter I train, the better I'll get."

I remember John Caldwell of Putney, Vermont, considered by many to be the patriarch of American Nordic skiing, relating an experience he had years ago in the Soviet Union, during the era of their international domination of the sport. He had been invited to visit a Soviet training facility and was intrigued to see sleeping rooms decorated with peaceful forest scenes and filled with soothing music. Apparently, the Soviets believed that they were approaching the limits of intensity and volume of physical training and therefore were shifting their focus toward maximizing the benefits of the rest and recovery cycle. Their logic makes sense; if the quality of the rest and recovery phase can be improved, perhaps the athletes will be capable of even greater workloads.

Athletes today are well informed about the value of staying adequately hydrated. Many of us cringe when we think of well-intentioned but misguided coaches of our youth who withheld water during demanding workouts to "toughen us up." If anything, the pendulum may have swung too far in the other direction, considering the current, mind-boggling assortment of sports drinks claiming to do everything but run the race for you. I have no doubt that some of the scientifically formulated sports drinks contain precisely the correct concentration of sugars and salts to move quickly through the stomach wall and into the blood stream, but I've found that many of the commercial sports drinks upset my stomach when I'm depleted of energy and flirting with exhaustion. Many athletes and sports medicine physicians will agree that old fashioned water is hard to beat for rehydration during an event.

A related tip that most endurance athletes learn from experience is to drink early and drink often. By the time you actually feel thirsty during a race or a hike, you are already well on your way to dehydration. Most major races these days have plenty of water stations, where the well-intentioned volunteers overfill every cup. I make it a habit of never passing a water stop without taking a cup, but I rarely drink more than one good mouthful before discarding the remainder.

Whatever your athletic goals for the summer, you can improve your results and minimize the chance of injury or illness by incorporating two simple principles: get plenty of rest and stay hydrated. Now I've got to go get a drink of water before my nap.

Sports on Our New Eaarth

I just finished Bill McKibben's new book, Eaarth. McKibben is the writer, outdoor enthusiast, and environmental activist who in 1989 brought national attention to the impending impact of global warming with his book The End of Nature. But while the rest of the world recognizes McKibben as an environmental scholar and activist, I know him as an avid Nordic skier and unofficial faculty advisor to the Middlebury College ski team.

Years ago, Bill got my attention during a presentation in our community when he stated, matter-of-factly, that three of Vermont's most widely recognized activities—admiring the brilliant autumn foliage, tapping maple trees to produce maple syrup, and the sport of skiing—could all disappear within our lifetimes. In his new book, McKibben asserts that it is no longer a question of "if" or "when" concerning global warming, but that the earth has already changed from the earth we remember in our youth. The evidence is all around us. The only uncertainty is what we, as residents of this new eaarth will do to minimize the negative influences of global warming.

If you find McKibben's observations compelling, as I do, you accept the probability that our lives will change dramatically in the years to come (though, thankfully, Vermont may not change as dramatically as Bangladesh, the island of Fiji or south Florida).

An obvious change will be the increasing value of a diminishing supply of oil. At what point will it no longer be economically feasible to run snow-making compressors and Piston Bullys all night to groom Alpine runs for the decreasing number of skiers who can afford $150.-a-day lift tickets and fuel for their cars that exceeds $5.00 a gallon? I would imagine that snowmobiling and ATV use would decline dramatically as well.

On a positive note, snowshoeing and cross-country skiing might experience a resurgence as Alpine skiers and snowboarders switch to a less costly winter activity. Expensive, fluorocarbon waxes might be abandoned for less costly options, and geographically remote competition sites might be passed up in favor of local or regional races. Currently, it is not uncommon for a Nordic racer from Vermont to compete in northern Maine, Quebec, New Hampshire, upstate New York, perhaps Wisconsin or Minnesota, and even in Alaska during one winter season. My guess is that in the future, most of our racing will be relatively local.

In fact, one intriguing probability that McKibben mentions in *Eaarth*, which may have implications for sports enthusiasts, is the internet. For some time now, the innovative Morrisville company Concept II has been conducting competitions on its popular rowing ergometer. Hundreds of avid rowers gather in a field house in Cambridge, Massachusetts, and work to exhaustion on machines that simulate the physical exertion of rowing on the nearby Charles River. Since the machines are equipped with small computers that record the force exerted by the participant, it is relatively easy, thanks to the internet, to transmit data anywhere in the world, like Cambridge, England, for example, where a similar group of rowing fanatics are pulling on identical rowing machines. The result, in effect, is an international rowing competition without the airfare.

With the Concept II competitions in mind, it's not too much of a stretch to imagine Nordic skiers in Alaska equipped with miniature GPS devices that compute the severity of the terrain and the speed of the athlete to be compared to similar data from a skier competing in Maine. Perhaps in the not-too-distant-future we will be selecting national and even Olympic teams from athletes who have never actually competed against each other due to the prohibitive expense of bringing all the contenders to a central location.

I don't hold out much hope for NASCAR and NFL football. Perhaps they can adapt to a post petroleum world, but how will they sustain their entertainment extravaganzas without the sponsorship millions from Sunoco, Exxon, Texaco, Firestone, Goodyear, etc.?

On the other hand, cycling and biathlon may finally gain national prominence. When thousands, perhaps even millions more Americans commute to work by bicycle, I'll bet there will be renewed appreciation for the endurance and skill of the Tour de France riders (provided of course, the organizers take the sport back from the unethical dopers).

And when increasing numbers of rural and suburban breadwinners return to the woods every autumn to bag a deer for the freezer, there will be intense respect for athletes who can hit a silver dollar-sized bull's eye at 50 meters after skiing full tilt for several kilometers.

A Troubling Observation

The final issue of Sports Illustrated every year features the unforgettable moments in sport that have occurred during the previous twelve months. It also pays tribute to notable sports personalities who have passed away. Since Sports Illustrated, to a significant degree, focuses on popular, team sports like baseball, basketball, football and ice hockey, many of the names in the 2010 issue were unfamiliar to me, although a few struck a chord.

I know it's bad manners to speak ill of the dead, but I have never had much respect for George Steinbrenner. In addition to having been the controversial owner of the New York Yankees for more than thirty years, Steinbrenner was also a member of the U.S Olympic Committee. His arrogant, in-your-face ownership style may have been tolerated or even admired in New York, but in my view he didn't set much of an example for sportsmanship.

My real gripe with Steinbrenner came during the 1988 Winter Olympics in Calgary. The Games got off to a rough start for the U.S. team, with injuries to promising Alpine skiers, tough luck for some of the skaters, and unrealistic expectations burdening the hockey team. Before the Olympics were half over, Steinbrenner, attending as a member of the USOC, sounded off to the press about the U.S. team's disappointing performance, especially in comparison to the traditionally successful summer sport athletes. Not only were his remarks poorly timed, but they illustrated how little he knew about the winter Olympic sports. Ironically, much of the perceived imbalance could be traced to his own philosophy, so evident in building the Yankee's dynasty, of just throwing more money at the problem. His comments came at a time when the winter sports were woefully underfunded compared to the summer sports.

Another sports celebrity we lost last year was Merlin Olsen, the legendary cornerstone of the Los Angeles Rams' Fearsome Foursome defensive line. Even if he hadn't stood 6 foot 5 inches tall and weighed 270, or been selected to play in the Pro Bowl fourteen of his fifteen years in the NFL, a name like Merlin Olsen would be easy to remember. But I had an additional insight into his remarkable athletic ability.

Ralph Wakely, of Salt Lake City, Utah, finished twenty-seventh, America's top result, in the 20-kilometer biathlon event at the '68 Winter Olympics in Grenoble. Even casual observers acknowledge that biathlon is among the most physically demanding sports on the Olympic program, and physiologists have repeatedly confirmed that Nordic skiers are among the most aerobically fit specimens on the planet. That wasn't much consolation when, a few weeks after the Games, Ralph met his brother-in-law, Merlin Olsen, for a friendly workout in the Utah stadium. As Ralph told the story, everything they did—100 yard sprints on the turf, bounding up the endless stadium steps, even a distance run on the track—"Merlin just smoked me!" Granted, Ralph was coming off an exhausting winter of travel and competitions while Olsen was in the midst of spring training, but still....

There are other sports figures who will be missed: Juan Antonio Samaranch, who led the International Olympic movement into the modern age, and John Wooden, the beloved UCLA basketball coach who set a standard for the profession few will be able to achieve. But among the individual tributes a disturbing trend emerged, an alarming number of athletes took their own lives. Of the fifty-four recently deceased athletes that Sports Illustrated deemed worthy of recognition, five, perhaps even six of them committed suicide. That's roughly 10 percent. For comparative purposes, the national average for suicide is in the range of 11 per 100,000 people, or roughly a tenth of 1 percent. I recognize that the magazine might choose to feature a young athlete simply because of the tragic nature of his or her death, but it still seems like quite a disparity from the national average.

Of course each case is different, but I'll bet there are some common threads. It wouldn't surprise me if the athletes who took their own lives displayed their athletic talent early on, perhaps to a point where it defined who they were. I could also imagine that at some point their natural talent failed them or they may have been sidelined with injury. No doubt substance abuse played a role in more than a few cases.

For many of us sport has become a way of life. But when the loss of the adulation, the money, and the celebrity status reduces athletes to suicide, we have lost a rational perspective on sport's appropriate role in our culture.

Growing Evidence That Lance Doped

Seven years ago, in 2004, I wrote a column in Vermont Sports titled, "I Want to Believe in Lance." At the time, the U.S. cycling icon was poised to win an unprecedented sixth Tour de France, but the publication of L.A. Confidential: Lance Armstrong's Secrets, by David Walsh and Pierre Ballester, accused Armstrong of using performance-enhancing drugs. Lance vehemently denied the accusations, stating repeatedly that "neither he, nor any of his U.S. Postal Service teammates had done anything illegal." Another frequent Armstrong retort to the nearly constant questions from the press about doping was, "I have been tested hundreds of times and I have never failed a drug test."

I should state here for the record, that I believe in the concept of "innocent until proven guilty." All of us received a vivid reminder of that concept not long ago when several Duke University lacrosse players were accused of sexually abusing a female entertainer whom they had hired for a party. Encouraged by a voracious media and an overzealous prosecutor, many of us convicted the athletes in the court of public opinion, only to learn later that the entertainer had fabricated her story and that the athletes were innocent.

Having said that, I am tired of athletes who stridently maintain their innocence until faced with overwhelming evidence against them, when they suddenly become repentant and admit to "making bad decisions." In general, successful athletes are not stupid people, especially where sports performance is concerned. Many are very sophisticated about training regimens, nutritional supplements, equipment refinements, etc. It is difficult for me to believe, with the possible exception of a few teenaged East German swimmers back in the 1960s, that top athletes aren't fully aware that they are doping when they inject themselves with something to improve their performance.

If you want to give Lance Armstrong the benefit of the doubt, what he stated in an interview I saw on television is probably true. According to a recent exposé in Sports Illustrated, Lance may have had access to a new drug called HemAssist, created to treat victims of trauma and severe blood loss. Since the drug was still in trials, and thus not yet on the banned list, Lance could technically state that he and his teammates had done nothing illegal.

It is also reasonable to assume that anyone as dominant as Lance Armstrong was in international cycling, is going to generate some envy and bruised egos. Consider the team dynamics of the Tour de France. A group of the world's best riders ally themselves behind a "favorite" whom they protect and pace to the victory. Certainly the motivation for most of these journeymen cyclists is to someday earn that coveted distinction of favorite, and win the Tour themselves. According to the Sports Illustrated article, a significant number of Armstrong's former teammates and support staff are coming forward, relating what they heard or observed. Could this all be a result of envy and jealousy, or is it perhaps an overdue sense of conscience and a desire to assuage their guilt?

Perhaps the most noteworthy recent development is the involvement of Jeff Novitzky, the FDA's investigator responsible for bringing to justice several participants in the BALCO illegal performance enhancement case. As a result of Novitzky's work, several people went to jail, including multiple Olympic medalist Marion Jones. In addition, a congressional subcommittee was motivated to hold hearings on the use of steroids in Major League Baseball. San Francisco Giants slugger and home run king Barry Bonds is still under investigation for perjury. The fact that Novitzky has turned his attention toward Armstrong suggests that the investigator suspects that the famous cyclist is hiding something.

This entire situation is especially tragic because, since his recovery from cancer, Lance has done so much to raise awareness and funding for cancer treatment. There is no doubt that the millions raised through Armstrong's Livestrong Foundation have significantly advanced research into the causes and possible cures for cancer. Equally important, as a cancer survivor himself, Lance has inspired people around the world who struggle with the disease.

In conclusion, I suspect Lance did what he thought he had to do to win, and in the long-standing culture of the Tour de France, that meant illegal performance enhancement. To his credit, he was careful how he answered the constant accusations, and he probably didn't actually lie. My guess is, if he admitted his youthful lapse of judgment, in the heat of battle so to speak, and vowed his continued commitment to fighting cancer, the majority of sports fans would accept his confession and be grateful for his help in the search for a cure.

A Great, Wet Day

Thetford's invitational Woods Trail Run has become firmly established in the cross-country running lore of New England. Swelling in recent years to more than 2,500 high school runners from as far away as Maryland, athletes seeded by their anticipated 5-kilometer finish time, in one of twelve different starts throughout the day, test themselves against 200 other runners in their heat, as well as the tough, hilly course through the forest. What we consider typical terrain for Vermont seems like the Himalayas for runners from suburban Connecticut or New Jersey.

I admire runners for a number of reasons. I'm impressed that they often train, and even compete, in relative obscurity, rarely receiving recognition in the sports pages. I like the way runners can spill their guts out in a sprint to the finish, then, seconds later throw a sweaty, congratulatory arm over the shoulder of the competitor who just nipped them at the tape. And I love how runners take any weather conditions in stride: sweltering heat, pouring rain, even snow. This year, participants at the Woods Trail Run endured torrential rain and the resulting muddy, slippery course. So, the loyal race volunteers donned their Gore-Tex, the visiting teams erected their colorful tents, the athletes adjusted their race strategies and the events went off on schedule.

Working in the finish area provides a unique perspective on the competitions. It is not uncommon to see the winners of the twelve different heats glide, almost effortlessly, across the finish line, scarcely out of breath. Many minutes later, the slowest runners in each heat jog across the line, impressive in their determination, perhaps a compensation for lack of physical ability. Between these extremes are the majority of runners, some elated by a terrific result, others crushed by the fear of "letting down the team."

This is the part of the race that typically contains the most drama. In one of the top seeds, it is not uncommon for more than one hundred athletes to cross the finish line in a minute. The greatest challenge for the finish line crew is to accurately establish the order of finish, and to maintain that order as the athletes decelerate and file into the chutes, where their numbers are recorded. You can imagine how stressful this job becomes if half a dozen highly motivated high school boys are thundering toward the finish in a pack, closely followed by scores of others. Then, crossing the line, one of the first pack slips in the mud, tripping two others who go down with him, while the approaching runners attempt to dodge and vault the fallen finishers… You get the picture. We refer to this scene as a "train wreck" and those of us recruited to work the finish line have nightmares about it. Consider how the rainy weather and a slick, soggy course increase the possibilities for such a disaster.

The other predictable entertainment occurring between the winners and the cabooses are the drama queens. Although there are typically more girls in this category, there are plenty of boys who earn recognition as well. These are the runners, almost always in the middle of the pack, who find some creative way to draw attention to themselves as they approach the finish line. A common ploy is the "sprint to the death," usually resulting in a total collapse across the finish line, an effort that would be far more convincing if the athlete hadn't comfortably jogged the entire course prior to the near-fatal sprint in front of the finish line crowd.

Then there are the floppers, usually girls, who make it through the race only to collapse into the arms of a volunteer. Often they are sobbing, sometimes they appear nearly comatose, but almost without exception, after a few minutes of attention and reassurance, they are once again cavorting happily with their teammates.

In spite of the grim weather and challenging running conditions, this was a banner year for the Woods Trail Run. No train wrecks, virtually no floppers and very few tears. There were several competitors who finished missing a shoe, a few with bloody knees, and everyone was covered with mud. As the old saying goes, "when the going gets tough, the tough get going." We were inspired by the gutsy performances of more than 2,000 tough kids in this year's Woods Trail Run.

Wrestling with Joe Pa's Legacy

For three days in June of 1988, the United States Olympic Committee co-hosted an academic conference at Penn State University. Current and former Olympic athletes, coaches and team leaders from both the summer and winter games were invited to attend. The curriculum included presentations on the 1980 Summer Olympic boycott, the use of anabolic steroids in amateur sports and the commercialization of the Olympics, among dozens of other fascinating topics.

I car-pooled to State College from Vermont with a couple of other coaches, and I remember being impressed by the size of the Keystone State. I recalled learning in a history class that Vermont's farming economy faltered after the Civil War, not only because of battlefield casualties, but also due to the irresistible attraction of the fertile fields of Pennsylvania, which lured Vermont farm boys from the steep, stony hillsides back home. Having attended Middlebury and coached at Dartmouth, I smugly thought I had seen the most beautiful college settings in the country, so the rural charm and striking campus at Penn State came as a pleasant surprise.

Even before the conference began, there was a buzz about Joe Paterno. As college coaches ourselves, we chuckled at the life-sized, cardboard representations of Paterno for sale in the college bookstore. Here was a football coach who had achieved rock star, celebrity status. Paterno was one of more than a dozen presenters the first day of the conference, and there wasn't a vacant seat in the auditorium. His talk seemed off-the-cuff, perhaps a little rambling, but clearly focused on his lifelong crusade for excellence, both on the playing field and in the classroom.

When he finished, a line of attendees who wanted to shake his hand formed quickly. I had a reason to join the line. Not long before the conference, a new Dartmouth athletic director fired the college's admired head football coach, who had a year remaining on his contract. Many of us thought he was getting a raw deal. To our delight, the coach took the contract dispute to court, where his friend and mentor, Joe Paterno, spoke

411

on his behalf, helping to win the case. When my turn arrived, I introduced myself, mentioned that I coached skiing at Dartmouth, and thanked him for supporting his former colleague. Paterno became animated as we shook hands and said something like, "Aw that was stupid. Why the college didn't just let him finish out his contract, I'll never know. He's a good coach and a great guy."

Later, I had the opportunity to speak with a Penn State Ph.D. candidate who had made a presentation on steroid abuse in collegiate athletics. I asked him how Paterno had become such an icon at the university. He responded by sharing a story. Several years earlier, the Penn State football program was rebuilding, having lost many of its top players to graduation. Planning and budgeting for the upcoming season had been completed recognizing that post-season play or a bowl game invitation was unlikely. But the younger players exceeded expectations, the regular season was successful and the team did play in a bowl game. When Paterno and the players returned to campus, the coach presented Penn State's share of the bowl game television revenue, a check for nearly $1 million, to the university library! The grad student concluded his story with a statement, "Name me another football coach, of a nationally prominent program that would have done that." Ultimately, Paterno helped raise $14 million to rebuild Penn State's library, his family contributing $4 million.

What struck me at the time of that conference, almost twenty-five years ago, as I write this, was Paterno's conviction that excellence in collegiate athletics and academics were not mutually exclusive. As a coach at Dartmouth, I often had the feeling the athletic department and the academic professors were at odds, competing for the precious time and commitment of the undergraduates. One particularly perverse example was a Russian professor who threatened to fail one of my skiers who requested an excused absence from two weeks of classes, to compete in the Biathlon Junior World Championships, in Minsk, Russia!

Somehow, at Penn State, Joe Paterno had helped to create an atmosphere where academic and athletic excellence could and did coexist.

Like everyone else, I was horrified by the revelations, in November of 2011, of the scandal involving former Penn State assistant football coach Jerry Sandusky. I suspect that even after extensive investigations and a lengthy trial, there will be much we will never know regarding who knew what, and when they knew it. The real tragedy, if verified, is Sandusky's abuse of vulnerable boys, but it's tremendously sad to see Joe Paterno's lifetime legacy tarnished.

Fallen Heroes

It might have been an uncanny coincidence, but the release of the Freeh Report to the Trustees of Penn State University appeared to confirm that the late legendary football coach Joe Paterno knew more than he had previously admitted about his former assistant coach Jerry Sandusky's destructive attraction to young boys. Within what seemed like a matter of days, Lance Armstrong announced that he would no longer contest the U.S. Anti-Doping Agency's efforts to strip him of his victories based upon mounting testimony and evidence that he used performance-enhancing drugs throughout his career. After more than a decade of defiantly fending off accusations and innuendos, Lance, somewhat abruptly, tossed in the towel, in effect conceding the charges against him.

The two stories are similar, primarily in the incredible stature of the sports figures involved and their precipitous falls from grace. It is all too common to hear of college coaches who bend recruiting rules to attract talented players, or overzealous young athletes caught for supplementing their natural abilities with performance-enhancing drugs, but Paterno and Armstrong were the standard-bearers of their professions. There could scarcely be a better example of the old adage, "the higher they fly, the farther they fall."

Much has been written about the scandal at Penn State since it became national news. It is widely recognized that during his forty-six-year tenure as Head Football Coach, during which he became the winningest collegiate football coach in history, Paterno also played a significant role in bringing Penn State national recognition, not only for athletics but for academic excellence and research as well. Although some at the university may have had legitimate concerns regarding the influence and stature of the football program, most in Happy Valley idolized Joe Paterno and proudly recounted the millions of dollars he and the football program contributed to the library and other academic programs.

Soon after the scandal broke, Paterno's home was besieged by the media. A frail old man with the signature coke-bottle eyeglasses stood pathetically on his front step and admitted that "he should have done more." He was referring to simply passing on to his athletic director the report of an assistant coach who had observed Sandusky sexually abusing a young boy in the Penn State football locker room. Although more may come out as investigations continue, it appears now, in 2011, that several Penn State administrators, including Paterno, failed to take decisive action, fearing the negative publicity it might generate toward Penn State Football.

Much has also been written over the past decade regarding Lance Armstrong's alleged use of performance-enhancing drugs in winning his unprecedented seven Tour de France victories. And the plot gets more convoluted as the story unravels. Lance has maintained for more than a decade that "he has never done anything illegal," and "has never failed the hundreds of doping tests he has taken." But for years, unethical athletes, coaches and sports scientists have been creating slight variations of proven enhancements simply to avoid using the drugs on the list of banned substances. And although Lance never failed a test, there have been several mysterious irregularities, test samples that disappeared, etc. In fact, part of the evidence against him to date involves samples taken years ago, but retested recently using more sophisticated, advanced, testing methods that reveal illegal performance enhancement.

Some might say, so what? The Tour de France has been notorious for doping for decades. For a time, doping was almost synonymous with endurance cycling. Is Lance a cheat if he is simply doing what had become tradition among the leaders of the sport? And consider the witnesses who have agreed to testify against him, nearly a dozen, many of them fellow riders who doped themselves, lied about it and eventually came clean.

I suspect that Joe Paterno tried to protect his beloved university and football program from a scandal, and when he fully understood the extent of Sandusky's crimes, Paterno's deep regret, sense of guilt and sorrow hastened his death from lung cancer.

I believe that Lance Armstrong is a fierce competitor who "saw how the game was played" and did what he had to do to win. I don't think that either Paterno or Armstrong are evil, they simply got swept up in situations that overwhelmed their judgment, their basic sense of right and wrong. Perhaps the real lesson here is that sport should remain healthy and fun and that our sports heroes are just normal people who have the good fortune of making a living playing a game. When sport becomes entertainment, generating millions of dollars and creating positions of power and influence, we inevitably get into trouble.

London Olympic Highlights

A full disclaimer at the start: I've had the amazing good fortune of attending eight Winter Olympic Games in a variety of roles from biathlon competitor to volunteer. Perhaps, because of that experience, I feel a stronger affinity to the Winter Olympics. The figure skaters may be the prima donnas of winter sports, but I can relate to them more easily than I can to the synchronized swimmers or the dressage riders. As a result, I wasn't glued to the tube for endless hours during the recent London Olympics. My wife and I did, however, catch enough of NBC's coverage to develop some impressions.

First, some thoughts about the television coverage itself. I smiled when I heard a radio personality criticize NBC for focusing almost exclusively on American athletes. How soon people forget! It doesn't seem that long ago that ABC was criticized for featuring primarily the leaders and eventual medal winners. At many previous Winter Olympics that excluded most of the American participants, who were fortunate even to be mentioned. Actually, I thought NBC did a pretty good job of covering the favorites, regardless of nationality, while also acknowledging the American participants.

Like the coverage of most professional sports in this country, NBC paired an experienced announcer with one or two "color commentators," in most cases former athletes. While it's helpful and interesting to have some insight into the nuances of the sport (for example, the platform divers hit the water with flat palms to make a hole in the water and thus minimize their splash), I felt some of the color commentators became smug and even arrogant in their evaluation of the competitors.

I know it is obscenely expensive to televise the Olympic Games, and that NBC claims to lose money every time, but the preponderance of commercials is agonizing. There were evenings when I was convinced that we were watching ten minutes of commercials for every five minutes of sports.

One final comment about the TV coverage. NBC deserves tremendous credit for allowing us to experience the growing excitement and emerging tactics in some of the events, which the spectator on the scene has no way of discerning. Aside from the annoying commercial breaks, we watched the men's marathon from start to finish, including Ryan Hall's agonizing withdrawal from the race and Meb Keflezighi's phenomenal surge from sixteenth place to finish fourth.

Although such a massive undertaking always has its critics, it seems to me that London set a new standard for hosting the Games. The organizers took a part of the city that had become an eyesore and revitalized it. They struck a balance between creating wonderful new facilities and temporary venues that will be dismantled after the Games. And if hosting the Olympics is an opportunity to showcase your city to a worldwide audience, the organizers made certain that we had plenty of opportunities to see the Parliament Building, the Tower of London and Buckingham Palace.

And how about those Opening and Closing Ceremonies? I've seen some terrific ones, especially Albertville in '92 and Lillehammer in '94, but the Queen arriving by parachute! It will be interesting to see how the Russians top that, two years from now in Sochi.

The unsung heroes of the London Olympics may very well be the security details. If they do their job well, everything goes smoothly and we are only vaguely aware of their presence. But in today's geopolitical climate, with the eyes of the world focused on London, I have to believe that there were dozens of lunatics and fanatics determined to spoil the party. The athletes and coaches of the world could focus on doing their best because relatively anonymous, dedicated, public servants had them covered.

Regarding the events themselves, there seemed to be the typical spectrum from unrestrained exuberance to heartbreak. Michael Phelps may actually be human after all, but as Ryan Lochte discovered, Phelps is still pretty phenomenal. What a welcome dose of joy high school swimmer Missy Franklin must be to her home state of Colorado, especially after the tragedy in Aurora.

Some have called the London Games the Women's Olympics, and the U.S. women's soccer team contributed to that impression. I had mixed feelings regarding last year's women's World Cup, believing that somehow Japan deserved the victory following the earthquake and tsunami that devastated their country. But there can be no doubt which team deserved this year's gold medal in women's soccer.

Of the dozens of memorable performances, the one that will stick in my mind is Meb Keflezighi, the thirty-seven-year-old who persevered through injury and personal hardship, simply refusing to give up. His fourth-place finish in the marathon was a significant victory by any measure.

Evolving Sports

Not long ago, I was made aware of how dramatically some sports can evolve and even transform through the years. Of course, a sport like marathon running has changed relatively little in the 116 years since a handful of stalwarts toed the line for the 26.2-mile race into Boston. Running clothing has certainly become more functional, shoes are definitely lighter and more comfortable, and training for the marathon is far more scientific and systematic. But the basic activity of running 26.2 miles has hardly changed in more than a century.

Not so with Nordic skiing. In the early 1980s the skating revolution threatened to tear the sport of cross-country racing in two. For centuries, extremely fit competitors in the northern latitudes had been kicking and gliding through the snow-covered forests and fields, testing themselves against each other and the elements. A vital component of this "classic" type of skiing was the unique property of the wax that was applied to the running surface of the skis, simultaneously providing grip or purchase as the skier weighted the ski to stride forward, and also glide as the ski broke free, sliding forward over the snow.

In the early 1980s, large snow-grooming machines were used to pack wide swaths of trail, especially in the increasingly popular, mass start ski marathons like the Vasaloppet in Sweden and the Birkebeiner in Norway. Innovative skiers, including Bill Koch from Guilford, Vermont, discovered they could travel faster over the packed surface by pushing diagonally off to the side, similar to speed skaters. The real breakthrough came when these racers realized they could dispense with kick wax entirely, prepare their skis purely for speed (like Alpine skiers), and skate an entire course significantly faster than with the traditional kick-and-glide technique.

For a couple of years the sport was in turmoil. At first skating was declared illegal and athletes using the technique were disqualified. Race courses were groomed to make skating difficult, if not impossible. But thankfully, sanity prevailed and the FIS (International Ski Federation) eventually recognized skating as a discipline distinct from the traditional "classic" kick-and-glide technique. Now, thirty years after the skating revolution, cross-country skiing enjoys more popularity than ever before, driven at least partially by an increased number of televised events at the Winter Olympics.

Which brings me back to my recent revelation. For the past two decades, the annual Vermont High School Cross-Country Running Championship has been hosted by Thetford Academy on the challenging Dan Grossman Woods Trail. It is a relatively convoluted, 5-kilometer loop, predominately through forest, encompassing more than 200 vertical feet from the low point to the high point of the course. Through the years, races have been held in stifling heat, pouring rain and even snow, but Vermont's high school runners typically finish the course with a sense of accomplishment, many having tested themselves to the limit.

Not long ago, I learned that Louisville, Kentucky, a city with a passion for a variety of sports, aspires to become a recognized center for cross-country running. There are plans to develop a cross-country running venue to rival the best courses in the nation. I was surprised and disappointed to discover that the courses currently regarded as "state of the art," including trails at Terra Haute, Indiana, and Madison, Wisconsin, are basically flat, containing less than 20 percent of the climb of the Thetford course. I have learned that the two factors driving cross-country running at the elite level these days are fast times and safety. In other words, top collegiate coaches avoid challenging, hilly courses because their athletes run slower times, and they prefer a smooth, fairway-like, grassy surface because they don't want their thoroughbreds tripping on roots and spraining ankles.

Ironically, a century ago, the original cross-country running events in England often required the athletes to vault fences and ford streams. Athletes who crossed the finish line muddy and bloody were simply part of the sport. I suspect that the gentrification of cross-country in America stems from running on golf courses, the only available terrain in many urban locations across the country.

My suggestion to the cross-country running community: Divide the sport into two disciplines as Nordic skiing did. The first could be fast and flat, basically, track meets on grass; while the second discipline could retain the historic traditions of the sport, running through forests and fields, over roots and rocks, uphill and down.

No Easy Answers

I wrote this column for nearly two decades and voiced opinions on subjects as controversial as overzealous Little League parents, gratuitous violence in ice hockey and illegal doping. But no columns I have written for Vermont Sports have stimulated the intense feedback of "Taking a Stand on Guns" in 2003 and "Too Many Guns," published in 2007, in the aftermath of the Virginia Tech tragedy. As I pointed out at that time, I am no stranger to firearms. As a member of the U.S. Biathlon Team from 1968 through 1976, I shot more rounds of ammunition in training and competition than the vast majority of sport shooters will fire during their entire lifetimes. Living in Alaska for a decade, I took full advantage of that hunter's paradise, filling the freezer with moose meat, Dall sheep, caribou, spruce grouse and ptarmigan.

As an infantry advisor to the South Vietnamese in 1970, I was rarely more than arm's length from my M-16, even when I slept. In fact, it would be accurate to say that I have had extensive experience with firearms in their three most widely accepted roles: marksmanship, hunting and self-protection.

In my view, all human life is precious, but the shooting rampage at Sandy Hook Elementary School seems even more senseless than Virginia Tech, Aurora, Colorado, and even Columbine High School because it is hard to imagine victims more innocent and defenseless than first-graders and their teachers. As news of the tragedy dominated our national consciousness, I was struck by an unbelievable irony; Newtown, Connecticut, is also the home of the National Shooting Sports Foundation, the association representing the firearms industry, whose mission is to "promote, protect and preserve hunting and the shooting sports." I must confess that my first reaction was, "Wow, talk about reaping what you sow."

As the industry's representative, the NSSF considers semiautomatic weapons (one shot for each pull of the trigger) the natural evolution of shooting technology. Semiautomatic weapons were originally designed for the military, but were quickly adapted for civilian use in hunting or marksmanship. Semiautomatic rifles and shot guns have been popular with hunters for about a century. But many of the avid hunters I know are shifting back toward bolt-action rifles, muzzle loaders and even archery to enhance the sporting aspect of deer, moose and turkey hunting. I don't know anyone who hunts with a Bushmaster XM 15 with a thirty-round magazine, one of the weapons Adam Lanza used to kill twenty-six students and teachers at Sandy Hook Elementary.

But my initial reaction was misguided. In fact, the NSSF has done much through the years to promote firearm safety. Since 1999, the organization has distributed, for free, more than thirty-five million gun locks, significantly reducing the accidental discharge of weapons in homes across America. The NSSF has worked with the Veterans Administration to provide every veteran returning from a combat zone gun locks and safety kits. And for many years, the NSSF funded a summer biathlon program that organized running and shooting events across the country. One aspect of that effort was to recruit a talented European coach, Algis Šalna, a 1984 Sarajevo Olympic biathlon gold medalist from Lithuania, who has inspired and motivated American athletes for more than two decades. Not long ago, one of Algis' protégés struck it rich. At the recent Biathlon Youth and Junior World Championship held in Obertilliach, Austria, seventeen-year-old Sean Doherty of Center Conway, New Hampshire, earned a gold medal and the distinction of World Champion in the 10-kilometer pursuit event. Sean had won a silver a couple of days earlier in the 7.5-kilometer sprint race, and followed up his gold medal performance in the pursuit with another silver medal in the 12.5-kilometer individual event. It was the first time an American biathlete has earned three medals at the same World Championships. A couple of weeks later, America's top biathlete, Tim Burke of Paul Smiths, New York, won a silver medal in the 20-kilometer event at the World Championships!

The U.S. biathletes have made steady progress internationally, and many believe a medal is possible at the Winter Olympics in Sochi, Russia. Some of the credit for this success should go to the National Shooting

Sports Foundation, which generously supported a successful summer program, and made it possible for talented coaches like Algis Šalna to emigrate to the United States.

As is the case with so many issues in our modern society, gun control is very complex. I don't believe the average American citizen has any need for an AK-47 or an M-16 with a thirty-round magazine in their closet. Most of the hunters I know rarely require more than three shots to drop the animal they are stalking. Meanwhile, Tim Burke, young Sean Doherty, and their teammates have brought honor to us all by skiing fast and hitting their targets.

As someone who has competed internationally, filled the freezer and defended myself in combat with a firearm, I have an appreciation and respect for rifles. But we obviously have to do a better job of making firearms, especially those with such an incredible capacity for destruction, less accessible to those with malicious intent.

Boston Strong

I've run the Boston Marathon six times during the past four decades and attended as a spectator at least half a dozen more. I've braved the traffic and crowds to give my family and friends a feel for the excitement at Heartbreak Hill, Cleveland Circle and the final stretch to the finish line on Boylston Street. My last three Boston Marathons, I was a member of the Dana-Farber Marathon Challenge, a group of more than three hundred runners who contribute over $4 million annually to one of the nation's premier cancer treatment centers. In fact, one of the last times I ran the race, I was asked to give an inspirational speech at the pasta feed arranged for the Dana-Farber runners the evening before the marathon. Talk about turning the tables. I met doctors, researchers, cancer survivors and patients who gave new meaning to the word "inspiration."

There are other marathons that have found their pace, and in some measure have surpassed Boston. For many years, the organizers of the Boston Marathon resisted the growing trend to pay elite athletes generous appearance fees simply to participate in the race and even more lucrative prize money for winning. World-class marathoners can only put it all on the line a couple of times a year, so many elite runners elected to skip Boston in past years in favor of generous cash prizes and luxury automobiles at marathons in London, Amsterdam and elsewhere.

But Boston is widely regarded among dedicated runners as the original marathon of the modern era. The 2013 Patriots' Day was the 117th consecutive running of the event. Although many other marathons, like New York, the Marine Corps in Washington, D.C., and Chicago have become so popular that the thirty thousand (or so) annual participants must be selected by lottery, Boston still demands that runners meet qualification standards. It is not a "come one, come all" event, but rather a gathering of dedicated running enthusiasts who have proven their ability and commitment by exceeding an age-appropriate standard for 26.2 miles on a certified course in the previous twelve months. I know several capable runners who struggle valiantly, sometimes year after frustrating year, to successfully qualify for Boston.

Another remarkable aspect of the Boston Marathon is the throng of enthusiastic spectators that lines the course from Hopkinton to Boston. Because of the race's colorful history and its traditional scheduling on Patriots' Day, an official holiday in Massachusetts, the 26.2-mile course is usually lined by cheering, flag-waving spectators. A highlight for many participants is running the gauntlet of screaming Wellesley College women soon after the halfway point of the race. After surviving the series of climbs in Newton culminating with the infamous Heartbreak Hill, it's highly likely you'll be offered a beer by a celebratory Boston College student around mile 21. Within a couple of miles of the finish, when you're barely holding on, if you're running for Dana-Farber, you'll get high fives from the bald kids currently undergoing cancer treatment.

I know a cancer survivor who has run the race for nearly twenty years, in the process raising hundreds of thousands of dollars for cancer research. I know a high school English teacher and cross-country running coach who has also participated in the Boston Marathon for two decades, in the process inspiring a couple of generations of high school runners. I have a friend and neighbor who, after decades of endurance events, was especially proud to run this year's Boston with both of his sons.

For all these reasons and many more, I was incensed that anyone would sabotage the Boston Marathon. I have to admit that, following 9/11, it had occurred to me that a major sporting event like the Super Bowl or the World Series would be a tempting target for a terrorist who was determined to strike at the core of the American way of life. But somehow, I had never imagined the Boston Marathon as target.

What is especially ironic, as the investigation unearths more details about the two suspected bombers, is that they emigrated to this country from a former Soviet state, took advantage of America's educational system and perhaps even our welfare benefits, before turning against us.

As President Obama said in his comments in Boston days after the bombing, "They picked the wrong city to attack." In the moments, hours and days following the disaster, there were dozens of stories of selflessness and courage coming out of the city. And my prediction is there will be more applicants for the 2014 Boston Marathon than ever before.

A Confluence of Sport

For my birthday this year, my wife, Kay, got us tickets to a Red Sox game. Although I've never been a fanatic baseball fan, growing up in southwestern New Hampshire, just down the river from Carlton Fisk's hometown, insured that the few times I've visited Fenway Park were special occasions.

This year was no exception. The excitement outside the stadium is contagious, amid the throng of spectators and entrepreneurs hawking programs, T-shirts and baseball paraphernalia. Entering the grandstands, I'm always impressed by the brilliant green grass contrasting with the red dirt of the infield and the perfection of the white base lines.

Because the players seem to be traded so frequently, $3 for a program provides interesting information about the current team members. For example, the Red Sox payroll on opening day was $151 million (fourth in major league baseball), while their opponents that day, the Colorado Rockies, had a team salary less than half that much. I found it interesting that while a maximum of nine players actually represent a team on the field, Boston's roster totaled thirty-four men, of which more than half are pitchers. The highest paid player on the team is John Lackey, a pitcher who will earn $15.25 million this season. The entry-level salary appears to be $490,000, which five players on the roster receive. Just so we don't feel too badly for these rookies, the average annual salary for teachers across America is $44,000, less than a tenth of what these ballplayers earn in a season.

If the action on the field lags, there is always entertainment to be found in the stands. What an amazing cross section of the population attends baseball games: from corporate titans in the luxury boxes, who spend most of the game focused on their smart phones, to rowdy, blue collar types, fueled by the plentiful beer, who are not shy about voicing their opinions on almost every play.

There were plenty of blue-and-yellow BOSTON STRONG T-shirts in evidence, reinforced by a prominent image on the right field wall.

Although life goes on (as they say), and thousands of Red Sox faithful were enjoying a warm, summer afternoon at Fenway, most attending the game also remembered the horrific events that made the Boston Marathon in April national news for several days. The bombings took place just a few blocks from the ballpark and it's not uncommon on Patriots Day, for Boston sports enthusiasts to watch the leaders finish the marathon then walk over to Fenway for the Red Sox game.

But the real buzz during the game we attended was the news coming in on people's smart phones that New England Patriots tight end, Aaron Hernandez, had been arrested in connection with the murder of an acquaintance. There was no shortage of opinions in the stands regarding his guilt or innocence. Some claimed to have seen it coming, given Hernandez's previous brushes with the law. Others expressed a sense of betrayal that the Patriots had embraced a troubled youth who had then squandered a remarkable opportunity. Oh, and the twenty-three-year-old Hernandez had just signed a $41 million, seven-year contract with the Patriots.

Although it didn't actually come up at the Red Sox game, the Bruins fought valiantly against the Detroit Red Wings in one of the finest Stanley Cup battles of recent years. After the series it was revealed that one of the Bruins' star players was competing with broken ribs (which he knew about) and a punctured lung (which he didn't know about).

In roughly the same time period, Doc Rivers, who had coached the Celtics for more than half a decade, would be leaving for California. The Celtics are entering a rebuilding phase and apparently, Rivers was not the right guy for that job.

As if all this sports news isn't enough, I just learned that there is an effort to promote Boston (and New England) as a candidate to host the 2026 Winter Olympic Games! Presumably the hockey, figure skating and speed skating would take place in the many rinks in the greater Boston area, with the snow sports contested on mountains in Maine, New Hampshire and Vermont. The proposal may not be as far-fetched as it appears at first glance. Even the Winter Olympics have become a monumental undertaking, with accommodations and facilities for the athletes being dwarfed by the requirements for thousands of journalists and security personnel. A world-class sports city like Boston might be just the ticket.

Sports and Life

438

No Fan of the NCAA

A series of incidents through the years has made me skeptical, and occasionally even hostile, toward administrative or supervisory organizations. One summer during college, I got a job with a large construction company involved with building Interstate 91. A prerequisite of the job was joining the union and paying a hefty membership fee, which was taken out of my pay. The little crew to which I was assigned built granite and masonry headwalls on the exposed ends of the drainage culverts that passed under both lanes of the highway. The construction company had three "pipe crews" digging up the roadway and installing culverts. Our three-man crew scrambled to keep up. One hot summer day a big Cadillac stopped above the wall we were building and the corpulent driver suggested that we "slow down, you're making the pipe crews look bad." I laughed, thinking the guy must be joking, but quickly learned he was the union steward and could have me fired on the spot.

After college and four years in the U.S. Army, I was offered a job teaching high school English and coaching running and skiing in Anchorage, Alaska. In those days, teachers in Alaska were among the highest paid in the nation, and thanks to a strong military influence in the community, teachers had excellent health care and retirement benefits. I had the good fortune of working for one of the most capable and beloved school administrators in the state. But officials of a national teachers' union forced a strike against the Anchorage School District. It quickly became contentious and acrimonious. Many union members in my high school refused to strike out of respect for our principal, and endured hostility and retribution from teachers who walked out. Nobody won, certainly not the students.

In my view, the National Collegiate Athletic Association, the organization charged with overseeing the fair and safe conduct of intercollegiate sports, has been eager to skim off vast amounts of money generated by collegiate athletes, while at the same time appearing strangely reluctant to take decisive action on the many serious issues undermining the integrity of collegiate athletics.

From the NCAA's perspective, there are revenue-producing sports (primarily football and basketball) and then there's everything else. The NCAA rulebook, which contains several hundred pages, is largely focused on issues related to football and basketball. There are relatively small, supplemental pamphlets that deal with sports like skiing, swimming, golf and tennis.

For decades, there have been persistent, troublesome issues in the NCAA Skiing Championship that have remained unresolved. Collegiate skiing involves a broad selection of institutions, from large state universities with many thousands of undergraduates to small private liberal arts colleges. Some of the large universities have their entire ski team on athletic scholarships, while many other schools don't provide athletic scholarships at all, and aren't even permitted to recruit off campus. This doesn't do much to create parity at the championships every March.

For more than a century, ski jumping has been the most visible and the most exciting discipline of the ski sports. The ski jumping competitions at the Winter Olympic Games are always among the first to sell out. In the early 1980s the NCAA dropped jumping from its championship program. Before the next season, virtually all of the collegiate, and most of the secondary school programs, across the country discontinued their ski jumping programs. There are still dozens of medals awarded at the Olympics for ski jumping and Nordic combined, but any American athletes striving for them have to get there pretty much on their own.

Recently, Sports Illustrated published a five-part exposé revealing the alarming and wide-ranging ethical lapses and rule violations of Oklahoma State University in their football team's recent rise to national success. Although I was disgusted by the alleged abuse of players and blatant disregard of the rules by coaches and team boosters, I am especially frustrated by the NCAA's apparent apathy to such abundant violations for such an extended period of time. What is even more unsettling is that the investigative journalists who wrote the Sports Illustrated series admitted that they focused on one program but that they suspected similar violations were common in colleges and universities across the country. When the TV commentator for the nationally broadcast college football game cheerfully announces that State U's offensive line averages 325 pounds, doesn't it make you wonder how they got that big and strong? It is not just the nation's obesity epidemic or the great food in the student union.

For once, I'd like to see the organization charged with keeping collegiate sports fair and safe have the courage to do its job.

Just a few weeks into the 2014 NFL season, the headlines are all about the disgraceful, off-the-field behavior of several high-profile players. Last summer, a videoclip from an Atlantic City hotel surfaced showing Baltimore Ravens running back Ray Rice dragging his fiancée from an elevator. The star player was suspended for two games for domestic violence. More recently, a second, far more disturbing video hit the internet showing Rice knocking his fiancée out with a punch to the face. The public outcry forced the Ravens to cut Rice from the team and the NFL to suspend him from the league indefinitely.

Before the Ray Rice situation subsided, an alarming story emerged from Minneapolis, where the Vikings' record-setting running back Adrian Peterson was accused of child abuse for beating his four-year-old son with a switch to the point of breaking the skin and leaving visible bruises. Then it seemed that the floodgates opened, with Sports Illustrated and other sources reporting a series of recent cases of violent, off-the-field behavior by NFL players.

Ray McDonald, a defensive end for the San Francisco 49ers, is being investigated for beating up his pregnant fiancée. The Carolina Panther's star defensive end, Greg Hardy, a player who will earn $13.1 million this season, is appealing a judge's ruling that found him guilty of "assault on a female and communicating threats." On September 17, Arizona Cardinals running back Jonathan Dwyer was deactivated after being charged with domestic violence. Back in November 2013, Vikings cornerback A.J. Jefferson was arrested for domestic assault by strangulation. And just so that we New England Patriots fans don't get too smug, let's remember that Aaron Hernandez will soon go on trial for murder.

This recent spate of alarming, violent incidents involving NFL celebrities prompts three observations, at least two of which could be considered quite positive. First, I'm reminded of some nearly forgotten college introductory psych course in which I first learned about the bell-shaped curve, which I've more recently discovered applies to almost everything. As a brief review, the bell-shaped curve is a graph representing that on either extreme of almost anything, there are relatively few individuals, while the vast majority are somewhere in the middle. Considering college applicants, for example, there will be a few students with the grades and test scores to be successful anywhere they apply. At the other end of the spectrum, there will be a few applicants who do not have the scores or high school grades to be successful in college. And the vast majority of applicants between the extremes have the grades and skills to be admitted to the college of their choice.

It's important to remember the bell-shaped curve in regard to the misbehavior of NFL football players. The vast majority of players are dedicated athletes and conscientious citizens. A smaller segment of NFL players are remarkable community advocates leveraging their celebrity to advance worthy causes, from youth sports to a wide variety of medical challenges. Unfortunately, a relatively small number of NFL players allow their wealth and fame to distort their perspective, and they behave in ways the general population finds unacceptable.

A second observation is an admission that we are all partly responsible. Many of us, perhaps a majority of us, harbor a fascination with violence. Would NASCAR racing be the most popular spectator sport in America if there weren't the occasional, multicar pileups or the flaming spinouts into the infield? We are grateful that recent enhanced safety measures ensure that most of the time the drivers walk away from those horrendous crashes, but honestly, wouldn't NASCAR be boring if there were no accidents?

NFL football is exciting because of the speed, athleticism and skill of the players. We cheer for a linebacker who fights through the offensive line, reaches the opposing quarterback, and slams him to the turf. Our heroes are receivers who get open, miraculously catch a pass drilled at them like a bullet, then hold onto the ball when blind-sided by a defensive cornerback with the force of a freight train. We are fascinated, engrossed, even enthralled by the violence. And while we compensate the athletes who entertain us very generously, it might be unrealistic to assume that they can simply turn on and off that level of violence. We have learned since the Vietnam War that soldiers forced to endure months of fierce combat often have trouble readjusting to civilian life. Although the NFL is not the life-and-death combat our military has faced in recent years, professional football demands a level of physical violence not common in other twenty-first-century occupations.

Finally, and perhaps most optimistically, our national culture is changing. One hundred and fifty years ago, during the western expansion, gunfights and random acts of violence were relatively commonplace. As recently as the 1950s, Americans in the South were lynched with impunity simply for the color of their skin. In 2014, national celebrities are disgraced, held to account and perhaps suspended from their powerful positions for striking women and children. A generation ago these incidents would not have been national news. Today, the Commissioner of the NFL may lose his $30 million-a-year job because he underestimated the public's disgust over the indefensible behavior of a few of his athletes.

It may be slow, but I believe we are making progress.

Not long ago, the sports world was giddy about a thirteen-year-old Little League phenomenon from South Philadelphia who struck out eight and walked none en route to a two-hit, shutout victory at the Little League World Series in Williamsport, Pennsylvania. The big deal that landed the young player on the cover of Sports Illustrated is that Mo'ne Davis is a 5 foot 4 inch, 111-pound girl. And baseball isn't even her best sport! She dreams of playing college basketball. Sports commentators across the country were dissecting Mo'ne's 70-mile-per-hour fast ball and raving about the perfect mechanics of her curve. Don't get me wrong, I think it's pretty terrific that Mo'ne can not only play ball with the boys, but that she can excel, and get national recognition while doing so, but another part of me wonders, what's the big deal? Many have recognized the potential for girls and women to excel in sports, if they are only given the chance.

My first indication may have been on the top of the Middlebury College ski jump in early 1965. As several of us, all ski team hopefuls, tried to work up our courage, the coach's spunky eleven-year-old daughter, Patty Sheehan, dropped her little Alpine skis on the snow and asked, "You guys gonna stan' up here freez'n all day, or are ya gonna jump?" Then she rocketed down the inrun and launched into the air. I was not surprised, years later, when Patty gained national recognition as one of the top golfers on the LPGA Tour.

In the summer of 1968, soon after I went on active duty in the army, I was assigned to Fort Benning, Georgia, the home of the infantry. At the height of the Vietnam War, there was no place in America more male chauvinistic than Fort Benning. This was before women served in the military other than as nurses or secretaries. Fort Benning was also home to the Advanced Marksmanship Training Center, a small facility that developed the best sport marksmen on the planet. Olympic, World and Pan Am Champions like Gary Anderson, Lones Wigger and Lanny Bassham honed their skills on the ranges at Fort Benning. In addition, one woman, Margaret Murdock, was assigned to the AMTC. Captain Murdock, an officer in the Army Reserve, trained with and competed against the best men in the world. At the '76 Montreal Summer Games, she made Olympic history by tying Capt. Lanny Bassham with the top score in the three position, small bore event.

In February of '76, I was a member of the U.S. biathlon team to the Innsbruck Winter Olympics. It was a disappointing Games for me, having been knocked out of the 20-kilometer individual event by a stomach flu and skiing a mediocre leg in the biathlon relay. Our team leader that year was a Finnish immigrant who arranged a "fun little relay" with the Finnish Olympians the day before the Closing Ceremony. With nothing riding on the outcome but bragging rights and a bit of national pride, I was shocked to discover that I'd be anchoring the U.S. relay and skiing against Helena Takalo, the twenty-eight-year-old Finnish housewife, who in the previous sixteen days had medaled in all three of her events (one gold and two silvers). It was a stride-for-stride battle for 5 kilometers, probably the hardest I'd skied all winter. As we sprinted for the line, I asked if she wanted to tie, "for the sake of international friendship," and got a scowl in response. It nearly killed me, but I beat her by a boot length.

I remember the media flap back in 1967 when Kathrine Switzer subtly concealed her gender when entering the Boston Marathon, which at the time was open only to men. Then, in 1972 Frank Shorter won the Munich Olympic marathon and launched a national running craze in America. Overnight community road races, 10k's, half marathons and marathons were hosting thousands of runners, and for the first time, many of them were women. I remember chuckling to myself when my running buddies commiserated about "almost being passed by a GIRL." Better get used to it, guys, I thought.

In the 1980s, I achieved a lifelong dream by qualifying for and then participating in the Boston Marathon several times. At first, I was able to run with some of the leading women, although I was laboring while they seemed to be floating effortlessly, scarcely touching the pavement. I still think Joan Benoit's Olympic marathon victory in 1984 is one of the most inspiring athletic performances of all time, but in one sense, I was not surprised. For decades, I have seen what girls and women can accomplish in sports when given the chance.

You go, Mo'ne!

The Last Great Race

It was spring 1972 and I was finishing up a four-year hitch in the Army, three years at the Biathlon Training Center in Alaska, interrupted by a tour in Vietnam. As the days grew longer and the deep winter snow began to melt, a call came down from headquarters that the commanding general needed some biathletes for a little ski tour. Several of us reported to nearby Elmendorf Air Force Base, where we boarded a helicopter along with the general and his aides for a short flight across the Cook Inlet and the Susitna River to the wilderness, west of Anchorage.

The U.S. Army had been asked to reestablish a legendary dog mushing trail from Anchorage to Nome, 1,100 miles to the northwest on the Bering Sea. The trail was first used during the 1898 gold rush, but it gained mythic stature in 1925, when heroic dog mushers relayed a 20-pound package containing diphtheria serum, 675 miles from Nenana to Nome in less than five days, rescuing the town from a deadly epidemic.

The general's mission that spring day was twofold. The obvious purpose of the trip was to inspect the progress of the infantry units that were slogging their way through the tundra on archaic "white elephant" skis and burdened by huge packs full of Arctic survival gear. His second purpose became evident soon after we landed, when a covey of eager infantry officers vied for his attention.

"Gentlemen, you can give me your briefing later. It's a beautiful day. Let's go skiing."

With a nod to the biathletes, indicating that we should lead the way, the general fell in line with the infantry officers scrambling to follow. Originally from Colorado, the general was an accomplished skier in excellent physical condition. But he had struggled in his efforts to elevate the combat readiness of the soldiers in Alaska, many of whom believed that future winter conflicts would be fought by helicopters and tracked vehicles rather than by riflemen on skis.

We followed the trail across frozen muskeg bogs and through thick stands of dwarfed spruce until there was no sign of the infantry officers behind us.

"This ought to be enough," the general announced with a grin. We stopped to catch our breath and admire the scenery. As we began to cool off, the others approached, red faced and sweating profusely.

"Well, men, looks like you've got this trail off to a good start," the general announced. "I've seen enough, let's head back."

We biathletes admired how effectively our commanding general, a man well into his sixties, demonstrated to his subordinates that they were poorly prepared for winter warfare.

Miraculously, considering the modest ability of the soldiers we met that spring day in '72, the trail was reestablished, and the following March, the first full-length Iditarod Trail Sled Dog Race was held. Every year since then, dozens of Alaska's toughest dog mushers line up on Anchorage's Forth Avenue for the ceremonial start, struggling to control hundreds of eager Huskies, dogs that live for the thrill of running.

A day later, the actual start takes place in Willow, north of the broad, glacially fed Kink Arm. The mushers head west through the majestic Alaska Range into the vast wilderness of the Alaskan interior. The weather is almost always a challenge. Often temperatures exceeding 20° below zero sap the dogs' energy and make the snow feel like sand under the sled's runners. Warm weather brings thaws and deadly overflows on the many frozen rivers that lace the route.

Wild animals are another concern. Susan Butcher, winner of four Iditarods, was forced to drop out one year when her team overtook a moose, which without warning, turned and attacked.

There are also the howling winds and blinding whiteouts along the shore of Norton Sound. Through the years, many mushers have credited their lead dogs with guiding the team safely through the maelstrom of snow to the finish line in Nome.

During the past three decades the Iditarod has experienced startling changes. Originally a macho test of wilderness survival lasting nearly a month, the race has become a nine-day sprint, with women like Libby Riddles and Susan Butcher frequently giving the men a run for their money. Once the domain of Native Alaskans and Sourdoughs (the nickname for gold rushers who kept a sourdough bread starter in their breast pocket so it wouldn't freeze), the 2004 Iditarod hosted eighty-seven teams from twenty states and a dozen foreign countries.

The event which Alaskans proudly call "The Last Great Race" actually lives up to its name.

New Year's Resolutions, Revisited

When I think about it, I'm aware that I seem to anticipate the New Year with a combination of renewed optimism and underlying misgivings. I'm reminded of the reoccurring Peanuts cartoon in which Lucy offers to hold the football for Charlie Brown, then, inevitably, snatches it away at the last instant. Every year, in spite of his previous experience, Charlie becomes convinced that THIS YEAR, Lucy might actually hold the ball in place so that he can kick it, yet every year she tricks him.

I've come to feel that way about New Year's resolutions. Every year I think about a few aspects of my life that could be improved and resolve to make some changes. Inevitably, I get a few days or weeks into the new year, forget or simply ignore my resolutions, then abandon the whole effort as a failure. This recurring scenario is especially frustrating because for many years I was a competitive athlete, followed by a couple of decades of fairly high-level coaching. Goal setting is a vital skill for successful athletes and coaches and was an important aspect of my competitive and coaching philosophy. What makes it even more embarrassing is that back in 1992, I wrote a book about Nordic skiing in which I included a section devoted to the importance of goal setting.

Even though I haven't competed for a while, it was helpful to glance back at what I had written twenty-three years ago for some help in setting New Year's resolutions that might stick. It is important for elite athletes to establish goals that are appropriate, possible, but also not easily within reach. As a college ski coach, I frequently had athletes express their ultimate objective as skiing in the Winter Olympics. While for some, this might have been a reasonable ultimate goal, for most of them a more appropriate immediate target might have been missing only one workout a week. On the other hand, I remember a very talented incoming freshman who, as an Alaskan high school student, had represented the forty-ninth state with impressive results in four successive Junior National Championships. I was surprised and a little chagrinned when he informed me (with the independence and self-confidence typical of Alaskans) that his goal for his first year at college was to return to the Junior Nationals for a fifth time, rather than to compete at the NCAA Championships.

Since positive feedback is an important factor in the successful achievement of any goal, I'm a big believer in multiple goals. While only a few, elite athletes can realistically aspire to win the events they enter, most avid or even weekend runners can tell you their P.R.s (personal records) at various distances. I spent years trying to improve my marathon P.R. of 2:43:05, but the many races where I fell short of that goal were not failures. Thankfully, most running and skiing events are divided into ten-year-age increments, so even if you finish well back from the winners, you still may place very well in your age group. Since we have no control over other competitors, I resist setting goals related to other athletes, even if we seem to be battling it out with the same age-group rival every weekend. A better approach would be to estimate a finish time that would assure us placing ahead of the rival and focus on that time as the goal.

An additional characteristic of successful goal setting is specificity. All too often, I heard skiers say, "I just want to go faster," or "I want to finish higher on the results sheets." The more specific and clearly articulated the goal, the more likely it will be achieved. When President Kennedy stated in the early 1960s that "we will land a man on the moon and return him safely to Earth before the end of the decade," there was nothing wishy-washy about the objective.

So, in 2015 I resolve to: #1, lose weight, #2, get more exercise and #3, reestablish a healthier balance between work obligations and family activities. Specifically, that means: #1, taking smaller portions and avoiding desserts, #2, scheduling at least an hour of outdoor, physical activity at least five days each week and #3, committing to at least one day per week focused exclusively on family activities and free of work-related obligations. Another powerful enhancement to any goal or resolution is to actually write it down and post it where it can be easily viewed.

"So, Lucy, are you really going to hold the football in place this time…?"

Original Publication

Some of the pieces included in this collection had a previous life either as a radio commentary or as a column in a newspaper or magazine.

The following originally aired on Vermont Public Radio's Commentary Series.

Pond Hockey, March 8, 1994
The Agony of Tennis, June 21, 1994
Glory Days on the Gridiron, September 20, 1994
Bee Hunting, October 25, 1994
Motorcycles, July 22, 1997
Skydiving, June 20, 1995
Pele, August 30, 1994
Hoops in Phung Hiep, December 12, 1995
Windsurfing, August 15, 1995
In the Hall of the Mountain King, November 22, 1994
The Cosmic Message, November 8, 1994
The Simple Pleasures of the Winnipesaukee Relay, August 9, 1994
The Finish Line, August 23, 1994
Running Through Mud Season, April 23, 1996
Competitive Gardening, July 30, 1996, September 17, 1997
Summer Weddings, October 22, 1996
The Centennial Boston Marathon, April 28, 1997
Sherman Adams' Long Walk, September 22, 1998
Giving Blood, November 12, 1998
In the Shadow of Mt. Everest, March 2, 1999
Eat Like There's No Tomorrow, October 28, 1998
Terror in the Beauty Salon, September 15, 1999
Acknowledging My Addiction, April 29, 2003
Memories of a Rookie Coach, May 9 1995
Monster Trout, March 30, 1995
The Shrine Game, September 5, 1995
Bird Watching, July 2, 1996
Summer Vacation, July 12, 1994
The Prom Dress, July 12, 1995
The Long Trail, Part 1, October 31, 1995

The following originally aired on Vermont Public Radio's Commentary series brunch.

Turning Point, Spring 2008
The Long Haul, April 25, 2009

The following were originally published in *Vermont Sports Today*.

Pond Hockey, January 1996
The Agony of Tennis, May 1996
Glory Days on the Gridiron, October 1998
Track and Field Friends, June 2002
Bee Hunting, June 1996
Motorcycles, July 2000
Sailing, July 2009
Skydiving, August 2000
Pele, October 1997
Hoops in Phung Hiep, March 1997
Windsurfing, July 1996
In the Hall of the Mountain King, November 1998
The Cosmic Message, April 2005
The Simple Pleasures of the Winnipesaukee Relay, September 1996
The Finish Line, November 1995
Running Through Mud Season, April 1997
Competitive Gardening, August 1997
Summer Weddings, July 1998
The Centennial Boston Marathon, April 2000
Sherman Adams' Long Walk, June 1999
Giving Blood, February 2001
In the Shadow of Mount Everest, September 1999
Eat Like There's No Tomorrow, August 1999
Terror in the Beauty Salon, June 2002
The Twenty-Seventh U.S. Marine Corps Marathon, December 2002
Acknowledging My Addiction, May 2003
The Moosilauke Triathlon, November 2004
Running the Vermont City Marathon, May 2005
The Solstice Hike, August 2005
Marathon Flashbacks, May 2006
Eight Old Guys Paddle North, July 2006

London Olympic Highlights, September/October/ 2012
Evolving Sports, Jan 2013
No Easy Answers, April 2013
Boston Strong, June 2013
A Confluence of Sport, August 2013
No Fan of the NCAA, November 2013,
Bad Boys in the NFL, November 2014
"Let's Hear it for the Girls", September/October 2014
New Year's Resolutions, Revisited, January 2015

The following were originally published in *Dartmouth Medicine*.

The Heart of an Olympian, Fall 2003
Of Snowstorms, Airplanes and the North Woods, Winter 2000
Dudley Weider's Denali Vacation, Winter 1999

The following was originally published in the *Middlebury College Magazine*.

Outward Bound from Tashkent, Summer 1990

The following was originally featured at Thetford Elementary School's Veteran's Day ceremony

Veteran's Day, 2008

Acknowledgments

This collection of stories and essays would not have been possible without help, encouragement and advice from a number of people: Betty Smith-Mastaler, who for decades was the demanding but supportive producer of the Vermont Public Radio Commentary Series, Kate Carter, the founder and skillful editor of *Vermont Sports* newspaper, as well as Angelo Lynn, the current publisher of *Vermont Sports*.

I am also especially grateful to Deborah Heimann who patiently copy-edited and helped me organize the stories, and to Emily Newton whose design expertise created an attractive book from a utilitarian manuscript. Sarah Clarke took care of all the details of publication. In addition, I'd like to thank the following for their help and encouragement: Judy Geer, Peter Graves, Matt Jennings, Willem Lange, Kay Morton, Bill McKibben, Andy Shepard, Jed Williamson, Perry Williamson, and Dana Grossman.

Sports and Life

466

About the Author

John Morton has participated in ten Winter Olympic Games as an athlete, a coach, the biathlon team leader, chief of course or, more recently, enthusiastic U.S. biathlon team fan. He has attended scores of national championships, world championships, biathlon world cup competitions, and the World University Games.

After 11 years as head coach of Men's Skiing at Dartmouth College, he wrote *Don't Look Back*, a comprehensive guide to cross-country ski racing. In 1998, he published *A Medal of Honor*, a novel about the Winter Olympics. In 2020 he published *Celebrate Winter*, a collection of stories and commentaries related to skiing and the Winter Olympics. He was a commentator for Vermont Public Radio and a monthly columnist for *Vermont Sports Today* (a monthly, regional newspaper) for almost two decades. His articles on the outdoors have appeared in more than two dozen publications.

Morton is also the founder of Morton Trails, and has spent the past 33 years designing nearly 260 recreational trails and competition venues across the country. Recent projects include design of a world class biathlon facility in Brillion, WI; design of a Nordic competition venue at Bogus Basin, ID; reconfiguration of trails for Dartmouth College in Hanover, NH, and Holderness School in Plymouth, NH, to accommodate snowmaking and lights, as well as several trail networks for private landowners in the Northeast.